"This book could be subtitled 'Dr. Lacan in British Columbia.' Burnham ventriloquizes the old master in his ideological and psychoanalytic readings of the poets of the Kootenay School of Writing, an absolutely crucial, compelling, and provocative poetry collective that emerged on Canada's West Coast in the 1980s. Burnham is right: it is the poetry that matters. The poems at stake here burn off the theory like the Vancouver sun piercing the city's notoriously grey skies."
—Charles Bernstein, Donald T. Regan Professor of Comparative Literature, University of Pennsylvania; author of *All the Whiskey in Heaven*

"This important new book points to the potential of poetry as critique in Vancouver's long moment of rising neoliberalis—a period that takes us from Bill Bennett and the 'Restraint Budget,' to the coalitional 'Operation Solidarity' of the 1980s up to the zombie urbanism of gentrification today. A particular energy leaps from Burnham's critical method, which is often as paratactical as the poetry from the Kootenay School of Writing poets that he closely reads: Joe Clark and Flora MacDonald appear alongside Lisa Robertson and Peter Culley, Jacques Lacan and Slavoj Žižek join Dorothy Trujillo Lusk and Deanna Ferguson. Burnham's accelerated materialist reading is not only a rock solid work of a literary history that locates KSW within North American poetics, but it is both brilliant and weird enough to be a crucial critical intervention into Canadian literary studies."
—Jeff Derksen, author of *Annihilated Time* and *Transnational Muscle Cars*

"When you choose to call a book about a regionally-based collective of writers *The Only Poetry that Matters*, you set yourself a remarkably difficult task. With a title so bold, so presumptuous, so contestable, the challenge is obvious. Fortunately, Clint Burnham doesn't leave his title stranded! Here, an attentiveness to materiality—in the archive, in the everyday, and of the signifier—combine to make a strong case for the Kootenay School of Writing's persistent impact on North American cultural politics and avant-garde writing since the collective's inception in 1984. For readers who can lay claim to a piece of this history, *The Only Poetry that Matters* promises an "archival jolt," with all the uncanny and pleasurable reverberations. For the rest of us, Burnham's study is a place to begin understanding why the cultural work and poetics of KSW really do matter."
—Kate Eichhorn, author of *Fond* and *Fieldnotes, a fore*

READING THE KOOTENAY SCHOOL OF WRITING

CLINT BURNHAM

ARSENAL PULP PRESS Vancouver

TH
E
ON
LY
PO
ETR
Y

TH
AT
MATT
ERS

The songs of The Slits, The Raincoats, Patti Smith, Young Marble Giants, The Au Pairs, Annie Lennox, L7 and P.J. Harvey lent me a generous diction and compositional rhythm.

—*Lisa Robertson* [1]

Soundtrack for those times held heavy recurrences of The Pogues, The Smiths, PiL, Queen Latifah, Neneh Cherry, Public Enemy, Madonna, Sonic Youth, Single Gun Theory.

—*Colin Smith* [2]

As I study this age which is so close to us and so remote, I compare myself to a surgeon operating with local anesthetic: I work in areas that are numb, dead—yet the patient is alive and can still talk.

—*Paul Morand* [3]

THE ONLY POETRY THAT MATTERS

ARSENAL PULP PRESS
Suite 101, 211 East Georgia St.
Vancouver, BC
Canada V6A 1Z6
arsenalpulp.com

The publisher gratefully acknowledges the support of the Canada Council for the Arts and the British Columbia Arts Council for its publishing program, and the Government of Canada (through the Canada Book Fund) and the Government of British Columbia (through the Book Publishing Tax Credit Program) for its publishing activities.

Editing by Anne Stone
Book design by Shyla Seller

Printed and bound in Canada

Library and Archives Canada Cataloguing in Publication

Burnham, Clint, 1962-
The only poetry that matters : reading the Kootenay School of Writing / Clint Burnham.

Includes bibliographical references and index.
Also available in electronic format.
ISBN 978-1-55152-429-0

1. Canadian poetry (English)--British Columbia--Vancouver--History and criticism. 2. Canadian poetry (English)--20th century--History and criticism. 3. Kootenay School of Writing--History. I. Title.

PS8159.7.V3B87 2011 C811'.5409971133 C2011-905447-7

for Michael Turner

Contents

INTRODUCTION

> Although these popular movements are often denounced by governments as 'anti-democratic,' they actually deepen democracy. Liberal democratic institutions are often described as the bridge between individual citizens and the state, but elections, parties and parliaments seem increasingly ineffective for this purpose. This is especially so whenever corporate profits sag. Indeed, 'the more serious these problems become the less can governments afford to allow the type and actual timing of their policy to be determined by whatever consensus does—or does not—emerge from the process of democratic politics.' Governments become desperate for private investments and try to by-pass normal democratic procedures. In the circumstances, people have to resort to unconventional means to make their influence felt. This is what extra-parliamentary politics is all about.
> —William K. Carroll 1984, 111[1]

This book is a reading of a moment, a reading of the 1980s, a reading of a time when poetry was political not (only) in terms of its content, but formally. A time when the politics of Vancouver, of British Columbia, meant large-scale demonstrations in the streets and the threat of a general strike. A time when a shut-down, rural university writing program was reborn as an urban hotbed of experiment and cosmopolitan theory, with as much in common with Gramsci as with the anarchistic Direct Action group. A time when a still coalescing American L=A=N=G=U=A=G=E poetry scene would find itself brought together in Vancouver, outside of the US (if not outside of America), giving birth to the Kootenay School of Writing like a teen mother gestating a fully grown child. A poetry movement—the KSW—that was as much about the street as the library, about art as literature, about politics as aesthetics, about community as the academy. And like that movement, this book straddles different worlds, is of the archive but also wants to be read in the café, is about (some) writers I've known for twenty years but abjures the interview for close reading. Because this is about the writing, about the poems, about not so much *what* they mean as what they *do* with meaning. And we can only figure that conundrum out if we don't dodge the bullet, if we meet the bristling, dense, playful, and yes, sometimes difficult, writing head-on.

So what I'd like to do in this introduction is three things. First of all, I want to flesh out the title of this book, unpack the various meanings of "matter," and do this not merely theoretically but through a reading of the work of Nancy Shaw, a key member of the KSW who passed away at the age of forty-five. For, as I will show again later in this book, it is in the reading of the work that we learn the most. This is to jump in feet first, but then to pull back, to quickly situate the KSW in a couple of different ways: in terms of the histories of poetry in Canada and the US, but also in terms of the political and social histories of Vancouver art and communities. Finally, I outline the structure of this book, how I look at the writing in different chapters, developing a psychoanalytic theory of poetry—drawing especially on Jacques Lacan, as well as Slavoj Žižek and Sigmund Freud.

What do I mean by "the only poetry that matters"? First, to think of "matter" in three different ways: as mater, or mother; as what matters or is important; and as material(ism). As *mater*, the KSW body of work is also a body in dialogue with feminism—both in the work by women inside and outside the grouping and in work by men that is itself constituted in relation to feminism. And, with a nod to the punk band The Clash, whose 1979 album *London Calling* was advertised as being by "the only band that matters," the body of KSW poetry as "what matters," as what is important in Canadian or contemporary writing: work that is, I would argue, the most vital body of innovative poetry today (emerging from a social milieu that still, almost thirty years on, continues to host and produce such work). In terms of materialism, again, this concept breaks down: first, material as the stuff of language—the books, magazines, publications—the pages and letters and bindings—the archivist's substrate. Then, materialism as a political concept, referring to the economic conditions for the production of culture, the exchange value promulgated under capitalism and the critique thereof (in the sense that Marxism can be said to be a form of materialism). Finally, the materiality of the signifier, which means the semiotic and psychoanalytic notions of discourse, of the laws of language and how writing can challenge those.

These notions play out in various ways in the chapters that follow. In my readings of work by Colin Smith (the chapter on Social Collage), Kathryn MacLeod (the chapter Empty Speech), and Lisa Robertson (the chapter on Red Tories), gender politics come to the fore. In the Social Collage chapter, the juxtaposition found in these post-lyrics (especially in Dorothy Trujillo Lusk and Deanna Ferguson) is analogous to the collage aesthetic found throughout punk—from Dick Hebdige's notion of the visual look (leather jackets and safety pins, Jamie Reid's collaged album cover for the Sex Pistols) to musical juxtapositions (between reggae, heavy metal, rockabilly). Here the materialism of the archival *substrate*—of the objects to be found in the KSW archive—is also discussed in terms of a political economy. And the Lacanian critique of language—especially as outlined in the Empty Speech chapter, maintains a tension between a political materialism and a materiality of the signifier.

Now, it may seem paradoxical to "explain" poetry by recourse to an even more difficult language, that of psychoanalysis. But my hope here is that the two discourses will illuminate each other, without either mindlessly simplifying or obscurely complicating. So let's turn to Nancy Shaw's work, and especially to some of the poems in her first full-length book collection, *Scoptocratic*, published in 1992 by ECW Press. The book's title already signals that we are in the realm of film theory, of Lacan's (male) gaze, and perhaps of feminism: scopophilia was a Freudian term popularized in the 1970s by writers in the British film journal *Screen*, and especially by Laura Mulvey in her 1975 essay "Visual Pleasure and Narrative Cinema." There, using Lacan, she argued that the symbolic order of cinema depended on a certain lack, a gendered lack, in the castrated female subject. That system then depends on a pleasure in looking, which is how the term "scopophilia" was first used by Freud in his 1905 text *Three Essays on the Theory of Sexuality* (1966, vol. VII, 156–57) and in being looked at; but this pleasure is also imaginary, or having to do with the image, with the recognition/misrecognition that occurs not only when we see ourselves in the mirror but in all of our relations with the Other.

So this sense of potential meanings in the title *Scoptocratic* points to the various filmic aspects of Shaw's text (and also its visual aspects, as in her photograph that graces the cover, in which we see a forest mirrored in a lake or inlet). "Unrealized Scenarios" (15–37) is the most ambitious of these "Cine poems" (the title of another text: 50–69), and it often reads as treatment for a *film noir*:

> The two men begin. Without having seen each other for quite some time, they recount a problem of some intellectual propensity, of trouble to them both. With each change of scene there is a new round of drinks. Other gestures that punctuate pertinent moments include: looking in the mirror, smoking cigarettes, smoothing hair or accentuating physical features, drinking without reply, walking the periphery. (20)

The text is occupied with the visual (from the colloquialism of "Without having seen each other for quite some time" to "looking in the mirror"), with the double (*two* men), but also, like much of *Scoptocratic*, with the textual or dialogic: the men "recount a problem," or its absence when there is "drinking without reply," or even speech's oral substitutions—smoking, drinking. Such filmic concerns are a matter for *Scoptocratic* both formally as well as thematically—via reference to such genres as a "Shooting script" (23*ff*), the "Scenarios," or, in the much more minimalist "Cine poem," the look of a few isolated words on the page (the page as screen). Thus page 52 features only:

cratic

In some ways this page then functions as a critique of scopophilia, by showing that the scoptocrat is, when shorn of his visual power, left as a nonsense word, meaningless, vulnerable to the reader's gaze.

There are certainly ways to read Shaw's book via film theory itself in terms of the *mater* that I see as key to the KSW program—and, as will be evident throughout this book, the feminist critique of language and power is key to the work by many, if not most, of the writers associated with the collective.[2] But we can also trace this feminism, this question of gender, as well as other senses of the "matter," though a less tendential text, one that sits awkwardly in *Scoptocratic*, no doubt in part because it is a collaboration: "Close to Naked" (70–76), which was written with Gerald Creede and first published in *Writing* 23/24. (Interestingly, in terms of the trajectory Shaw's work was to take—including posthumously—collaboration was an important strategy, resulting in *A Sunday Drive* [1993, a catalogue essay with Lisa Robertson], *Busted* [2000, with Catriona Strang] *Light Sweet Crude* [2008, with Strang], and *Cold Trip* [2009, also with Strang, a libretto].)

But "Close to Naked" is an important text not only because it brings together Shaw's erudite, and coolly elegant, approach with Creede's more brutalist, pulp fiction/poverty *noir*, but also because of how it makes this unlikely synthesis work at the level of formal disjunction as well as thematic readability. The poem is concerned with the spatial/urban:

> We always hung out in someone else's neighbourhood. (70)
> In the old family neighbourhood, others watch faithfully. (72)

But also with language *qua* material signifier:

> A blouse, abuse, a pose, arouse, something on paper. (71)
> Whore is ontological. Whore is until. (73)

With the difficulty of communities and institutions:

> Zealous reformers in the community centre seemed to bask in the suspicion that they might be. (73)
> On the cornerstone of the community centre, while the cement was still wet, some kid had written Fuck God and drawn a heart around it. (76)

And also with the fantasy of culture, of film, and perhaps even *film noir*:

> He'd had enough of intrigue. A movie night, a barbecue, a mixed dance. [...] All the closeups are body doubles. (70)
> She'd been made an accomplice to the affair. [...] Film tactics. (72)
> Body double. Voice over. (75)

In its doubling, in its voice-over a body double (but also a voice that is over, or done), such a text, and indeed such a text by such different writers, is so thoroughly a matter of literary miscegenation that it brings to mind an earlier text in the avant-garde, Gertrude Stein's "Lifting Belly." Indeed, in opening a discussion of the position of the

Kootenay School as an institution in relation to the more hegemonic academy, it is worth noting that University of British Columbia English professor Peter Quartermain not only taught courses on Stein at the KSW in the 1980s (see Chapter Five), but wrote about her work in a book published the same year *Scoptocratic* saw release: *Disjunctive Poetics: From Gertrude Stein and Louis Zukofsky to Susan Howe*. For Stein's quite astonishing "Lifting Belly" is a text that, if in some ways a love poem, is also one in which there is a dialogue, as if love itself were to be a matter of speech, of countering one proposition with another. Stein begins by declaring, "I said lifting belly," and then "I said it I mean lifting belly," and when asked by an interlocutor, "What did you say lifting belly," affirms through the question "Did you say, oh lifting belly," and even if subject to doubt ("I am so discouraged about lifting belly"), she counters that "Lifting belly is so able to be praised," indeed, is a matter in need of validation ("You mean lifting belly is all right"), and also that "Lifting belly makes a sound," for not only is lifting belly "kind and good and beautiful," but, Stein reaffirms, "Lifting belly is my joy," and, indeed, "is perfect." But it perhaps is not perfect, for we are only ten pages into a fifty-page poem, and it is the poem's—and indeed Stein's—method to return again and again to this matter, signalling the provisionality of what "lifting belly" as a phrase may be or mean, a provisionality that, Quartermain contends, makes "Lifting Belly" referential yet obscure, inaccessible yet coherent, a text in which an "unassigned voice" privileges a pre-existing narrative where we must trust language patterns, recurrences, and variations, and the situation of the telling, even while uniformity and predictability is always being undermined. Crucial to Quartermain's reading is the assertion that the reader cannot "distinguish inner from audible speech," that there are different speakers, but those speakers blur into each other. (Quartermain 1992, 29–32)[3]

I am arguing that just as Stein's text can be read in a dialogic manner, as Quartermain does so brilliantly in *Disjunctive Poetics*, so too is

Shaw and Creede's text referential yet obscure, inaccessible yet coherent, a text in which *more than one* "unassigned voice" suggests a pre-existing narrative (in the preponderance of antecedent-less pronouns—he and she—for example). Too, the speakers blur into one another in "Close to Naked." But this formal—or dialogic—aspect of the text, which, in my reading, aligns the poem to a certain strand of the (American) avant-garde, that is, to the *mater* of us all, is also joined by a global strategy in "Close to Naked." This strategy has more to do with the materiality of the signifier, a matter I will return to later in this book with respect to other writers as well: I mean the notion of the ideologeme. This term comes to us from Fredric Jameson, from his argument in *The Political Unconscious* that texts work at the level of the signifier as bearers of political, or ideological, meaning. I discuss this strategy in a number of KSW texts (including "Close to Naked") later in this book, but let's have a brief preview of what Jameson means and see if it can help us to think about the materiality of the text in this poem. Jameson's ideologeme refers to the smallest possible unit of political belief or action that mediates "between conceptions of ideology as abstract opinion, class value, and the like" and literary materials (1991, 87). The example he gives from Nietzsche and nineteenth century novels is *ressentiment* as a class ideology. But such ideologemes find their material life in the utterance, in the material of language. "Close to Naked" intervenes into ideologemes via the utterance, as in the following instances: "Raindrops on roses and whiskers on killers" (Creede 1989, 70), "Kick out the raspberries. Kick out the plum" (71), "the boys spent more time in the bar than in jail" (71), "No explanations were in order" (73), and "Out of sight, out of jail" (73). The first two examples from "Close to Naked" are parsed from popular music—"My Favorite Things" from *The Sound of Music* and "Kick Out the Jams" by Detroit garage rockers MC5. In both cases an inversion takes place at the level of the utterance: "kittens" become "killers"—a metonymic shift of the signifier—and "jams" becomes "raspberries" and "plums"—metonymy again. In the third example, we may expect the last word of the phrase to be "school," in which case this would be a judgmental utterance about boys wasting their time drinking instead of studying; but in comparison to jail, the bar doesn't look so bad. Or, indeed, no explanations are now in order (the original phrase, "explanations are in order" is an example of language being used as a form of power); the final phrase, repeating the content of the bar/jail line, uses the original utterance's anaphora (the repetition of "out of . . ." to suggest a parallelism) to different ends.

This reading of Nancy Shaw and Gerald Creede's "Close to Naked," then, suggests some of the ways in which I will argue, in this book, that the KSW is "the only poetry that matters." This is work that engages with gender and continues an avant-garde tradition embodied by such figures as Gertrude Stein. The poetry also is embedded in a political economy of counter-traditions, of marginalized spaces and bodies in the history of Vancouver. And it does this work via the materiality of the sign, via language itself not only representing a political alternative, but performing that alternative.

Some of these questions of materialism—the economic, especially—are explored in the fifth chapter of this book, when I look at the archive, but I want to situate the KSW in terms of a political economy of Vancouver history as well as a Canadian-American literary history. When I was working on the various chapters, I submitted two of them to academic Canadian journals. The procedure that is usually followed in such publications is for the submitted essays then to be sent out for peer review in a system known as "double-blind": the reviewer would have received my essay stripped of any identifying marks, and I, as author, would not know the identity of the reviewer. In the case of one of the chapters, it came back with the following comments:

> . . . the question of significance in this critical work remains

> chiefly determined by whether the author can adequately demonstrate what Lacanian psychoanalysis can in itself add to literary criticism's interpretation and assessment of the poetic works featured in the piece and the Kootenay School of Writing in general as an important Canadian literary movement. Certainly current Canadian literary canons tend to marginalize the history and cultural importance of this particular Vancouver-based practice. Few university presses and peer-reviewed academic journals feature work or criticism on the school—a neglect that is due in part to its geographical distance from Canada's literary establishments in Toronto and Montreal, its radical politics and its penchant for revisionary aesthetic forms. Hence, serious critical interrogation of this somewhat neglected lineage of poetry and aesthetic theory remains overdue, and the author's work is clearly an attempt to address this deficit.[4]

I think that this reviewer is correct in arguing that the KSW has been marginalized in both the mainstream or canonical formation of Canadian Literature and in its reception and critical construction via academic discourse. So in providing a literary-historical context for the Kootenay School, I have to speak to two audiences at once: first of all, those who are familiar with, and indeed interested in, the tradition of the Anglo-American literary avant garde, a tradition that runs, in the first half of the twentieth century, from Stein and Pound and Zukofsky and Niedecker to the New American poetries of Olson, Creeley, Duncan, and Spicer; this tradition was then contested in a Canadian context by the TISH poets (George Bowering, Daphne Marlatt, Fred Wah, Frank Davey) and in the American one by the L=A=N=G=U=A=G=E writers (Charles Bernstein, Bruce Andrews, Susan Howe, Bob Perelman, Barrett Watten); more recently, "post-Language" writers, sometimes denoted as conceptual or Flarf writers, include the Americans Kenneth Goldsmith, Juliana Spahr, Vanessa

Place, Mark Nowak, Rob Fitterman, Rod Smith, and the Canadians Rachel Zolf, Sina Queryas, Christian Bök, Kate Eichhorn, and Darren Wershler. This is all just a list of names, a list that is hardly exhaustive or uncontroversial, but which functions as a placeholder. It can stand in contrast to readers who may come to this text from other traditions, whether from more conservative twentieth-century modernism and anti-modernism (which may run from Eliot and Frost to Plath and Lowell and the contemporary "workshop" or *New Yorker* poem or follow a less hegemonic trajectory) or the various strands and counter-hegemonic traditions of so-called "identity" poetics, from the Harlem Renaissance of Hughes to Brooks in the 1950s and then the Black Arts Movement and Canadian iterations in George Elliot Clarke or, closer to home, Wayde Compton, and the gendered poetics of Adrienne Rich and Margaret Atwood and Lowther; *or* the various anti-academic and sometimes populist forms from the New York school (Frank O'Hara but also Ted Berrigan and Ron Padgett) and its late-century epigones in spoken word and rap poetics to the Canadian small press and visual poetry movements, including Stuart Ross, jwcurry, Daniel f. Bradley, and other carriers of the Coach House torch.

But as the regional power imbalances cited in the reader's review of my essay above suggests, there is no "United States of poetry," no liberal chorus of eclecticism, and no discussion of poetry can indulge in the fantasy of "covering all the bases." The stakes may seem small in the poetry world, but the power disparities (whether around the question of representations of "raced" or gendered subjects or academic and critical reception) are, as in other social formations, nonetheless formidable.

And this literary history is then also contested on the ground and in the streets of Vancouver, the city where the Kootenay School has worked since the mid-1980s. Here is a brief recap of a history that is familiar to any reader of the KSW anthology[5]: in the 1980s in British Columbia, a conservative government—the Social Credit party, which had ruled the province almost uninterrupted since World War II—got onto the Thatcherite/Reagonomics bandwagon and enacted legislation that would introduce "fiscal restraint." Which is to say, the government decided to cut its spending, and part of what that meant was shutting down a small liberal arts college in the town of Nelson, in the south-eastern corner of the province: David Thompson University Centre, or DTUC. The college had a lively creative writing program, including Colin Browne and Tom Wayman as instructors, a rotating roster of visiting writers (David McFadden, John Newlove, Margaret Atwood—apparently British novelist Ian McEwan even dropped by for a party at some point), and a budding group of students. When the college was shut down, protests happened locally—protests were going on all over the province, it was an exciting time—but in the end many decamped for Vancouver, where they transferred their energies to building a new entity, the Kootenay School of Writing (named after the region of British Columbia in which DTUC was located).[6]

As a collective, the KSW began on the run, as it were, as the offshoot of 1980s-style neoliberalism[7] (as David Harvey and others have come to call the tendency in the late twentieth century to roll back modest post-war gains of social democracy in the name of globalization and consumer choice)—but it also took root in an already existing, and lively, Vancouver political and artistic culture. This was a city that since the 1960s had seen a rise in independent, non-profit art galleries, known in the Canadian art world as artist-run centres; a city that also was well-known for its clashes between civic authorities and hippies in the '60s and '70s; a city that had an exciting punk scene that gave rise to any number of acts, bands, and personalities, from the U-J3RK5 and D.O.A. to the Subhumans and Art Bergman (see Armstrong, Keithley); a city that nurtured a resilient anarchist culture, giving rise not only to squats, militant veganism, and a protest culture, but also the urban guerilla tactics of the Direct Action group, whose firebombing of porn shops, arms manufacturers, and hydro towers led to the brief media controversy of the "Squamish Five" (see Antliff, Hansen); and a city that, after the flourishing of the TISH poets in the 1960s, had seen their retreat to the academy, leaving the scene to the determined activities of their fellow-travellers in the urban milieu, including the Vancouver Co-op Radio host and *BC Monthly* publisher Gerry Gilbert, red-diaper-baby-gone-hippie Maxine Gadd and, maybe, a few writers beginning to pick up on the new writing happening south of the border, some in exile from Vancouver Island (Kevin Davies and Peter Culley, both of whom had novelist Jack Hodgins as a high school teacher), and others, such as Dorothy Trujillo Lusk and then Gerald Creede, just doing their thing, waiting for something to happen, making something happen.[8]

This is a quick sketch of a social context for the KSW (which I go into more detail about via the archival research in Chapter Five; while, in Chapter Three, I deal more with the KSW in relation to the twentieth-century poetic tradition); I conclude this introduction with a brief synopsis of the five main chapters that follow. In the first chapter, "Tripartite Taxonomy," I argue that the work of the KSW falls, in terms of poetic method, into three categories: the social collage method, the Red Tories, and that of empty speech. This chapter is where I range over a variety of poets in each group, and introduce arguments and readings that are then explored in further depth in the three chapters that follow. In effect, the Tripartite Taxonomy chapter is like a home page with links; as a form of experiment, I develop readings that are then elaborated upon in the following chapters. In this regard, I was thinking especially of comments that Walter Benjamin makes early in his study of German baroque tragedy, the *Trauerspiel*, in which he writes that "the value of fragments of thought is all the greater the less direct their relationship to the underlying idea" and "the writer must stop and restart with every new sentence" and, further, that the content of the work of art "is revealed in a process which might be described metaphorically as the burning up of the husk as it enters the realm of ideas, that is to say a destruction of the work in which its external form achieves its most brilliant degree of illumination" (1985, 29, 31). With this context, in the first chapter, the fragments of interpretation bear a relationship to the more extended work of the following chapters and, in reverse analogy, those later chapters' engagements are with, for the most part, fragments of poems, or single poems from larger bodies of work. The reader, like the writer, must stop and start—must jump to links—and then this book as a whole is consumed in its reading, as its critical exegesis consumes the poetry proper. (To be more explicit: there are various segments of the "Tripartite Taxonomy" chapter that are repeated, almost verbatim, in the following three chapters. Readings of Kathryn MacLeod's work thus are repeated in the second chapter, of Deanna Ferguson's in the third chapter, of Lisa Robertson's in the fourth chapter. The purpose of this method is to transform the book from an inert object into one that, like the poetry it examines, is alive with intertextual reference, with allusion, influence, and the anxieties thereof.)

This reference to Benjamin introduces him as a curious fellow-traveller to the more orthodox Lacanian apparatus of this study: as, for the most part, it will be Lacan, and his latter-day commentators Bruce Fink, Slavoj Žižek, Malcolm Bowie, and Jodi Dean, to whom I turn for theoretical accompaniment in these readings of KSW poetry. But Benjamin has also joined this party. In part, this is because of my own engagement with his work over the past three or four years, going back to a homophonic translation I undertook in 2007–08 of his *Berliner Kindheit um neunzehnhundert*, published in 2009 by BookThug as *The Benjamin Sonnets*. More recently, I have been teaching *The Arcades Project*, and so it was almost inevitable that this poetic, obscurantist, Marxist critic should come along for the ride.

In the "Tripartite Taxonomy" of the first chapter, I make some references to the Lacanian ideas that I develop in this book, but we really get into it in Chapter Two, on empty and full speech. In terms of engaging with Lacan, I should offer some biographical justification or at least context: In the fall of 2007, after ten years of bouncing around Vancouver from one academic institution to another as a sessional instructor, I was given a limited term appointment at Simon Fraser University (SFU) and was about to sign the paperwork for a tenure stream position when a group of clinicians and academics in Vancouver started a Lacan Salon, a reading group that has been meeting every two weeks since. This intensive reading practice—of essays from *Écrits* and from various *Seminars*—then seemed to provide me with a new entrée into the KSW corpus and history. On the one hand, it offers a much more supple way of reading texts than the tendentious politicized reading practices that surround the school (and here I must be impolite and single out the introduction to *Writing Class: The Kootenay School of Writing Anthology*; and on the other hand, the combination of Lacanian theory and KSW poetics offers a way to use the one to explain or introduce the other. My theoretical approach—what I later came to call my *lapproach*, a way of combining the *la* with the approach, a nod to Lacan's *llangue* or *lalangue*—was to map out or taxonomize the writing of the KSW into three groups or tendencies or formal approaches: the Red Tory neopastoralism of Lisa Robertson and Peter Culley (which I look at in terms of Lacan's Imaginary, or the dialectic of screen and mirror, as well as Žižek on lack and loss and left melancholy); the social collage/disjunction form to be found in the work of Jeff Derksen, Deanna Ferguson, Colin Smith, and Dorothy Trujillo Lusk (this work I talk about in terms of the Real, or the notion of capitalism as unsymbolizable, especially as theorized in terms of Lacan's four discourses—the hysteric, master, analyst, and university—in *Seminar XVII*); and the concerns of procedural constraints and Blanchotesque absence in Susan Clark, Kathryn MacLeod, Dan Farrell, and Melissa Wolsak (this work I interrogate in terms of the Lacanian Symbolic, or his theories of language to be found in his work of the 1950s).

This all takes place in the next four chapters. The fifth chapter concerns the KSW archive, to be found at SFU's Contemporary Literature Collection, and concerns the materiality not only *of* the archive—the financial and socio-political context for KSW as an institution—but also *in* the archive—its material form as substrate, as papers, as five years' worth of weekly collective minutes on legal writing pads, for instance. Here I examine the archive and also ask what does the archive ask of us—in Lacanese, *Chè vuoi?* What do you want? Does the archive want to be read, or to be left alone, undisturbed? Who is the subject of the archive—the collective subjectivity of the poets of the KSW? The archivist? The researcher? And so on. My book then culminates with another chapter of close readings. In this case, the readings are an attempt to bridge the gap between the formally radical KSW work and the equally political work writing that developed simultaneously (here the work of Tom Wayman, but also Colin Browne, as key figures in the collective in the 1980s, must be underscored). While still in a psychoanalytic mode, this chapter looks to a work by the American poet Clark Coolidge—*Own Face*—and a poem by Canadian Tom Wayman—"The Face of Jack Munro"—in terms of what Žižek has to say about the face as the gentrification of the Other.

This book owes an economic debt to Simon Fraser University for a President's Research Start-up Grant (2008–11). I am also indebted to the Department of English for its support of my work, including funding for Jason Starnes' production of the index (thanks, Jason), and to my many colleagues with whom I have discussed this project, including Ronda Arab, Michael Barnholden, Susan Brook, Paul Budra, Steve Collis, David Chariandy, Jeff Derksen, Peter Dickinson, James Fleming, Tom Grieve, Jamie Hilder, Christine Kim, Carolyn Lesjak, Jon Smith, and Jacqueline Turner. Research help by Donato Mancini was especially important in the early days of this project. The staff of the Contemporary Literature Collection and Special Collections at the SFU W.A.C. Bennett Library was very helpful in granting me access to the KSW archives, and I am especially thankful to Tony Power for his work above and beyond.

I am also grateful to members of the Lacan Salon for their intellectual challenges and companionship, including Hilda Fernandez, Ted Byrne, Alessandra Capperdoni, Paul Kingsbury, and Jesse Proudfoot. Writers, artists, activists, and academics here and elsewhere whose example always inspired include Aaron Vidaver, Am Johal, Andrew Klobucar, Chris Stroffolino, Christian Bök, Christine Stewart, Colin Browne, Colin Smith, Dan Farrell, Dorothy Trujillo Lusk, Fred Wah, George Bowering, Gerald Creede, Ivan Drury, Jason Starnes, Jim Green, Kathryn MacLeod, Kim Minkus, Lisa Robertson, Lori Emerson, Lorna Brown, Louis Cabri, Margery Fee, Mark Laba, Melissa Wolsak, Peter Culley, Rob Manery, Robyn Laba, Roger Farr, Roy Miki, Shawn Millar, Susan Clark, Terry Johnson (RIP), Tom LaViolette, Wayde Compton, and Wendy Pedersen.

Thanks also to the crew at Arsenal Pulp: Brian Lam, Robert Ballantyne, Shyla Seller, Susan Safyan, Cynara Geissler, and to Anne Stone for an awesome job of editing. Versions of some chapters of this book were read in 2009 by Hilda Fernandez, Steve Collis, and Rob Manery: thanks, but I'll still take credit for mistakes. Comments made by reviewers for *English Studies in Canada* and *Open Letter*—where earlier versions of chapters three and two, respectively, appeared—were also useful. An earlier version of Chapter Three was also published in draft form by Vancouver Publication Studio: thanks to Keith Higgins for the work on that (and to Matthew Stadler, whose franchise it is ...), and also to Brian Kaufman for putting a chunk of the introduction into *subTerrain*.

I gave a talk on the process of writing Chapter Two at the Candahar Bar in 2010: thanks to Michael Turner and Reid Shier for the opportunity. Students at Emily Carr University, Capilano College, the University of British Columbia, and SFU were helpful in feedback (and, sometimes, the production of readings). Some less formal institutions and sites that hosted—wittingly or not—the production of this book include Humanities 101, gene café, the Millennium line of Metro Vancouver's Skytrain system, the Carnegie and other locales of the Vancouver Public Library system, Artspeak, the OR Gallery, and the Western Front. Thank you to Julie Sawatsky and Devon Sawatsky Burnham for knowing that any acknowledgment of their contributions can only be an empty gesture, however necessary.

CHAPTER ONE

A Tripartite Taxonomy

> By 1856 and the writing of *The Confidence-Man*, wild and whirling words, the whole persistent multitude of Melvilles and Shaws felt that something had to be done, that there had to be some disposition, once and for all, of this man whom some tolerated and others feared, and of whom most were ashamed and all seemed weary. The money for this trip came from his father-in-law, Justice Shaw. This time Melville did not go away on his own; he was—though guardedly—sent away. In England, to book passage on a Mediterranean steamer, he visited Hawthorne. Hawthorne describes him as 'looking much as he used to do (a little paler, and perhaps a little sadder), a rough outside coat, and with his characteristic gravity and reserve of manner.' The two men spent a day by the sea near Southport, sheltering themselves from the wind in a hollow among the sandhills. They had what Melville calls in his journal simply 'good talk.'
> —Charles Olson, *Call Me Ishmael*, 90–91

When I began work on this project, it seemed to be important from the start to break with any monolithic view of either Language Poetry or the poetry written under the rubric of the KSW.[1] In that spirit, I began a rough division within the body of KSW work according to technique and method. First of all, I reduced my field of interest, focusing on work by writers from the mid-1980s to the early 1990s—the period in which the school saw a rapid and intense period of social, political, and poetic formation. I divided the poetry into three camps or tendencies: the concerns of procedural constraints and Blanchotesque absence in Susan Clark, Kathryn MacLeod, and Dan Farrell; the social collage/disjunctive form to be found in the work of Kevin Davies, Deanna Ferguson, and Dorothy Trujillo Lusk; and the Red Tory neopastoralism of Lisa Robertson and Catriona Strang. This "tripartite taxonomy" then became useful as a way to broaden my thinking about the writers and their texts. So the development of this approach (which I also have come to call, in terms of its Lacanian focus, my *lapproach*) is to be seen in the three chapters that follow this one. But this chapter—some of which is then repeated, in more refined or elaborated form, in the chapters that follow—is, as it were, a rough draft of criticality.

I. Procedural constraint (absence): Farrell and Wolsak

We read poems to understand them: "difficulty" shows that comprehension is the *objet a* of reading. If *only* I had all the biographical, historical, literary, political, formal knowledge, then I would *know*, nay *understand* the poem. With KSW writing, the stakes are different: desire shifts to drive! That is, *we enjoy* not knowing: this is surplus knowledge, where the problem is that the references go in so many directions at once, they cannot be pinned down. Look at the opening lines of Dan Farrell's poem "Intent," from his 1994 collection *Thimking of You*:

> Late in the dream my sides shorten they ha
> d course. I came to accuse him of my cold
> act but my testimony goes off. It came to

> that? It came to catch that. Every opposit
> e towards him hid in the privily spur. A c.
> (n.p.)

The first and most evident form of "meaning" here has to do with form: with the arbitrary ending of lines in the middle of words and then new lines beginning with letters that "finish" the previous words but arbitrarily. The "d" at the start of the second line and the "e" at the start of the fifth could as easily have been cut off from another word—but for how they complete "ha" at the end of the first line and "opposit" at the end of the third. The disjunction, then, between and within words, opens meaning up: a surplus meaning is performed here, rather than a fixed or restricted meaning. What this means is the following. According to standard structuralist or semiotic theory, signs acquire their meaning conventionally: language works by assigning signifiers to signifieds. Thus "late in the dream" has a fairly fixed meaning: a temporal designation. But Lacanian theory argues that there is always something left over, something sticking out, something that doesn't quite fit into the symbolic order of language. And poetry is the place where that extra is brought into play. And this is especially true in language poetry. A Lacanian reading of the poem would first of all point out that meaning is always being deferred in language, and all that poetry does is to make this deferral more evident. While any use of language may seem arbitrary or tricky if we consider it with enough vigour, with a conventional use of language, meaning *is* arrived at sooner or later: thus we can imagine someone saying "late in the afternoon I had a beer," where "I had a beer" is the activity that takes place and so, gives meaning to the phrase "late in the afternoon." Or we can even imagine a patient (an "analysand"), lying on the couch in the analyst's office, muttering away "late in the dream my sides shorten they ha-" and then suddenly sneezing just as he or she is about to explain why, in the dream, it seemed as if the sides of his or her body had suddenly shortened. But what is surely striking here is that in this very rude interruption of language (an interruption that, as in the optical illusion:

MARY

HAD A

A LITTLE LAMB

we rarely notice in everyday life), in this cutting off of speech, we suddenly arrive at surplus meaning, surplus language. And so,

> Late in the dream my sides shorten they ha

does not necessarily mean that the last word of the line is only *part* of a word, after all: it may be an exclamation of delight, the patient or poet's joy at such a fine or fun line. Even if the pattern in the poem seems to be to leave off words and add the probable endings to the next line, since the lines are only approximately the same length (and not the same character length, as if this were a typeset version of a typewriter poem), there are still other possibilities. This line could be in a Scot's dialect, from the poetry of Robbie Burns or Tom Leonard or the novels of Irvine Welsh.

But, again, am I knocking on an open door in making such a stark declaration of the difference between what goes on in Dan Farrell's "Intent" and what goes on in everyday language? Doesn't the kind of language we find in text messaging or advertising or graffiti also include such abrupt endings? Or, if this is so, and if such formal aspects of language are not restricted to poetry, then is the privileging of poetry misguided: should we not perhaps have a more catholic argument for how language works?

Perhaps. But let's hold these thoughts in abeyance for a while, and explore instead how Farrell's poem allows us to think about both lack of reference and constraint in terms of surplus meaning and the *objet a*. This second term in Lacan refers to the small 'a' other (or *autre*):

not the Big Other of language, the symbolic order, or God, but rather the *objet a* that is a remainder or trace of the Real, of some intense satisfaction that is either from "before" we enter into the Symbolic (not in a strict chronological or developmental sense, but in a conceptual sense) or from somehow in or beyond the Real. Here, it's useful to consider Lacan's famous topographical model of the torus or the doughnut: if the Symbolic order is the doughnut of language, then the hole in the doughnut, which is both in the doughnut and outside it, is what shapes the Real. (Canada's famous Timbits, of course, are the perfect example: they are the remainder, what is left over, and then, ingeniously, transformed into a commodity, into the symbolic). The *objet a* is the object-cause of desire; it is not so much what we want as what we want to want, or what keeps us wanting. Meaning is the paradigmatic *objet a* of literature, and especially of poetry. And since we want to keep desiring, the reading of texts in which meaning itself always eludes the reader, such as Language writing and KSW texts, can become pleasurable (perhaps even a matter of *jouissance*). After a while, reading Farrell's text (mischievously titled "Intent"—the only discernable intent here is to frustrate meaning) is enjoyable not only in spite of the lack of meaning, but because of it: freed up of the tyranny of reference, language can simply be. "ha" doesn't mean had or ha or hand or anything else: the letter is the letter in its materiality. The letter is not in the Symbolic, but in the Real.

But let's pull back a bit from this foray into psychoanalysis and return to the work of another poet whose text I think of in terms of the procedural, or constraint, or minimalist-absence.

> ... messy liquids ... uninvited failure
> a collection of substantial size ...
> your nipples visible through t-shirt ...
> ... exchange an old one for a new one ...
> brief morality ... angry about "the masterpiece"
> unmaking the bed. evasive.

... completion or celebration, erected
out of boredom ... my right point of view ...
relax/antagonize ... complete the sentence
... his hard line ...
(MacLeod in Klobucar and Barnholden 1999, 77)[2]

This excerpt from MacLeod's poem, "The Infatuation," foregrounds the separation of words graphically: in this case, through the use of ellipses. Like Emily Dickinson's dashes, the ellipses separate and join; their best-known appearance in twentieth-century literature is no doubt in the novels of Louis-Ferdinand Céline. Writing about style and language in Céline, Merlin Thomas commented on his use of what he calls the "three dots": "[T]hey divide his text into rhythmical rather than syntactical units, permit extreme variations of pace and make possible to a great extent the powerful hallucinatory lyricism of his style" (1979, 89). This is in some ways what is going on in "The Infatuation." Loosely, the poem may be said to be about a love affair: "keep it hard the whole time" appears in the first verse-stanza; "gentle male companion ... inspired tongue and finger" in the second; "don't push his buttons ... damp shirt" in the third; "... a complete withdrawal ... making you touch me ... isolated study of the male organ" in the third; "unmaking the bed" in our excerpt, the fourth; "you don't need courage with a mother" in the fifth; "I deliver you" in the sixth; "virile girls for men" in the seventh; and "... sexual arsenal ... delicate subversive ... punitive silence, sentenced to naked women ... dreams of a long cock betrayed him" in the eighth and final verse-stanza (1999, 76–79).

However, this putative content or narrative is subverted by the formal constraint of the ellipses. In the excerpt's first line, we have the ellipsis, then "messy liquids," then another ellipsis, and then "uninvited failure." By opening the verse-stanza or section of the poem with the ellipsis (which happens three other times in "The Infatuation"), MacLeod suggests something missing, something absent. Like Kevin

Davies' square brackets, the punctuation here speaks. "Messy liquids" and "uninvited failure" may suggest the material conditions of sexual intercourse—*coitus interruptus*, perhaps, or premature ejaculation, or even the messy liquids of sperm, lubricant, spermicide, and so on. But the text itself is messy, in a way, with all of these dots visible, like the nipples "visible through t-shirt."

The ellipses also suggest the rhythm that Thomas detects in Céline, here a languorous pace, one that is laid-back in a way that conflicts neatly with the precision of the images. One can imagine MacLeod genially listing off these observations or phrases, a listing that itself becomes a commentary of sorts on the law of equivalence. By this I mean the Marxist insight that under the commodity form, all objects, no matter how different they are in themselves (a pen and a coffee cup have intrinsically different use-values: you can't pour coffee into a pen and you can't write a letter with a coffee cup), can all be compared to each other economically (in terms of their exchange value: a coffee cup may cost eight dollars and a pen $1.99, so the cup is worth roughly four pens). Our labour itself is commodified under capitalism: thus, while my work as a university professor may seem to be quite different from that of a hospital nurse, our salaries can be compared (and, indeed, we both do forms of what is now called affective labour: thus my teaching must include "student-friendly" gestures so students don't feel bad if they don't understand something; too, the nurse is expected to attend to the patient's comfort while teaching the patient how to regulate his or her body).

By foregoing the syntactical crutch of conventional poetry—the stable, albeit ironical 'I,' and the grammatically regular sentence—language poetry makes evident how language itself is commodified: not simply, in a Naomi Klein sense, as a brand-name or logo but, more profoundly, as a discourse. This is the most important meaning of the "equal signs" in the title of the journal *L=A=N=G=U=A=G=E*. Thus in MacLeod's text, *all phrases are equivalent*. "Messy liquids" are the same as "uninvited failure," which is the same as "a collection of substantial size" and "your nipples visible through t-shirt" and "exchange an old one for a new one" and "brief morality" and "angry about 'the masterpiece'" and "unmaking the bed. evasive." and "completion or celebration, erected out of boredom" and so on. The rhythm of the poem, then, ensues from its parading of equivalence.

But this rhythm can be misleading in two different ways. First, if we ignore the gaps, and second, if we overlook the variations in punctuation. As I said in relation to Davies' brackets, the punctuation here has a role to play. In the genre of academic quotation, ellipses signify that words are missing; in other conventions, they simply mean a segue of some kind, a transition. In general, the disjunctive nature of MacLeod's poem suggests the first meaning, but the great disparity between one phrase and another (say, between "a collection of substantial size," an abstract, neutral description, and "your nipples visible through t-shirt," a more concrete, intimate statement) also means that we cannot hope to fill in the missing text. For in some ways this is all simulacra, and it is unlikely that MacLeod simply took an existing text and left out words to create this poem. The ellipses, then, are the simulation of absence: its signifier.

A penultimate reading of the ellipsis: in his essay "Discourse in Poetry: Bakhtin and Extensions of the Dialogical," Michael Davidson argued for a social-semiotic reading of how "contextual frames" worked in contemporary poetry. Specifically, he said that in such writing: "[T]he discontinuity between one line or sentence and the next is both a qualification of causal, narrative logic and an assertion of the paradigmatic nature of reference. The gap between elements is asserted as a sign itself, not simply as a caesura between two elements in a theorem. The gap calls attention to contextual frames within each unit, frames which overlap and interpenetrate like sedimentations in geological strata" (1983, 146).

In addition to the argument I've already made on how this signal form of punctuation, which joins and separates, which signifies absence as well as transition, is so meaningful after all, something new that Davidson brings to the table here is the idea that the "gap"—for our purposes, the ellipses—brings attention to "contextual frames." By this I think he means the notion of ideology as a discursive construction, or the significatory processes by which ideology functions.

II. Social collage

By collage, I mean work that operates with a high level of disjunction, and by *social* collage, I mean that this disjunction operates as a critique of the hegemonic role of meaning in late capitalist society. Collage, then, also signifies the breakdown of the signifying chain, whether at the level of the sentence (i.e., from sentence to sentence or phrase to phrase there is little narrative coherence) or on down to the word/signifier/phoneme. The argument then is that such writing constitutes an attack on how capital presents itself linguistically: that coherence is the ideological structure whereby capital interpellates the subject, that is, how we are addressed, and indeed created, as persons in our roles as readers, teachers, lovers, etc.

Here are some examples of this writing:

> Forget it forget it & write about US. Despot a viscous mesh apparent; these walls return a favour—i.e. bum. Bum, I will meet him in 45 minutes my will disintegrate amen. Taken short shrift so change the lesser nouns, mewling—"Some job" i.e. weasel thrust apparent to talk around your ears "the world". Totems of thought. The gorge.
> (From "Oral Tragedy," Lusk in Klobucar and Barnholden 1999, 139)

– {yellow} {flowers}
{& mingle more}

{incomplete} {enough to} {force} {weather}

{to}
{*do*}
{you}

{possible} {government} {surveillance}

{miserable} {exile} {guards} {public} {rooms}

{a blank}
{roasted}
{newspaper}

{Electricity yet}
{dog-eared}

("From *Pause Button*," Davies in Klobucar and Barnholden 1999, 58)

Sometimes the subordinate clause is while you still have friends. Causality abets restless energy; ensues credit. If stool the size of an infant's head is removed from one's cadaver, it's a sign. Adjust connective degenerations. What appears to the eye and touch after twenty or thirty years is the same after forty or sixty, singing, cords, casts, stuck to the bottom. (From "Swoop Contract," Ferguson 1993, 51)

There are two ways of thinking about work of this ilk. First of all, we can locate this technique in terms of post-structuralist critiques of language: notions of intertextuality (texts always refer to other texts, and are palimpsests), of the "open" or "writerly" text (meaning is not some inert thing *in* a text to be discovered/consumed by the reader, but is created or constructed by the reader), of language as a signifying chain (meaning is always being deferred). Then, we can locate a politics in this technique, a politics *both* at the level of content (references to domination and resistance, the latter often highly ironized) and as form (arguments that these very techniques, in their shifting of meaning from the author to the reader, are liberatory manoeuvres: a textual politics).

But let's see how these ideas work "on the ground," as it were, in reading these excerpts critically. Disjunction works at a fevered pitch in Dorothy Trujillo Lusk's "Oral Tragedy," which was first published in a chapbook of the same name from Tsunami Editions in 1988. The opening sentence of our excerpt (page 37) demands not only that the reader "write about US" (which, as a student recently reminded me, could be read as "write about the US"), but that s/he "forget it" not once but twice. Now, forgetting is, of course, the modernist gesture *par excellence*: if one is to "make it new," one has to almost by default forget what is old. But the repetition of the demand makes it both insistent and hectoring—tones or affects that are to be found throughout Lusk's work. Immediately, however, the next sentence retreats from sensibility: "Despot a viscous mesh apparent; these walls return a favour—i.e. bum." Replete with the punctuation marks of complex syntax—a dash, a semicolon—the sentence begins flirting less with meaning than with sound—the continued "s"s of Despot, viscous, and mesh. And the words themselves flirt with contiguous signifiers: despot with depot, viscous with vicious, mesh apparent with heir apparent. Then, for walls to "return a favour" makes walls themselves into some kind of subject. This writing evacuates traditional subjectivity even while it shows how we attribute subjectivity to—how we anthropomorphize—the inanimate world around us. Here we can imagine leaning against a wall and perhaps the wall leaning against us or at least against one's bum; the meaning of that last word quickly shifts at the beginning of the next sentence. Now "Bum" is an interpellation, as in "you bum" or "that bum." Is this bum the "him" that will be met "in 45 minutes"? This next sentence ends with a paraphrase, perhaps, from the Lord's Prayer: "my will disintegrate amen" instead of "thy will be done … amen." Subjectivity is evacuated and intentionality is eroded. But then agency is restored, in a sense, with the beginning of the next sentence: "Taken short shrift." This skews the normal usage of "short shrift," as in "I was given short shrift": now, a lousy pittance is taken, perhaps without asking.

Such a reconstruction of meaning can blind us to how meaning never actually resides in the work, in the writing. In Lusk's "Oral Tragedy," each sentence seems, as it meanders along, to have indeed forgotten "it," to have forgotten what the writing started talking about: from mesh to bums to disintegrating will, from shrift to mewling to "the world." Each sentence disintegrates under the force of association and the signifier, each sentence is given or takes short shrift, each sentence changes the lesser nouns—each noun becomes a pronoun, a shifter—each sentence quotes mindlessly, repeats heedlessly, talks around your ears as if they were not there, is a totem of thought both in the sense of a badge of honour and of a stratified hierarchy. Each sentence makes the gorge rise in an acid reflux of regurgitated text.

It may seem that I am a hostile reader of Lusk's work. But what I think this writing does, what a poetic sentence like

> Taken short shrift so change the lesser nouns, mewling—
> 'Some job' i.e. weasel thrust apparent to talk around your
> ears "the world"

does is to free the sentence from its own imprisonment, from the linear thrust of meaning in which meaning is, finally, something one has to "get" and then consume and then know. And this works specifically in terms of a concept I will elaborate upon below in my discussion of Deanna Ferguson: the idea of the signifying chain.

Lacan's notion of the signifying chain holds that language functions as a structure to give meaning to signifiers; and further, that those signifiers constitute how memory works (or, in the case of repression, does not). In one formulation of the role of signifiers, things are remembered for the subject by the "signifying chain"—by words (Fink 1997, 20). And in a parallel to Lusk's text, Lacan notes the case of "the man who withdrew to an island to forget—to forget what? he forgot—so the Minister, by not making use of the letter, comes to forget it ... But the letter, no more than the neurotic's unconscious, does not forget him" (2002, 24–25).

The signifying chain works in the following way. Take the ordinary sign: "Thank you for not smoking." We do not know what "thank you" means—what we are being thanked for—until the end of the sentence, of the signifying chain. "Thank you for not ..." what? We may know the dictionary meaning of "thank you"—of common gratitude—but we do not know its meaning in this sign until the chain is complete. "Smoking" gives meaning to "thank you."

Looking at Deanna Ferguson's excerpt (page 38), then, we can add a second meaning to the notion of the signifying chain: not only does a sentence only "make sense" once it is complete, but when sentences are removed from their context they do not make sense. Thus, for the reader of the entire poem, "stuck to the bottom" at the end of the Deanna Ferguson quotation would resonate with, or echo, the line from the poem's opening paragraph: "Failing tomato juice, macaroni stuck to the bottom, she squawked" (50). But that reference or resonance or echo does not mean that the phrase "stuck to the bottom" now *means* food or macaroni is stuck to the bottom of a pot; what the reference *means* lies in the technical or formal device of 'collaging in' a phrase from earlier in the poem; it *means* that the stuff of the poem is drawn from itself as well as from other texts, other meanings. Ferguson's poem is an intertext; its text is dialogic. Meaning in the sense of a fixed, definable essence is resisted, is never arrived at.

It's also important to realize that it is not just this kind of poetry which is subject to the signifying chain—all language is. We can return to the "Thank you for not smoking" sign, for instance, and note that there are further indeterminacies at work: for not smoking *what*? (Indeed, in the context of Vancouver, a city in which lately one is more likely to be censured for smoking tobacco than marijuana, the question is not merely mischievous.) Or for not smoking *where*? *When*? Ever? Or just right now, right here? This opening up of the signifying chain, these questions which we ignore in our everyday use of language, is what this writing is engaged with. And the refusal of meaning going on here is also connected to how some critics have seen Lacan's own writing function. As Bruce Fink argues in *The Lacanian Subject*:

> [I]t is precisely insofar as understanding involves nothing more than situating one configuration of signifiers within another that Lacan is so adamant about refusing to understand, about striving to defer understanding, because in the process of understanding, everything is brought back to the level of the status quo, to the level of what is already known. Lacan's writing itself overflows with extravagant, preposterous, and mixed metaphors, precisely to jolt one out of the easy reductionism inherent in the very process of understanding ... Thus the gist of Lacan's claim that meaning (meaning as what you imagine you have understood) is imaginary. By assimilating something, you have the sense of being someone, or you imagine yourself as someone (an ego or self), who has accomplished a certain difficult task; you picture yourself as a thinker. (71)

So *understanding* a Deanna Ferguson poem or a Dorothy Trujillo Lusk poem—or an Al Purdy poem or a Rita Wong poem—entails fitting the challenge the poem poses into one's system, a challenge to one's sense of language, of self, of the world. To crudely sum up the examples of Ferguson, Lusk, Purdy, and Wong: disjunctive poetics, the use of the profane, the vernacular, ecological politics—*aha!* now I've got it. But the writing being described in the present study is doing something different, and its domestication or colonization by analysis and exegesis will do this writing a disservice if the truly radical nature of the disjunctive, of the social, is not given its due.

Let's return to Ferguson's excerpt, which begins with a meta-linguistic statement that rapidly becomes absurd: "Sometimes the subordinate clause is while you still have friends." The phrase "subordinate clause" is itself a noun phrase (as are my words "meta-linguistic statement"): ironically, this sentence does not have a subordinate clause. But the *frisson* of domination contained in the neutral linguistic marker "subordinate" is then continued with the foreboding "while you still have friends." Speech is connected to the social. The declarative statement that follows suggests that these are descriptions of some pre-existing condition, be it linguistic, political, or physical: ideas of causality and energy suggest the latter, for instance. But the disjunction between and within the sentences makes us suspect that the text is to be read as non-referential: what "ensues credit," for instance? Rather, we are reading a certain tone or affect that then continues with the cool description of a "stool the size of an infant's head" being removed from "a cadaver." The medical language here—"stool" instead of *shit*, "cadaver" instead of body or *corpse*—connects with other such words and phrases in the poem, including "proctitis" (inflammation of the rectum—*OED*), "the common cold," "professional·muscle," "dirty-minded dentist," the obvious "we know medical companies are interested" (50) and "more and more medicine," culminating in "Cell formations on file dead on DNA" (51). And the detached language is immediately turned around with the flat statement that if all of this happens, "it's a sign." A sign in a medical sense or a sign in a linguistic sense? Or, again, a meta-linguistic sign? Once again we have play going on with the signifying chain: this is a sign *of what*? The passage then shifts registers slightly, to a demand: "Adjust connective degenerations." Again, demands abound in the poem: "Find suitable vents" [50], "Code functional disorders," "Test the theory" [51], "Lunch forward," "Yell timbre," "Carry the baby," and "Forever calculate" [52]. These medical resonances, these demands, then return to the flat declarative and tautological sense of the beginning of the sentence as "What appears to the eye and touch after twenty or thirty years is the same after forty or sixty." This is a form of entropy perhaps (the entropic is an important concept in contemporary art, deriving from the influential Robert Smithson). But this sentence rapidly spirals out of meaning or control with the following: "... or sixty, singing, cords, casts, stuck to the bottom."

What disjunction does in the work of Ferguson and her colleagues is to open up language, the Symbolic, the big Other, to what cannot be contained or symbolized or signified. This is the non-meaning that results from play with syntax, as in the paragraph's first sentence, the non-meaning that results from lack of referentiality, as in the "Causality" sentence, the break in the signifying chain that leads to the deflationary rhetoric of the cadaver sentence, and the formal method that is commented upon with the impossible demand to "Adjust connective degenerations."

But these issues also connect to how poetry functions generally in our society, in the West perhaps. Poetry is forever constituted in terms of meaning, meaning being its *objet petit a* (see page 33 for a discussion of this concept), Poetry is always lacking in meaning, lacking in understandability—which is why, on the one hand, high school students are perpetually puzzled by it (perhaps also because of teaching methods which give the reader the sense that she or he has to "get it") and, at the same time, why the same adolescents write so much of it.

In Ferguson's work, however, pleasure (in Lacanian terms, *jouissance*), must be taken in *not* getting it. We may, for example, attempt to reconstitute sentences for more conventional meaning: perhaps the first one would then read "Sometimes it's best to be nice to people while you still have friends." The second one might end "it's a sign of intestinal distress." The third might read "Adjust connective tissues." But this is only to show us what is *not* in the text: our pleasure in reading such a text lies in its closeness to meaning. Proximity might be a better word, suggesting, too, the "prox cards" used in large corporate buildings to gain entry to locked-down areas. But the lack of meaning here is a trace of the Real in the sense that Ferguson's poetry shows how words that possess meaning ("connective," "bottom") can be deployed without meaning: signifiers unhinged from signifieds.

Let us now turn to the third poet whose work exemplifies social collage. The Kevin Davies' excerpt from *Writing Class* (see page 38), is taken from his book *Pause Button*, indeed, from a section of that book which is itself entirely within massive square brackets, each bracket taking up the centre of a page. Immediately we have a series of disruptions of the page and of the voice: the entire 'poem'—if it makes sense to call these thirteen pages (including the brackets) a "poem"—is itself bracketed, that is, excluded or perhaps added (as when we either bracket something from our discussion, or use square brackets to indicate an addition to a quotation). The square brackets, then, are not only both inside and outside the "poem," but they also indicate that the poem itself is either to be left out of the reader's consideration, to be bracketed, or that the poem is an addition to the larger text, to the book *Pause Button*. This same indeterminacy or negation is carried on within our excerpt, which, like the entire section, consists of words or phrases in "braces," {and}, which in mathematics or set theory delimit or specify a set. And surely all of these levels of bracketing and sets alert us to pay attention to the signifier, and to hold as contingent any connection between words, whether at the level of the line, phrase, sentence, or any other form of syntax that is supposed to lead to meaning.

This is not to say that there is no meaning in the text; indeed, in a 2000 interview with Davies, American poet Diane Ward spoke of *Pause Button*'s "generous give and take with information," adding that "by its pauses and what is 'stopped' (framed) by them, it respects many possible sources of information and allows for their ability and right to self- and systemic-critique of content" (Davies and Ward, 5).[3] Note that Ward sees a "give *and* take" of information (my emphasis)—so "{yellow} {flowers}" can connote both yellowness (in a Wittgensteinian sense) and flowers, *and* yellow flowers. What it cannot connote, or at least this would be my argument, is that we should just read "yellow flowers" and ignore the line's separation of words into signifers *qua* signifiers. So, too, "{& mingle more}" one supposes—or, here, grasps at straws—may be a reference to a Shaw/Creede line (from "Close to Naked"): "He called running the perimeter of grade school recess, 'mingling with the guests'" (Shaw 1992, 70).

And when the lines seem to work together—either grammatically, as in "{incomplete} {enough to} {force} {weather}" and "{miserable} {exile} {guards} {public} {rooms}" or in terms of sense, as in "{possible} {government} {surveillance}"—it seems churlish or orthodox to insist that there is *no* meaning involved. Rather, the brackets here contribute to meaning, especially in the "{miserable} {exile}" line where, presumably, the isolation of the signifiers bears a resemblance to the isolation of the {exile}, doomed to working as a security guard.

But there are a number of gaps being suggested here, as well. First of all, the thirteen-page braced poem, centred on the page as it is, in some small way suggests the symmetrical look of a Rorschach test, the pictures made by folding a page of ink in half. While the words themselves are not mirrored, a mirroring is suggested in this section's pages: in each line's centred length, and in the congruent white space that precedes and follows each line—and so, a larger, symmetrical image is apparent on each page. Then, as such signifiers in the Davies quotation as "{incomplete}" and "{possible}" suggest, the question of inside/outside and addition/exclusion also work at the level of the line. At this level, indeterminacy abounds: perhaps the given words on any line are merely part of a larger text that has been obscured, so "{possible} {government} {surveillance}" is taken from the phrase "it's possible that the government is against the surveillance of its citizens," rather like how a desperate movie marketing campaign will plunder negative reviews for positive signifiers. Finally, how are we to read or interpret these three lines:

{to}
{*do*}
{you}

This question—how are we to make meaning?—anticipates what I will, in Chapter Three, refer to in terms of what Lacan designates as the analyst's discourse in his *Seminar XVII* and, in my later chapters, as what both Žižek and Lacan consider in terms of the Italian phrase "*Chè vuoi?*" or "What do you want?" (Lacan 2002, 690*ff*, Žižek 1989, 87*ff*). That is, in terms of this last formulation, our question when we encounter a text of this enigmatic density is—what does the text want, what does it want from me, what does it mean? Does this text want "to do me," and if not in the sense of having sexual intercourse with me, then how? What does Kevin Davies want? And so, turning to how Lacan talks about the analyst's discourse in his seventeenth seminar, we'll consider an interview with students that took place in May 1970, when Lacan was told "[w]hat you say is always decentered in relation to sense, you shun sense." He replied: "This is precisely why my discourse is an analytic discourse. It's the structure of analytic discourse to be like that" (Lacan 2007, 146). Dominiek Hoens elaborates:

> The analytic discourse qua social bond works with and somehow *creates* desire, that is, a desire caused by an object that is neither imaginary nor symbolic. This implies that the subjects involved in analysis relate to each other neither as imaginary equals, nor as individuals occupying the place and position guaranteed by the symbolic order. They relate as radically different, that is, as singulars. The promise of the analytic discourse seems to be that in the current context of the replacement of the particular (master's discourse) by abstract universality (university discourse), there is a scene where, and a social bond in which, the singularity of the subject qua desire can have a place. (in Clemens and Grigg 2006, 93)

I will come to the intricacies of Lacan's four discourses in Chapter Three, as noted (and to the question of "*Chè vuoi?*" in the fifth chapter, on the archive), but Lacan's cryptic comment and Hoens' reading can be used as a way of concluding these remarks on Davies' work. Lacan is arguing that in the clinical situation, the analyst functions as an object of the patient's desire—not merely or only sexual or erotic, but more fundamentally in terms of transference. "What does the analyst want?" becomes "What do I want?" Our desire is always the desire *of* the Other. Trying to bring this clinical insight about desire into a teaching context (at least, Lacan says this is "perhaps precisely" what he does) means not making sense. Lacan goes on to say, "I adhere to it as much as I can, without daring to say that I strictly identify myself with it" (2007, 146). Returning to Davies, if his poem—which is also "decentered in relation to sense"—establishes a form of the "analyst's discourse qua social link," this is because the relation between reader and text is neither an imaginary one (I do not see myself reflected in the lyric I/eye of the poem) nor one guaranteed by the symbolic order (we are not quite sure if this *is* a poem, *is* literature, or if perhaps this text reminds us that poetry or literature are provisional terms for texts and acts and relations that stand outside the normative forms of communication). So here, in reading this poem, in confronting our status as subjects with/of desire, we find a place of resistance to neoliberalism, to the university discourse. (This last will seem like a jump—but it is only to give you a bit of a taste of the third chapter of this book, where such connections between texts, psychoanalysis, and politics will be made more directly.)

III. Red Tories and neopastoralists

With the writers Lisa Robertson, Peter Culley, and Catriona Strang, a different aesthetic, a different practice, is at work. Here is it a question of a usable past, of a genealogy of poetry that attempts to extract, out of modern (the Romantics for Culley) and pre-modern (the Medieval for Strang) traditions, a vocabulary and genre suitable to the present moment. I discuss Culley's work later in this book, but for now, let's begin with the following passage from Catriona Strang's *Low Fancy*:

> In light of my lewdster's GRIEVOUS thrashing at the hands of a pretty popular kind of war, it seems important to emphasize that they were neither PESTILENT nor insane. Compelled by enjoyment, they dreamt up their own splendour, and there is no need to reiterate that their methods opted for potency. My rabble did not TRIFLE within the greasy constraints of their vocabulary. Their voracious blasphemies irritated an established snare to the horizons of its diablerie; it is my own devious duty to strive towards an emulation of such eminent heresy. (1993, 59)

Or from Lisa Robertson's "How Pastoral: A Prologue":

> I needed a genre for the times that I go phantom. I needed a genre to rampage Liberty, haunt the foul freedom of

> silence. I needed to pry loose liberty from an impacted marriage with the soil. I needed a genre to gloss my ancestress' complicity with a socially expedient code; to invade my own illusions of historical innocence. The proud trees, the proud rocks, the proud sky, the proud fields, the proud poor have been held before my glazed face for centuries. I believed they were reflections. (in Klobucar and Barnholden 1999, 108)

Strang's text plunders the thirteenth-century manuscript *Carmina Burana*, a collection of drinking songs and critiques of the Catholic Church perhaps best known via Carl Orff's 1936 libretto of the same name. In Strang's translation, the signifiers are rent asunder, rendered into more signs, in a plunderphonic wonder that pays attention both to Benjamin's "Task of the Translator" and Lacan's distinction between metaphor and metonymy, preferring the condensation of the latter to the substitution of the former. The text is both social and private ("a shifting and private technique in the face of indifferent (if urgent) stimulation," as Strang writes earlier [1993, 19]), a low *fantasy* that is as carnivalesque as it is uncomely, as discourteous as it is courtly, a "low curse" and a "cunning murmur" (both 1993, 47).

But Strang is also concerned with the fissure between the translated text and the translator; here two comments by Benjamin—from his 1921 essay "The Task of the Translator"—are surely pertinent. First, he argues, a translation comes from a work's "afterlife," marks its "stage of continued life" (254) and then it points to an impossible ideal: "the predestined, hitherto inaccessible realm of reconciliation and fulfillment of languages ... that element of translation which goes beyond transmittal of subject matter" (257). This first notion of an afterlife is similar to Benjamin's later development of "messianic time," or the anti-historicist argument that events in history only come to make sense when we understand them according to the urgent political context of today (think of the remixes of the Bangles' "Walk like an

Egyptian" during the Arab uprisings in early 2011). We will see how Benjamin's concept is also similar to Freud's *Nachträglichkeit* or retroactivity—a dream or other symptom only comes to acquire meaning late, all too late. So the lewd lasciviousness that Strang translates/finds in the *Carmina Burana*, which she discovers in the stain of language as much as in "[c]ompelled ... enjoyment," is evidently at one with a certain late twentieth-century feminism. Too, she earlier remarked that her "anonymous striplings harmonized neither reason nor ingenious introspection" (1993, 22), a disavowal of harmonizing (and its well-nigh Jamesonian "imaginary resolution of a real contradiction") that must be read in terms of Strang's over-all project. For *Low Fancy* is also a very high art production, a collaboration with Strang's partner, the jazz musician François Houle, who provides scores in the text. And following immediately upon the critique of harmonizing is a page-turner that shifts from "Next night I'll bop / and suss this dizzy leave" (ibid., 23) to "Nudge a turn day in, day out" (24). That is, in terms of the Symbolic language of jazz, a shift from the Real of bop and Dizzy Gillespie to the Imaginary of Tin Pan Alley ("Day In, Day Out" as recorded by Nat King Cole, Ella Fitzgerald, or Billie Holliday).

"I needed a genre for the times that I go phantom. I needed a genre to rampage Liberty, haunt the foul freedom of silence." As with Strang, when we turn to Robertson, we are dealing with cultural capital, with Pierre Bourdieu's idea that cultural taste establishes, polices, and maintains social distinction and class barriers. In Robertson's texts, use of certain literary codes establishes *bona fides*. Robertson also accumulates cultural capital through historical capital: period pieces, the personification of Liberty, and auto-critique. This need of a genre is also Lacan's "demand" (that which is left when the need is met); is it performative? That is, who is this "I" and who is this I to need a genre? Why? What does a genre do? In *The Political Unconscious*, Jameson has it that "[g]enres are essentially literary *institutions*, or social contracts between a writer and a specific public, whose function is to specify the proper use of a particular marked cultural artifact" (1981, 106).

So we are not talking about the free-floating signification of postmodernist textuality; we are, rather, talking about finely crafted sentences, the ironic use of archaic language—again, a form of cultural capital—that is engaged, nonetheless, in a critique of genre, of the pastoral. As Robertson writes elsewhere in *XEclogue*: "Ontology is the luxury of the landed. Let's pretend you 'had' a land. Then you 'lost' it. Now fondly describe it. That is pastoral." Here we have three crucial statements. First, the question of whether ontology (the philosophy of being, or perhaps being itself) is a classed signifier. Second, the constructed nature of the pastoral, of nature and homeland (a tradition going back to Gertrude Stein and *The Making of Americans* and *The Geographical History of America*). But this much is orthodox post-structuralism, which is not to underestimate the sheer will of poetry necessary to reach that plateau. Third, we have the question of the relation between the text's (indeed, Robertson's *oeuvre's*) cultural capital (via archaic language) and her critique of the same. It is this relation—which in secret we would call dialectical, not to say a contradiction—which is like the quandary in Catriona Strang's work, where the very low fantasy of drunken monks alleviates what is also actually a key text of high culture. For, in effect, Robertson's contradiction removes the very basis of its formulation: its critique of the pastoral amounts to a critique of cultural capital. Or, is the contradiction resolved by Robertson's text being able to accrue cultural capital whilst disavowing it? This is where the text bears most heavily the political weight of its contradictions.

CHAPTER TWO

Empty and Full Speech

> The potential weak point of any kind of contextualization is its thin textual specificity. Contextualization and cultural studies sometimes do not resist an extractive attitude to texts and may elide or erase the specificity of linguistic texture. This issue is particularly acute and meaningful where poetry is concerned. There the challenge is both to contextualize poems and to mediate between their historical and social dimensions and their textual specificity, so that a critical, culturalist reading attends to the detail and can analyze dissonances, slippages, affirmations, and quirks within a range of verbal acts from discourses and semantic layering to the phoneme. That is, one wants any study of poetry to engage with poetry as such—its conventions and textual mechanisms, its surfaces and layers—and not simply to regard the poetic text as an odd delivery system for ideas and themes. As Jean-Jacques Lecercle reminds us in his theory of the opacities of the "remainder," there are culturally evocative, apparently excessive materials beyond the semantic meaning created by a word. These ideas about the density and layeredness of texts point to a post-formalist, yet formally articulate cultural analysis of poetry.
>
> —Rachel Blau DuPlessis 2001, 6–7

I. What I am doing and what I am not doing

In this chapter, I will be looking at the poetry of Susan Clark,[1] Kathryn MacLeod, Dan Farrell, and Melissa Wolsak. My approach—what I have also come to call my *lapproach*[2]—will be primarily Lacanian: especially, I am interested in using these writers' works to elucidate Lacan's theories of language from two key essays in the 1950s, working first with his distinction between empty and full speech, and then with his more structuralist theory of language: not so much to ask why such intensely innovative and formally adventurous poetry came to be written at this time and in this place, but rather, to ask what interpretive problems such poetry poses for the critic, for the reader, for other poets.

Before turning to reading the poetry, I would like to briefly situate the material conditions of the various texts I read here: that is, their status as books, chapbooks, magazines, and anthologies. While the Duplessis quote that begins this chapter might be seen to permit such a bracketing of historicism, what I am *not* going to do here is to provide a richer or more robust introduction to the sociopolitical historicization of this work, though it is both sorely lacking in Canadian academic discourse and, when it has been attempted in other fields, usually inadequate (but see Chapter Five for an archival approach to this history). Nor am I going to work through a reading of Lacanian theory to provide a corpus of keywords and paradigms that can then be called upon for the work of interpretation. Instead, this turn from a historical account to one interested in the status of texts *qua* texts will demonstrate, I hope, that KSW works need to be encountered in the milieu in which they were first published, a milieu that itself contains a history all too often reduced to matters of large-scale political events. Similarly, my quick introduction of theoretical matters will leave their elaboration to the practice of interpretation, allowing for an encounter between the theory and the text, and not merely the application of a reified theory to an idealized text.

As an example of the rich material terrain of KSW literary production, consider the following sites of production for Kathryn MacLeod's work: in April, 1986, the poem "Without Loss at Opposite" first appeared in the magazine *JAG*; in October of that same year, the poem "Circus Darkness" appeared in *Writing* 16; in 1987, the poems "Scrim," "Overqualified," and "Vile, Moral" were published in *Raddle Moon* 5; in 1989, a text "from *Houseworks*" saw release in *Writing* 23/24, and the anthology *East of Main* reprinted "Scrim" and "Overqualified." In 1990, another text "from *Houseworks*" appeared in *Motel* 3; in 1991, the poem "The Infatuation" in *The Capilano Review*; in 1992, "Oh, theory" and "Asylum" saw publication in *Raddle Moon* 11; in 1996, her book-length collection *mouthpiece* was published by Tsunami Editions, including work from *Writing*, *Raddle Moon* 11, *Motel* and elsewhere; and the 1999 anthology *Writing Class* included "The Infatuation" and "One Hour out of Twenty-four" (both from *mouthpiece*) and "Asylum."

This list spans thirteen years and includes magazines that were essentially photocopied typescript, often saddle-stitched or stapled at the corner (*JAG*, early *Writing*, *Motel*); those with more polished offset printing in book form (*Raddle Moon*, *The Capilano Review*, and later *Writing*); two key Vancouver anthologies (*East of Main*, *Writing Class*); and a stand-alone book (*mouthpiece*). All of these sites were local or regional. *JAG* billed itself as a magazine for DTUC émigrés (the David Thompson University Centre whose shutdown precipitated the formation of the KSW); *Raddle Moon* itself had moved over from Vancouver Island to Vancouver[3]; *Writing*, long the house magazine for the KSW, was at first published out of Nelson at DTUC[4]; *The Capilano Review* was based at Capilano College (now University) in North Vancouver and *East of Main* situated itself resolutely, and perhaps controversially, in the eastern half of Vancouver.[5] MacLeod's work also appeared in American magazines alongside fellow-travellers of KSW or post-Language poetry: *Big Allis* (New York), *How(ever)* (San Francisco), *Avec* (California), and *chain* (Buffalo).

Institutional and cultural capital issues are also apparent in this survey of MacLeod's work: Canadian sites were either in the academic institutions (*The Capilano Review*) or had moved from inside to outside (*Raddle Moon* began as a University of Victoria magazine; *Writing* made a similar shift); similarly, in the US, *chain* was associated with the writing program at SUNY Buffalo. This migration into and out of the academy is utterly key to understanding the KSW poetics, I would argue: the KSW is determinedly bohemian. And while MacLeod's work was published in the two book anthologies of avant-garde Vancouver poetry (*East of Main* and *Writing Class*), it was not included in two other key anthologies: the special issues of *West Coast Line: The New Vancouver Writing Issue,* no less, in 1990 and *Raddle Moon 17: 22 Vancouver Poets* in 1999.

When I was working on this chapter, my office at Simon Fraser University faced the University Library; indeed, I could see the outside edge of the building's top floor where the Contemporary Literature Collection (CLC) was housed, a collection that included many of the small magazines in which MacLeod's work first appeared. Wanting to examine some of these, I went over to Special Collections at around four p.m. on a weekday afternoon, forgetting that that collection closed at four-thirty. I was, however, able to see copies of *Motel*, which came from the collection of retired SFU professor, poet, and critic Roy Miki. Charmingly, or perhaps as a trace of racialized misrecognition, Miki's name was spelled "Mikki" on *Motel*'s address labels—both when handwritten for the first issue, and then computer-generated. *JAG* magazine was what I really wanted to see, but it was not in the CLC—rather, the library's online catalogue told me it was in the Lam Collection, in the sub-sub-basement (shades of Bartleby! or, rather, the sub-sub-librarian of *Moby-Dick*). So I then went down from the seventh floor of the library to this sub-sub-basement, where the Lam Collection turned out to be a series of moveable shelves. At the far left, the shelf went up to the end of "J"—but it did not, in fact, move. Luckily, *JAG* was near the end of the shelf and just visible, between something with *Italian* in its title and a German *Jahrbuch*. I had to lean in, over dusty disassembled shelves on the floor, to pull out the bound issues of this holy grail, this *objet a*. The magazine, this iteration of mid-1980s Vancouver poetry had, that afternoon, been functioning as the object of my desire—which is not to say that I really wanted the magazine (although I did), but rather that, as Lacan argues, the magazine took the place of the *objet a*: this structural place that not only taught me to desire, but protected me from the abyss of my desire. Now that I know where the magazine is (on Jason Wiens' recommendation—via Facebook—I requested that the issue be moved to the CLC), it no longer functions in that way.

II. Empty and full (1): Dan Farrell, Susan Yarrow, and empty speech

In a funny, perceptive, but also passive-aggressive article on the work of Susan Clark, Edward Byrne argues that Clark's writing "*is* post-romantic. It's delirious not realist, excessive not minimal, dialectical not analytical, philosophical not sociological" (2008, 10). My argument in this chapter will be that, on the contrary, Clark's (and MacLeod's and Farrell's and Wolsak's) work is both excessive and minimal. I would like to sketch out what I mean by "both excessive and minimal" in terms of Lacan's theories of language from the 1950s, reading texts by these poets that deal first with this notion of absence/excessiveness and then the question of procedural poetics.

First of all, this is writing that refuses reference, refusing either the readability of a Jeff Derksen poem (which, as in "from International Muscle Cars," asks "How is this 'my world' / any more than the typeface/of the Boston Pizza logo (mimetic) / or the eggman (realism) of Humpty's Family / Restaurant" [1998, 98]) or the erotic affect of Lisa Robertson's *XEclogue* ("This is how Lady M enters: Sinuously flanked by Roaring Boys who pan her stance with flicks of birch" [1993, n.p.]).

The poems I look at in this chapter are minimal in the rejection of reference, but maximal (or excessive) in textual production, in how they make the production of signifiers into their own non-referential site. This play of minimal and excessive, then, may be further elucidated with a turn to Lacan's early theories of language.

Two key essays of Lacan's from the 1950s are "The Function and Field of Speech and Language in Psychoanalysis" (in 2002, 198–268) and "The Instance of the Letter in the Unconscious, or Reason since Freud" (in 2002, 412–41). In the first essay, given as a talk at a psychoanalytic conference in Rome in 1953 (and thus often referred to as the "Rome discourse"), Lacan introduces the distinction between "full" and "empty" speech, a largely Heideggerian dualism he uses to talk about the clinical situation, contrasting the *empty speech* of a patient babbling on about nothing as a way to avoid getting at the real neurosis or trauma, with the *full speech* of a moment when a patient actually begins to talk about what is happening in his or her difficulty. In the second essay, a talk delivered at the Sorbonne in 1957, Lacan has much more comprehensively moved into a Saussurean or structuralist problematic, and here discusses signifiers and signifieds, the signifying chain, and the sliding of the signified under the signifier. Especially relevant for our purposes is Lacan's discussion of the *point de capiton*, the "button tie," and its role in retroactively fixing meaning in any given utterance.

In the "Rome discourse" Lacan is doing two things that are germane to our purposes here in talking about poetry. He is stressing the importance of psychoanalysts paying attention to speech in the clinical situation, in analysis. And, he is saying that there are two different kinds of speech that take place in that situation. For Lacan, then, empty speech is that "in which the subject seems to speak in vain about someone who—even if he were such a dead ringer for him that you might confuse them—will never join him in the assumption of his desire" (2002, 211).

In this vein, consider the following from Dan Farrell's "1988" chapbook *ape* [6]:

> a tiring
> the exhausting
> We set up the demons and let the turtles roam. There the
> day in the day's tingled.
> (n.p.)

There is an emptiness, an absence at work in these lines (which comprise—with more space than this quotation shows between the first two lines and the second two—an entire page of the chapbook). "A tiring" what? "The exhausting" what? The "day in the day's tingled" how? Is there a chronological shift from the present participles ("tiring" and "exhausting") to the past participle ("day's tingled")? Which is not to argue that poetry must make rational sense, but rather that the poem's departure from sense takes place in terms of this emptiness, an emptiness that is also temporal.

We can see the same strategy at work in Susan Clark's writing, such as in a text (published under the name of Susan Yarrow) with the title "From 'Not not'" (how's that for emptiness, or at least full-fledged Freudian[7] negation?):

> —I was in the middle and couldn't see—
> "a" instead of "I"
> Is there nothing unimportant on which I can wipe my
> hands?
> (1990, 77)

Is my argument, then, that the work of Farrell or Yarrow is empty of meaning, and therefore morally or politically empty? If we listen to this poem, and "a" is substituted for "I" in the line "I was in the middle and couldn't see"—so that we have "a was in the middle and couldn't see"—does this simply fetishize lack of meaning, emptiness, under the guise of showing the poetic procedure or process?

I want to try to answer these questions by returning to Lacan, whose distinction between empty and full speech does appear, at first glance, to be clichéd 1950s existentialism, rife with an appeal to authenticity and second-hand Sartre. And this is how Dylan Evans frames the difference: "Lacan draws on Heidegger's distinction between *Rede* (discourse) and *Gerede* (chatter) to elaborate his own distinction between 'full speech' (*parole plein*) and 'empty speech' (*parole vide*)" (2005, 191). But I don't think that that is quite how Lacan makes the distinction. He remarks, in the "Rome discourse:"

> Indeed, however empty his discourse may seem, it is only so if taken at face value—the value that justifies Mallarmé's remark, in which he compares the common use of language to the exchange of a coin whose obverse and reverse no longer bear but eroded faces, and which people pass from hand to hand 'in silence.' The metaphor suffices to remind us that speech, even when almost completely worn out, retains its value as *tessera*. Even if it communicates nothing, discourse represents the existence of communication; even if it denies the obvious, it affirms that speech constitutes truth; even if it is destined to deceive, it relies on faith in testimony. (2002, 209)

Which is to argue, then, that in Farrell's text, "a tiring" and "the exhausting" are shown in their emptiness, not because they do not refer to anything immediately present—such is the condition of poetry, or perhaps language—but because they "represent the existence of communication," because their lack of meaning is itself a form of meaning. Here we have texts that are, *pace* Byrne, minimal. And this minimalism is related to the worn-out nature of language, of speech, to its status as fragment or *tessera*, as seen in the fragments in Farrell, but also in the splintering of the sentence that Yarrow's em-dashes signify: "—I was in the middle and couldn't see—."

But let us engage with my claim that there is an emptiness here and with what it means to read in this way. After that, we will turn to Lacan's other theories of language (first full speech, and then the full-dress structuralism of "The Instance of the Letter") and what they can do to help us read the work of Farrell, MacLeod, Wolsak, and Clark/Yarrow. But for now, I would like to stay with Susan Yarrow's "From 'Not not.'" The piece itself appeared in the inaugural (1990) issue of *West Coast Line*, a journal emanating from Simon Fraser University that combined, under the editorial work of Roy Miki, his former poetics journal *Line* and Fred Candelaria's *West Coast Review*. This first issue of *West Coast Line* was subtitled "The New Vancouver Writing Issue" and had work by many writers associated with the KSW: from Deanna Ferguson and Colin Browne to Dennis Denisoff and Dorothy Trujillo Lusk; it also included work by such Vancouver artists as Mina Totino (the cover), Kathy Slade, Jin-me Yoon, and Stan Douglas, and a review essay on Tsunami chapbooks by Fred Wah.

This editorial context suggests various reading strategies with which one might approach Yarrow's text. Byrne's Vancouver-centric one (which is to say, situating Yarrow's work in terms of its exclusion from the *Writing Class* anthology) is exemplary in this regard. So if my turn to a Lacanian infrastructure is sensible in some ways (Lacan being in the canon of European theory), it is perverse in others. Unlike Byrne, I am not so much interested here in Clark's editorial work at *Raddle Moon*,[8] or her position in or out of KSW proper; rather, I am proposing a way of reading her work in synchronicity with others in that poetic orbit.

So what does this notion of empty speech have to say about "From 'Not not'"? The poem itself is structured as twelve pages, from "page 7 [following '...our delicate gluttony, without harm']" (which appears on page 76 in *West Coast Line*) to "page 18," which ends "(see also: 'plute')" (on 81). The variety of typographical and punctuation devices in Yarrow's text make it deliriously difficult to quote. Not only are the "page" references in small caps, but the note after "page 7" is, in Yarrow's poem, in square brackets; when quoted, the square brackets makes the words within look like my own intervention (and brings to mind Kevin Davies' text from *Pause Button*, discussed in the previous chapter). This postmodern play with the page, with type and signifiers, is thus about the very possibility of quotation—both the poem as quoting from another text (whether or not it is called "Not not"), and the poem in turn being quoted. In a certain way, a poetic line like

> PAGE 7 [following '...our delicate gluttony, without harm']

is a wonderful example of empty speech. For this is a poem that, whether or not it actually is referring to another text which has in it the lines "...our delicate gluttony, without harm," makes its reference into a gesture or text that itself will be emptied out by further citation. "From 'Not not'" anticipates its own citation, its own status as empty speech, in its opening lines.

The poem is thus in some way about citation, about engaging with the speech of the Other, the speech of another text. But the poem also refuses clear indicators of citation: lines may be flush left or indented; enclosed in parentheses or set off by em-dashes; short and on their own or almost prose-paragraphs. Here are a few other lines from the poem:

> As the weather in the province's far north or some words overheard enlarge us. (77)
> A month gapes. Her tangled face. Friendly, allowable violence. (All this *time* I've refused, but also sequence.) (78)
> Writing with some urgency atop a great pile of different papers, somehow 18th-centuryish. Those famous men were cramped for space. (79)
> —The longer sentences are often voiced but unaddressed— (81)[9]

In these passages, emptiness may be thematic ("A month gapes," the sense of the size of British Columbia and its far north), structural (overheard words), a matter of absence (the presumably unread "great pile of different papers") or psychoanalytic (in sentences that are "voiced but unaddressed," there is the question of to whom the poem or speaker is talking).

But if such emptiness is constitutive to this poem, what happens when I take it seriously? What happens when a critic or reader listens to empty words, reads them and, perhaps, echoes them back? Or is that what criticism does? Is criticism simply a matter of filling in the emptiness, providing referential footnotes (as in my sense that "the weather in the ... far north" refers to British Columbia)? Lacan talks about precisely this issue, the analyst reflecting back the analysand's empty speech, and what he has to say about it contributes to my feeling that even as he is sketching out its distinction from full speech he does not want to totally abandon the value of empty speech. Make no mistake: as will become evident, Lacan lays his money on full speech; but I get the feeling that his clinical experience does not let him totally dismiss empty speech:

> Responding to the subject's empty speech—even and especially in an approving manner—often proves, by its effects, to be far more frustrating than silence. Isn't it, rather, a frustration that is inherent in the subject's very discourse? Doesn't the subject become involved here in an ever greater dispossession of himself as a being, concerning which—by dint of sincere portraits which leave the idea of his being no less incoherent, of rectifications that do not succeed in isolating its essence, of stays and defenses that do not prevent his statue from tottering, of narcissistic embraces that become like a puff of air in animating it—he ends up recognizing that this being has never been anything more than his own construction [*oeuvre*] in the imaginary and

> that his construction undercuts all certainty in him? For in the work he does to reconstruct it *for another*, he encounters anew the fundamental alienation that makes him construct it *like another*, and that has always destined it to be taken away from him *by another*. (2002, 207–08)[10]

Finally, if we read these writers of absence in terms of empty speech, the rejoinder may well be that we are paying too much attention in trying to interpret writing that insists on its nonreferentiality (see Byrne); our answer of course, which is the answer of the stereotypical English lit professor or critic or scholar, is that it is our job to "read too much into it," to see meaning where none may lie. Parsing Lacan, our job is first to look at these "sincere portraits" produced during empty speech as "being no less incoherent"; then to uncorrect (or, in the jargon of the Word program, "undo") these "rectifications that do not succeed in isolating its essence." Next, to undo the "stays and defenses that do not prevent his statue from tottering," while perhaps thinking of stays as akin to the corset; and thus to fully engage in the "narcissistic embraces that become like a puff of air." Which is to say, for the poet, "in the work he does to reconstruct it *for another*" or for the reader, "he encounters anew the fundamental alienation that makes him construct it *like another*" in terms of the tradition, "and that has always destined it to be taken away from him *by another*" or the anxiety of influence. Lacan's poetic repetition here, *for another/ like another/by another*, moves us into a different direction, finally: into the realm of the community and the tradition, the national and the local, other poets and poetic contexts.

III. Empty and full (2): Kathryn MacLeod, Dan Farrell, and full speech

We are heading in the direction of Lacan's full speech, the speech that the patient makes of her history (Lacan refers to the hysteric "Anna O," a patient of Freud's colleague Josef Breuer who invented the term "talking cure" [2002, 211]). For Lacan goes on immediately, in his "Rome discourse," to make two arguments around full speech. The first argument is that full speech can be heard in that part of a discourse that is most significant, that is read against itself, in which a mistake reveals all, or where silence stands in for the whole. The second argument is that it is the breaking off of discourse (silence, breaking off—we still seem to be in the land of empty speech, of absence and tessera, don't we?) that brings about full meaning. So Lacan argues that full speech is both a matter of the substance and its framing. But he also uses the language of poetics in this argument, referring to the interruption of the patients' discourse as "scansion." So let's return to MacLeod's "The Infatuation" to see how this "full speech" works with some actual poetry[11]:

> ... messy liquids ... uninvited failure
> a collection of substantial size ...
> your nipples visible through t-shirt ...
> ... exchange an old one for a new one ...
> brief morality ... angry about "the masterpiece"
> unmaking the bed. evasive.
> ... completion or celebration, erected
> out of boredom ... my right point of view ...
> relax/antagonize ... complete the sentence
> ... his hard line ...
> (MacLeod in Klobucar and Barnholden 1999, 77)

"The Infatuation" foregrounds the separation of words graphically: in this case, through the use of ellipses. Like Emily Dickinson's dashes, the ellipses separate and join: they are a form of Lacanian interruption.[12] As in the earlier discussion (see page 34), the poem may be said to loosely be about a love affair, from its first verse-stanza: "keep it hard the whole time," to its final verse stanza: "... sexual arsenal ... delicate subversive ... punitive silence, sentenced to naked women ... dreams of a long cock betrayed him" (1999, 76–79). Again, this referential content or narrative is then subverted by the formal constraint of the ellipses through which MacLeod suggests something missing, something absent. Like full speech, the punctuation here speaks. "Messy liquids" and "uninvited failure" may suggest the material conditions of sexual intercourse—*coitus interruptus*, perhaps, or premature ejaculation, or even the messy liquids of sperm, lubricant, spermicide, and so on. But, again, the text itself is messy, in a way, with all of these dots, visible like the nipples "through t-shirt."

Once more, the ellipses suggest the rhythm that Thomas detects in Céline, here a languorous pace, one that is laid-back in a way that conflicts neatly with the precision of the images. One can imagine MacLeod genially listing off these observations or phrases, a listing that itself becomes a commentary of sorts on the law of equivalence. By this I mean the Marxist theory of commodification, where the quantitative exchange-value trumps use-value. Thus it is that in foregoing the syntactical crutch of conventional poetry—the lyric I, the grammatically regular sentence—this poetry makes evident how language itself is commodified: not simply, in a Naomi Klein sense, as a brand-name or logo, but, more profoundly, as a discourse. As equivalence is signalled by the "equal signs" in the title of the journal *L=A=N=G=U=A=G=E*, so in MacLeod's text, is the equivalence of all phrases signalled by ellipses. "Messy liquids" are the same as "uninvited failure," which is the same as "a collection of substantial size" and so on. The rhythm of the poem, then, ensuing from its parade of equivalence, acquires a meaning.

Earlier, we discussed how this rhythm can be misleading in two different ways: first, if we ignore the gaps, second, if we overlook the variations in the punctuation. Ellipses signify, in the genre of an academic quotation, that words are missing; in other conventions, they simply mean a segue of some kind, a transition. The disjunctive nature of MacLeod's poem in general suggests the first meaning, but the great disparity between one phrase and another (say, between the abstract description of "a collection of substantial size" and the more intimate and concrete image of "your nipples visible through t-shirt") also means that we cannot hope to fill in the missing text. "The Infatuation" can be read as an intervention into a pre-existing discourse, a forcing out of the significant. The ellipses are the simulation of absence, then: its signifier.

To expand our earlier reading, a second problem with just thinking about the ellipses is that we may ignore other forms of punctuation in the text: in this excerpt, the use of quotation marks around "the masterpiece," the periods after "bed" and "evasive," the virgule between "relax" and "antagonize"; the use of italics elsewhere in the poem and, no doubt the most subtle or complicated issue, the use of double sets of ellipses. The quotation marks around "the masterpiece" do a number of different things: they make it difficult to quote the words or the punctuation itself (similar problems lie in Susan Yarrow's work, as I argue above); they suggest that the masterpiece is not really a masterpiece; and they suggest that the phrase "the masterpiece" is a direct quote (a suggestion which may support the second reading, that the masterpiece is only putatively such). The periods in "unmaking the bed. evasive." *undoes* the role/rule of ellipses in the poem, and also is a kind of evasiveness. Too, the virgule between relax and antagonize suggests the on/off binary nature of the slash (i.e., either relax or antagonize—at first, we may think of the substitution function of the slash) that is also rather passive-aggressive (do you mean "relax" or "antagonize"?—although, given the right context, one person's relaxation might antagonize someone else).

Earlier, we considered a penultimate reading of the ellipsis: in his essay "Discourse in Poetry: Bakhtin and Extensions of the Dialogical," Michael Davidson argued for a social-semiotic reading of how "contextual frames" worked in contemporary poetry. Specifically, he said that in such writing the "gap between elements is asserted as a sign itself, not simply as a caesura between two elements in a theorem" (1983, 146). And in addition to the argument I made on the meanings of this signal form of punctuation, which joins and separates, which signifies absence as well as transition, we pointed to something new that Davidson brought to our discussion. That is, the idea that the "gap"—for our purposes, the ellipses—brings attention to "contextual frames." By this I think he means the notion of ideology as a discursive construction, or the significatory processes by which ideology functions.

But my earlier use of this argument from Davidson is both overdetermined and serendipitous. Davidson's essay appears in *Codes of Signals: Recent Writings in Poetics*, a 1983 collection edited by Michael Palmer, and a copy of which I purchased in 1985 at the New Poetics Colloquium organized by the KSW in Vancouver. I had turned to Davidson's essay as a way to bring some Bakhtinian theory into this text. In 2009, when I was writing this section of the book, I mentioned the Davidson text to Jeff Derksen in a conversation. To my unreasonable joy, Derksen said that that essay was a key text in the mid-1980s for KSW writers—"in the bar," he added—the bar being, for Derksen, an important site of poetic investigations and dialogue. Which is not to say that now that I know the essay was being discussed I feel it warrants inclusion in my chapter, but nonetheless, this can function as my own private fetishistic disavowal—*I know very well that theory forbids the use of biographical minutiae, and yet here I can use it to bolster my argument.*

Now, if MacLeod's poem shows us in a deliberate way what happens when things are left out or cut off by displaying the marks of that castration, a Dan Farrell poem works from the other end. Let's look once more at the opening lines of Farrell's poem "Intent," from his collection *Thimking of You*:

> Late in the dream my sides shorten they ha
> d course. I came to accuse him of my cold

> act but my testimony goes off. It came to
> that? It came to catch that. Every opposit
> e towards him hid in the privily spur. A c
> (Farrell 1994, n.p.)

Again, the first and most evident form of "meaning" here has to do with form: with the sudden ending of lines in the middle of words and then new lines beginning with letters that "finish" the previous words but arbitrarily.[13] The disjunction between and within words, you will recall, opens meaning up: a surplus meaning is performed, rather than a fixed or restricted meaning. What this means here is two different things.

First of all, we now bring to our reading a sense of Lacan's claim that the punctuation of a therapeutic session (Lacan's famous "ten-minute sessions"[14]) could generate meaning: "It is, therefore, a propitious punctuation that gives meaning to the subject's discourse. This is why the ending of the session—which current technique makes into an interruption that is determined purely by the clock and, as such, takes no account of the thread of the subject's discourse—plays the part of a scansion which has the full value of an intervention by the analyst that is designed to precipitate concluding moments. Thus we must free the ending from its routine framework and employ it for all the useful aims of analytic technique" (2002, 209).

As I noted previously, Lacan's use of the word "scansion" suggests this passage's usefulness to a critique of poetry. But perhaps I have it wrong. Is Lacan not arguing here specifically *against* the arbitrary intervention (the "routine framework") that Farrell employs in "Intent"? I think not; rather, the proper analogy for the usual ending of a psychoanalytic session (the fifty-minute hour, the "routine framework") would be when, in a typically type-set page of prose, certain words are broken up—as, on page 209 of Fink's translation of *Écrits*, we have "con-", "inti-", "reinte-", "sub-", "com-", and "descrip-". What Farrell's technique does is to make such moments into full speech, to transform the arbitrary sundering of words into meaningful and poetic signifiers.

As discussed earlier, according to standard structuralist or semiotic theory, signs acquire their meaning conventionally: language works by assigning signifiers to signifieds. Once more, "late in the dream" has a fairly fixed meaning: a temporal designation. But Lacanian theory argues that there is always something left over, something sticking out, something that doesn't quite fit into the symbolic order of language. And poetry, and especially language poetry, is the place where that extra is brought into play (for a more thorough discussion of this approach, see page 31). But what is surely striking in Farrell's interrupted language, in his cutting off of the speech, is how we suddenly arrive at surplus meaning, surplus language.

Again, the creation of meaning by what comes later in the sentence illustrates or is a connection between two different aspects of Lacan's theory. His discourse on full speech, and on the role of the interruption, is connected to his theory of logical time and, more specifically, the Freudian notion of *Nachträglichkeit*, or retroactivity.[15] That is, for Lacan, meaning in a sentence is always retroactive, or arrived at later. His diagram for this is as follows:

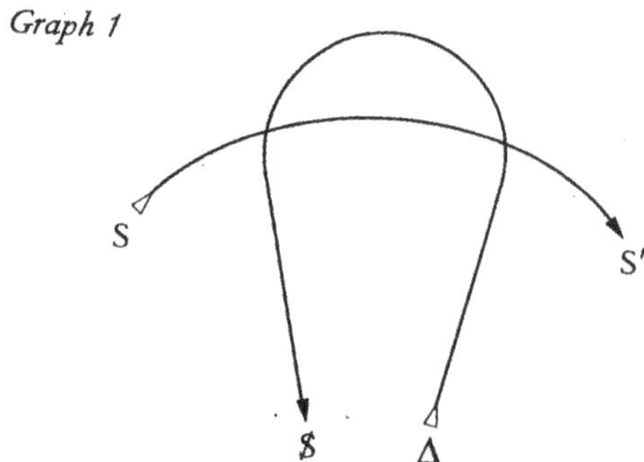

GRAPH 1. (Source: Lacan 2002, 681. Copyright W.W. Norton and Company, used by permission.)

As Lacan explains, we assume that language proceeds from S to S′, from one subject to another or, following syntax, from the beginning to the end of a sentence. But the arc from the triangle cuts through language. The triangle moves counter to the syntactic line, and begins with ¾, which represents our status in the Real (as beings before language, but also some mythic pre-intention) and loops back to the $, which represents the barred or split subject (the idea that we only exist in language and are therefore always castrated beings of lack). The movement of this triangle's arc, counter to the current of syntax, shows us that the meaning of the first word in a sentence (the second place of the arc) is determined by the second word. This process is then Lacan's button-tie or *point de capiton*.[16]

Again, Farrell's "Late in the dream my sides shorten they ha" does not necessarily have to mean that the last word of the line is only *part* of a word, after all: it may be an exclamation of delight, the patient or poet's joy at such a *fune* line (a fine or a fun line). And yes, even if the pattern in the poem seems to be to leave off words and then add their probable endings to the next line, since the lines are only approximately the same length (and not the same character length), there are still other possibilities.

IV. The structuralist turn: Yarrow, but then Melissa Wolsak

Susan Yarrow's poem "From 'Not not'" begins with a quote from Samuel Johnson's *Lives of the English Poets*:

> *It is possible,*' says Hooker, '*that by long circumduction from any one truth, all truth may be inferred.* (Yarrow 1990, 76)

The epigraph that opens Yarrow's poem is presented without a closing quotation mark, placing her entire poem into the category of what Richard Hooker said. But the form of rhetorical logic being presented here by Johnson/Hooker, that of circumduction, has a little resemblance to Lacan's structuralist theory of language propounded four years after the Rome discourse in his 1957 essay "The Instance of the Letter in the Unconscious, or Reason since Freud." I am referring to Lacan's notion of the signifying chain, and to the key distinction he makes between metaphor and metonymy (borrowing from, and perhaps mangling, Jakobson). As a theoretical frame for a final discussion in this chapter, that of a Melissa Wolsak text, I would like now to turn to Lacan's essay.

Lacan's semiotic or structuralist theory of language can be summed up in the following manner: first, in an extreme version of Saussure, the signifier is absolutely distinct from ("barred" from) the signified; then, meaning is dependent upon both the syntagmatic axis (or the realm of grammar) and the paradigmatic chain (or the realm of semantics), but not in a linear fashion (meaning is retrospective: see my discussion of Freud's *Nachträglichkeit* or Lacan's *point de capiton* previous). The signifying chain, then, is the "links by which a necklace firmly hooks onto a link of another necklace made of links" (2002, 418); finally, Lacan's metaphor and metonymy refer to Freud's notions of the dreamwork and the processes of condensation and displacement in particular. So, first of all, the signifier (the word) is to be distinguished from the signified (the concept it gives rise to) and, according to Saussure, there is an arbitrary relation between the two. But bringing in Lacan's penchant for topographies and diagrams, the line in the S/*s* formula (for Signifier/signified) is as absolute as the one, say, between the conscious and the unconscious.[17] For Lacan, the bar between the signifier and signified is as real as the rails of a train, as terrible as the phallus. Therefore meaning is, in Derrida's sense, a matter of both difference and deferral:[18] the meaning of cat is that the sign is different from hat or mat, and it is continually deferred because we never get at a signified, we only get at another signifier, another word. But also the following: meaning, once it is used in language, is never contained in a sign in any kind of grammatical or poetical or textual context:

> For the signifier, by its very nature, always anticipates meaning by deploying its dimension in some sense before it. As is seen at the level of the sentence when the latter is interrupted before the significant term: 'I'll never...,' 'The fact remains ...,' 'Still perhaps ...' Such sentences nevertheless make sense, and that sense is all the more oppressive in that it is content to make us wait for it.
>
> But the phenomenon is no different, which—making her appear, with the sole postponement of a 'but,' as comely as the Shulamite, as honest as a virtuous maiden—adorns and readies the Negress for the wedding and the poor woman for the auction block.
>
> Whence we can say that it is in the chain of the signifier that meaning *insists*, but that none of the chain's elements *consists* in the signification it can provide at that very moment. (2002, 419)

Let us put some of this to work, then, and look at a few lines from Melissa Wolsak's *The Garcia Family Co-mercy*:

how does he.
                    get his fur, to go like that
          pimpernel   upsurge
            lupins   wading
                    Minnie   and her lips
(Wolsak 1994, n.p.)

The first two lines instantiate Lacan's notion of the signifying chain: we do not know who this "he" is or what he is doing; and we want to know how he's doing it. But the full stop period after "he" draws our attention to the gap between that phrase and the next line, a line that is itself subdivided by a comma. The meaning, then, is something like: "how does he"? "How does he" what? "How does he get his fur?" "How does he get his fur" as in does he buy it or shoot an animal for it? No, as in how does he get it "to go like that," to be draped or fuzzy or stinky. And of course, the meaning that unfolds does not lie in this variety of meanings, our arrival at each meaning, or even in the plethora of meanings. In *Lacan to the Letter*, Bruce Fink has argued that Lacan does not so much say that there is no meaning as there is all too much meaning (2004, 88). Rather, the meaning of this passage is how meaning itself is dependent on language. The meaning of "fur" is not an animal's outer covering but a signifier occupying a place in the structure of words on the page. The meaning of fur is contiguous (in more than one way); that is, it lies in proximal relations. For example, consider the poem's use of the word "upsurge": "fur" is both spatially close on the page to "upsurge" and phonetically similar (the look and sound of the phoneme "ur"). In a similar vein, "pimpernel" and "upsurge" and "lupins" and "Minnie" and "lips" are connected metonymically by the "p" and "in" and "up" and "pi"/ "ip" and "im"/"Mi" and so on (for more on such play with phonemes, see Jakobson's essay "Linguistics and Poetics," where he discusses Poe's turn of "Raven" into "never" [2008, 157–58]).

So far, this seems like uncontroversial formalism, but Lacan goes further in a way that is useful to how we think about Wolsak's poem. For he argues that the sliding of the signifier, as we have seen here, the metonymic slippage (here, in the decomposition of the signifiers into their constituent letters and sounds), is also how desire works. Desire, he writes, is "caught in the rails of metonymy, eternally extending toward the *desire for something else*" (2002, 518). Which is to say that desire and language are always tied up in each other. As if in confirmation of this, when I discussed my interpretation-in-process with Melissa Wolsak in July 2009, she provided me with wonderfully relevant information on the process of writing the poem. That was a busy, but also casual, conversation and evening—we were at the launch of a book of mine—and when we chatted via Facebook a few days later I told her I wouldn't use the background information without checking with her first (at the back of my mind was anxiety over the ethical release forms I was supposed to give anyone I interviewed according to SFU research protocols—was a conversation in a bookstore liable to such legalistic interdiction?). But whatever wonderful information Wolsak passed on to me has, to the chagrin of literary history, disappeared into the ether.[19]

CHAPTER THREE

Social Collage and the Four Discourses

The reason it is difficult to talk about
the meaning of a poem—in a way that doesn't seem
frustratingly superficial or partial—is that by
designating a text a poem, one suggests that its
meanings are to be located in some 'complex' beyond an accumulation of devices & subject matters.
A poetic *reading* can be given to any
piece of writing; a 'poem' may be understood as
writing specifically designed to absorb, or inflate
with, proactive—rather than reactive—styles of
reading. 'Artifice' is a measure of a poem's
intractability to being read as the sum of its
devices & subject matters. In this sense,
'artifice' is the contradiction of 'realism', with
its insistence on presenting an unmediated
(immediate) experience of facts, either of the
'external' world of nature or the 'internal' world
of the mind; for example, naturalistic
representations or phenomenological consciousness
mapping. Facts in poetry are primarily
factitious.
—Bernstein 1992, 9

A note on method

After the previous chapter's deep immersion in the Lacan of the 1950s, it may be useful to return to the question of why I have turned to Lacanian psychoanalysis as a way of reading the work of the Kootenay School of Writing and, in that regard, perhaps address the question of historical and ahistorical readings. First of all, my turn to psychoanalysis is in response to a double lack. On the one hand, in the readings of contemporary poetry, there is very little to be found that engages with Lacan to any great extent. On the other hand, the great resurgence of Lacanian theory and criticism since the 1990s (owing to Slavoj Žižek's output and to the "clinical turn" that saw a new translation of *Écrits* and many of the *Seminars*) has tended to look at popular culture (especially film) or politics, but not poetry. This double absence is curious, not least because of the importance of Lacanian and Lacanian-feminist readings to such significant avant-garde forbears as Gertrude Stein.[1] Nonetheless, the strength of both these discourses—Lacanian theory on the one hand, and KSW and other L=A=N=G=U=A=G=E-based schools on the other—suggested that an intervention into both could be a useful new critical practice.

My designation of this absence as "curious" is not adequate as a scholarly inquiry into critical fashions[2] and there may be another reason for this lack: the misconception that Lacanian or psychoanalytic readings are ahistorical and, therefore, apolitical. For a number of reasons, I think that this is a misreading of Freud and Lacan (not to mention such obviously political and left commentators as Žižek and Jodi Dean). Both Freud and Lacan have made important statements on the political and historical nature of psychoanalysis; their bodies of work and writings can and have themselves been historicized, especially in terms of "early" or "late" Freud or Lacan; and, especially with respect to Lacan's theory of the four discourses, which arose in the late 1960s in the context of the student protests of May 1968 in Paris, these are obviously discourses that are very much based on a political intervention into late capitalist society. So I would like here to expand quickly on these qualifying statements, before turning to the interpretive work of this chapter.

Freud's statements on politics or history can be thought of in two ways: first of all, he was very much interested, even as early as *The Interpretation of Dreams* (1899), in how political events made their way into the subject's dreams—even if such matter was merely content for the dreamwork (for its condensation and displacement, its translation and revision). He never saw the everyday, be it political or more mundane, as unimportant—this was the raw material which the analyst, as much as the patient, had to work with (see also McGrath for a social history of "the politics of hysteria"). Obviously the "Rat Man" case study, so named for one of this patient's obsessive thoughts, would be a very different piece of writing if not for the military context of late nineteenth-century Central Europe. In Freud's later period, and especially in *Civilization and its Discontents* (1930), the historical situation of Western society—even if viewed through a Eurocentric lens—is undeniably foregrounded as Freud philosophizes on our compulsion for order and desire to maintain sexual proprieties. But there is another way in which both Freud and Lacan are always, unremittingly, historical, and this lies in their attention to the everyday life of the patient, to a social history (albeit one that, in Freud's case, was especially constrained by the middle-class nature of his client's demographics). Thus Lacan notes in the "Rome discourse" that the "unconscious is the chapter of my history that is marked by a blank or occupied by a lie: it is the censored chapter" (2002, 259), and goes on to speak of the "archival documents" of childhood memories. These references are more than metaphors in Lacan's practice; they remind us of how historical investigation itself, over the past half-century, has come to view the social in terms of a bottom-up popular history, one that is as much derived from the archives as from official statements. There is also the historicization of Lacan or Freud (like Marx) into different intellectual periods (the late Freud shifts from the unconscious to the ego, the late Lacan from structure to *jouissance*)[3]; this demarcation suggests that commentators on these thinkers are interested in situating these thinkers historically. But then, as shown by Althusser's distinguishing between the early, "humanist" Marx (of the *1844 Manuscripts*) from the later, "scientific" Marx (of *Capital*), where the "break" or rupture owes much more to the tradition of historian of science Georges Canguilhem than to any linear narrative of history, merely periodizing Freud or Lacan is not a guarantee of a historicist approach. But in some ways my argument for Lacanian criticism possessing a historical dimension is in danger of being disingenuous, for surely, in some ways, the strength of psychoanalysis lies in its isolating of the features of language and structure. This is Žižek's argument, in *Organs without Bodies* when, invoking Deleuze, he counters the "historicist [commonplace]" that works of art must be studied in their historical context and posits, on the contrary, that it is only by taking works out of their context, that we can properly appreciate their true workings (2004, 15). And so in what follows, I seek to engage in what may be a contradictory practice: a psychoanalytic reading that engages with historical and political context, but without ever reducing the poetry of the Kootenay School of Writing to a mere epiphenomenon of history.

Lacan's four discourses

Jacques Lacan's theory of the four discourses—promulgated in his *Seminar XVII* of 1969–70—stands slightly after the midpoint of his intellectual development regarding the topics of power and its domination of the subject.[4] In the 1950s and early 1960s, much of Lacan's theory moves from the Hegelian and Heideggerian motifs of the mirror stage and empty and full speech toward an emphasis on *jouissance* that emerges in his work in the 1970s. Throughout this movement there were distinct explorations: the structuralist moments of "The Instance of the Letter" and the "Subversion of the Subject" essays in *Écrits*; the seminars on ethics and the four fundamentals of psychoanalysis (*Seminars VII* and *XI*, respectively) which explore the dominating role of language and the "big Other" of the Symbolic, but also presage a growing role for *jouissance* as first *Das Ding* and then *objet petit a* (again, *Seminars VII* and *XI*). This *jouissance* would, in his later work in the 1970s (especially *Seminar XX*), descend into the radically unstable conception of *lalangue*. In this complex trajectory, *Seminar XVII* offers a unique moment, for here larger or extra-clinical questions are deliberated as he theorizes the great shift from the master's discourse (authoritarianism in its traditional sense, up to and including modernism) to the university discourse (the production of knowledge for its own sake, the rationalized or administered or bureaucratic society; but also the demand to enjoy). In recent years, the university discourse has come to play an important role in critiques of US imperialism and neoliberalism (see, in particular, Žižek's *Iraq* and Jodi Dean's *Democracy*). In this chapter, I read the radically heterogeneous formal make-up of KSW writing in terms of two of Lacan's four discourses: the university discourse and the hysteric's discourse.

Lacan presented *Seminar XVII*, *L'envers de psychanalyse* (variously, the underside or other side or reversal of psychoanalysis) in 1969–70, or in the immediate aftermath of May '68. And it is the turbulence of the 1960s student movement and worldwide protests against imperialism, capitalism, sexism, homophobia, racism, and indeed, the university, that should be considered to be one of the central contexts for Lacan's thinking in this seminar (we will see soon enough how this institutional critique is germane to our thinking about the Kootenay School of Writing).[5] Concerned, as always, with the analytical situation, with the role of language, and with the representation of psychoanalytic concepts (hence the recourse to diagrams), Lacan theorizes the discursive positions from which one speaks, and the full implications of such discourse in terms of power, comprehensibility and, crucially, social revolution—all reasons, then, why such concerns should be useful in considering the poetry and poetics of the KSW.[6]

Lacan's *Seminar* theorized that there were four discourses: the master's, the hysteric's, the analyst's, and the university's. Key to understanding this system is the premise that the first discourse is the master's discourse—the discourse from which the other three stem.[7]

$$\frac{S_1}{\$} \quad \frac{S_2}{a}$$

The master's discourse. (Source: Lacan, 2007, 29. Copyright W.W. Norton and Company, used by permission.)

So the master's discourse is the starting point, as is "the Subject presumed to know," because of their origin in the transferential matrix.[8] Too, the master is the classical holder of power. Here the master is signified by S_1 or the master signifier. In the formula, then, the master faces or addresses the other, the slave, which then is knowledge, or S_2. That is, the master *steals* knowledge from the slave or proletariat—steals it to produce surplus *jouissance* or (Marx's) surplus value. This operation "produces," as "excess" or loss, the *objet a*, the object of desire, the bit of the Real. This *jouissance*, Lacan argues, is what the master cannot know—at one point in *Seminar XVII* he refers to "Yahweh's ferocious ignorance" (133–40). Finally, what the master must repress, must disavow, must keep in his unconscious, is that he is also a split subject, that his demoninator is $; he is the subject of desire: "Human, all too human."

In the algebraic structure through which Lacan maps out the discourses, the lower right corner, the site of loss or production, is in some ways a blank spot—rather like the empty spot in a tile game; thus the discourses participate in a "revolution" as the master's discourse is transfigured into the hysteric's discourse: the S_2 shifts down to the bottom right, *a* to the bottom left, $ up to the top left, and S_1 to the top right.[9]

$$\frac{\$}{a} \quad \frac{S_1}{S_2}$$

The hysteric's discourse. (Source: Lacan 2007, 29. Copyright W.W. Norton and Company, used by permission.)

The hysteric's discourse is the formula in which the hysteric speaks as split subject, as barred subject, as $. When protestors gathered outside the Vancouver Art Gallery to declaim against the provincial government's cutbacks to the arts (as I and a thousand others did in early September 2009) or the 2010 Winter Olympics, or when American right-wingers packed town halls in the summer of 2009 to protest against health care reform, they/we/I were engaged in the discourse of the hysteric. We were addressing the master, the master-signifier, S_1, the provincial premier, the IOC, Obama. But the hysteric's discourse also produces knowledge, S_2, a knowledge that is prized more here than in any other discourse, a knowledge that is also a matter of loss—examples might range from the oral histories that emerge in such ephemeral, political moments to the role of historical hysterics like Freud's Dora, or Anna O, whose symptoms "produced" psychoanalysis. And what is also disavowed by hysterics, it should be noted—and this is key—is the pleasure that they take in their stance—the *a* below the barred subject. Protestors enjoy being protestors, right-wingers enjoy having a liberal president, activists enjoy their activism. Indeed, as if to illustrate the dialectic of opposites (from Hegel's infinite judgment to Jameson's dialectic of opposing lacks), positivist psychology recently came to much the same conclusions in a study arguing that activists are, indeed, happy in their activism (Klar and Kasser 2009).[10]

Next up is the analyst's discourse, where we find in the driver's seat *jouissance* itself, or the *objet a*:

$$\frac{a}{S_2} \quad \frac{\$}{S_1}$$

The analyst's discourse. (Source: Lacan 2007, 29. Copyright W.W. Norton and Company, used by permission.)

In the analytical situation, the analyst is the object of inscrutable enigma for the analysand—the analyst occasions the abyss of the other or the *Ché vuoi?* (What do you want?) moment. You go to your shrink sure that he or she is going to answer your questions, solve your neurosis, and he or she just sits there—perhaps you can't even see the analyst's face as you prattle on about your father or your mother or the neighbour who woke you up. You want to please the analyst or, more accurately, your desire *qua* desire of the Other means that you want to want what the analyst wants, you want the analyst to desire you, you want the analyst: the analyst is the object of desire. And this *objet a* then addresses the analysand *qua* hysteric, *qua* $ or barred subject. Analysis, as Fink remarks, hystericizes the analysand, "pointing to the fact that the analysand is not the master of his or her own discourse" (1997, 136). What is produced, in this discourse, is the master signifier, or S_1 in all its ineffable mystery—the mispronounced proper name, the Freudian slip, the language that reveals more than one subject is speaking. Finally, what the analyst cannot know is his or her unconscious, is knowledge *qua* knowledge, S_2. The position S_2 takes in the lower left of the formula is, it should be noted, truth; it is only in the analytical discourse that knowledge takes the form of truth.

The final diagram represents the discourse of the university:

$$\frac{S_2}{S_1} \quad \frac{a}{\$}$$

The university discourse. (Source: Lacan 2007, 29. Copyright W.W. Norton and Company, used by permission.)

This is in part because of Lacan's thinking that the university had replaced the master in late capitalism: now we are all technocrats, now we are rationalized subjects, now there is simply the demand for more and more knowledge, more and more scientific knowledge, rational knowledge, critical knowledge. In this discourse, S_2, or knowledge, is the agent. Knowledge speaks. And it addresses the subject *qua objet a*, the subject or human being reduced to bare life, to the quivering student before the professor, the vulnerable lab rat, the terrified human subject—think of Sharlto Copley's character, Wikus Van De Merwe, in the 2009 film *District 9*, as he's being operated upon by medical researchers.[11] What is produced, or lost, in the university discourse is that quivering subject as divided subject, hysterical subject, subject who acts differently than he or she knows: $. Finally, what the university discourse disavows, what knowledge cannot bear to know is that it is underpinned by power, by the master-signifier, or S_1: the Foucaultian argument *par excellence*.

Two final aspects of Lacan's four discourses: as he notoriously remarked in *Seminar XVII*, the hysteric demands a master so that she can dominate him; that is, the hysteric's demand is for domination. Speaking of the student protests, Lacan commented, "The regime is putting you on display. It says, 'Look at them enjoying'" (*Sem. XVII*, 208). Here, he points to how the protests *and* the state's response constitute that same shift—from the master's discourse to the university discourse—from an economy of restraint to one of consumerism, from the Super-Ego of the terrible "No!" to the obscene Super-Ego of the still more terrible "Enjoy!" But before we move on to thinking about how to read KSW poetry in these terms, it might be useful first to orient these categories or discourses with some canonical modern and postmodern poetry.

The discourse of the canon

In this regard, then, I would like to begin with a genealogy of New American poetry: the work of Ezra Pound, Allen Ginsberg, Charles Olson, and Susan Howe, for example. Evidently, Pound's poetry falls into the discourse of the master, as in the beginning of *Canto LXXXI*:

> Zeus lies in Ceres' bosom
> Taishan is attended of loves
>   under Cythera, before sunrise
> and he said, "Hay aquín mucho catolicismo—(sounded
> catoli*th*ismo)
>   y muy poco reliHon"
> and he said "yo creo que los reyes desaparecen"
> (Kings will, I think, disappear)
> That was Padre José Elizondo
>   in 1906 and in 1917
> or about 1917
>   and Dolores said: "Come pan, niño," eat bread, me lad
> Sargent had painted her
>   before he descended
> (1986, 517)

Pound is speaking the master's discourse in both the obvious, common-sense way we think of the master—the one who knows, akin to the subject supposed to know, one in command of various languages (and how to pronounce them), one who has mastered poetic and mythological traditions, painting and poetry. Too, the master addresses the slave (here, the reader?); he is concerned with passing on this knowledge and, in so doing, produces that knowledge as an object, the *objet a* of desire—that desire to know Pound, to understand Pound and the modern tradition, the "Pound era" or epoch or episteme. Finally, this master signifier, this Pound, also disavows his own status as being, as signifying subject, as speaking subject or split subject. (We might think of this disavowal as that which returns to haunt Pound in his hysterical stage, particularly the Mussolini broadcasts.) Part of this disavowal has to do with the master's relation to knowledge, which is, properly speaking, the property of the slave: "What does philosophy designate over its entire evolution? It's this—theft, abduction, stealing slavery of its knowledge, through the maneuvers of the master" (Lacan 2007, 21). Further, this theft of knowledge has nothing to do with the master wanting to know: "A real master, as in general we used to see until a recent era, and this is seen less and less, doesn't desire to know anything at all—he desires that things work" (ibid., 24). To stay specifically with modernism, this theft of the knowledge of the slave can be seen in the appropriation of popular culture. Joyce's incorporation of newspaper styles and popular romances in the "Aeolus" and "Nausicaa" chapters of *Ulysses*, and of folk rhythms converted into a nonsensical Imaginary in *Finnegans Wake*; Pound's incessant turn toward the pedagogic (*Guide to Kulchur* and *ABC of Reading*) but also his and Wyndham Lewis's flirtations with fascism; the moment in Woolf's *Common Reader* when she is tempted by the "rubbish heap" of popular fiction; and Eliot's *The Waste Land* becoming, as David Ayers has remarked, "unreadable because it is familiar" but also, again, its incorporation of the popular ("Hurry up please its time," "Ta ta. Goonight," etc.).[12]

With Ginsberg, then, we are firmly in the realm of the hysterical subject, the hysterical discourse (keep in mind that these are discursive positions, and not clinical diagnoses, though Pound, as a historical being, was certainly often acting as the hysteric). Ginsberg's poetry appeals to various masters—from Pound and Whitman to the US itself, the latter in the blood-chilling "Moloch" section of *Howl*:

> What sphinx of cement and aluminum bashed open their
> skulls and ate up their brains and imagination?
> Moloch! Solitude! Filth! Ugliness! Ashcans and unobtain-

> able dollars! Children screaming under the stairways! Boys
> sobbing in armies! Old men weeping in the parks!
> (2006, 6)

Here we have, evidently, the split subject speaking. Witness the problem of subjectivity in the poem (it is not just "the best minds of my generation," but that "I have seen the best minds ..."). Here is a speaker who disavows his own *jouissance* (the pleasure of the activist, of the denouncer) when addressing the master, the US ("Moloch"). A speaker who is also producing knowledge, the knowledge of America in the 1950s, its horrible repressed citizenry. Witness, too, the hysteric's divided subjectivity—Ginsberg was caught between the tradition of Christopher Smart, William Blake, and Walt Whitman, on the one hand, and the fallen ruins of American subcultures (William S. Burroughs' Times Square hustlers of the 1940s, the San Francisco Renaissance) on the other. And as such, the hysteric is not, Lacan argues, motivated by a desire for that knowledge. Rather, "her truth is that she has to be the object *a* in order to be desired" (Lacan 2007, 175–76).

With Olson, especially in his documentary turn in *The Maximus Poems*, we have the discourse of the university: and so, after a listing of provisions, we read that:

> The above is calculated from Capt Richard
> Whitbourne's list of outfit and pro-
> visions for a winter station at Newfoundland
> as of 1622; it compares to Rev John White's
> statement of the cost of maintaining the 14
> Dorchester Company men at Cape Ann
> (1972, 119)

Here, knowledge is master, but this is knowledge that disavows its own power position, its master-signifier (Olson's troubled relationship with Melville and Shakespeare in particular). Here, too, raw data becomes poetry, and addresses our desire for more and more knowledge (hence, in a way, becoming akin to how the master's discourse works) but what is produced by this desire to know is the split subject: the reader of postmodernism who can no longer linger in the groves of a white male academe. The university discourse addresses, or works on, the subject as bare life, as *homo sacer* (in Žižek's appropriation of Agamben). Here I think two moments from Olson's biography are *apropos*: on the one hand, his attempts at working on fishing boats in his youth, where he was inevitably disgusted by the REAL fishermen's non-Melvillean desires for women, for *jouissance* ("cunts and clap, crabs and syphilis": Clark 2000, 32). Then, in the obverse of this, in *Call Me Ishmael* (which really should be titled *Call me Male*: here is Olson at his most hysterical), Olson reads Melville as having outed the truth in Shakespeare: "In his copy of the PLAYS, when Shakespeare muzzles truth-speakers, Melville is quick to mark the line or incident" ([1958], 42). This is the university discourse: disavowing (or unconscious of) its own truth, but praising its discovery elsewhere (perhaps Olson is Freudian in this regard—seeing Melville as having committed patricide against his Shakespearean father).

How does our overdetermined survey finally result, with the L=A=N=G=U=A=G=E movement? Take this passage (the reproduction of an entire page) from Susan Howe's *The Nonconformist's Memorial*:

As if all history were a progress
She was coming to anoint him
A single thread of narrative
headstrong anarchy thoughts
Actual world nothing ideal

In Peter she is nameless
The nets were not torn

The Gospel did not grasp

(Source: Howe 1993, 7.)

Now, *pace* Howe scholar Steve Collis, I would argue that Howe's position is not so much that of the archivist as the analyst. The archivist is surely the obsessive, the neurotic who seeks to keep all of his or her papers, to collect them in some order that compensates for a lack. But then in Collis's anarcho-scholastic take on the archivist,[13] the notion of using the words of others or moving "through the words of others" (the title of Collis's study of Howe), situates Howe properly with the status of the pervert (who seeks to satisfy, or be the instrument of, the desire of the other—i.e., the passive-aggressive status of collage and appropriation art). But these are clinical designations; to return to our four discourses, with Howe we have the discourse of the analyst working in the following ways. First of all, there is her work on the page with the inverted lines. Note that in the following pages from Howe's book, the text is almost unreadable because of how she works with the page, laying lines of text upon one another. These inversions make the text itself the object of desire, akin to the analyst whom we suppose to know our troubles. Howe addresses the text to the reader, so this is a readerly text, a text that is about reading other texts such as the Bible and also about its own reading (all "open" texts are therefore the discourse of the analyst—although, as we will see, this has troubling ways of enabling neoliberalism). What is produced is the master signifier, or a brand of "the L=A=N=G=U=A=G=E movement" *qua* commodified literary object. (Here it should be noted that, while she has been anthologized as/with L=A=N=G=U=A=G=E writers, Howe herself resists the label). Ceaselessly, Howe provides an imaginary resolution of the contradictions in American capitalism, finding a dissenting tradition in the tradition *qua* tradition; but finally, what is disavowed is that very knowledge, that very "tradition in the tradition *qua* tradition."

This survey of the four discourses as a way to read poetry is not meant to be historical or teleological: I am not arguing that Olson follows Ginsberg in the same manner as Lacan says the four discourses revolve from one to another, nor am I saying that Howe is the culmination of a tradition that begins with Pound. As important as the relations between the four elements—S_1, S_2, $ and *a*—within each discourse is the relationship between the discourses themselves; as Oliver Feltham has argued, Lacan's account of the movement from one to another is both complex and contradictory. The hysteric produces the analyst and is a product of analysis; the master transitions into the university but also subvents it; Lacan argues that "the analytic practice is, properly speaking, initiated by this master's discourse" (2007, 152), but also, earlier in the same seminar, discusses the progression from one to the other in terms of quarter-revolutions. What I am now interested in discussing is the "social collage" tendency in KSW writing in terms of the four discourses and, ultimately, in terms of the very neoliberalism that not only gave birth to the school but turns out to be its secret love-hate object.

In her study of Lacan's discourses for legal theory, Jeanne Lorraine Schroeder argues that in the hysteric's discourse, the marginalized subject finally speaks: "Now—and only now—the barred subject acts as an agent. Up to now she has been acted upon as the subject subjected to discourse. The master ordered her, the university lectured her, and even the analyst, supposedly on her side, interrogated her. Now she finally has a voice. The hysteric's discourse is the discourse of the barred subject" (2008, 148).

Radical poetry, then, and especially radical poetry that takes the language of poetry or the language of power or the language of capital as its subject, speaks with the discourse of the hysteric. Radical poetry addresses the master—the master *qua* master-signifier, and also the master as power itself. But writing in the KSW vein does more than this: it also takes on the power structures of the university, assuming the trappings not just of institutional power but also the jargon of inauthenticity that characterizes the syntax and vocabulary of postmodernism. And this shift between the hysteric's discourse and the university discourse may account, on the one hand, for the resistance to the KSW registered in some left circles (Fawcett and Wayman) and, on the other hand, the vexed internal contradictions that occasioned the role of feminism in and out of the KSW.[14]

But the KSW bears another, familial, relationship to the university discourse. Like psychoanalysis, the Kootenay School of Writing is and is not a school, and has a vexed relationship with the academy; like the Vancouver school of photoconceptualism, the KSW has complex and problematic relations with counter-institutions in the region's artist-run centres and other formations.[15] That is to say, the KSW cannot be thought of simply as "outside" the academy, nor can it be dismissed as merely academic poetry. These claims take their basis both from the historical context in which the KSW was developed in the 1980s and from the theoretical perspectives (and parallels) offered by psychoanalysis. The parallels are both geographic and conceptual: from the 1950s to the 1970s, Lacan's seminar moved from one medical or academic space to another: sometimes in a hospital (Hôpital Sainte-Anne: 1953–63), sometimes at the ENS (Ecole normale supériure: 1964–69), and finally at a law school (Faculté de droit du Panthéon: 1969–80).[16] Much more migratory was the KSW, originating as it did at David Thompson University Centre in Nelson, BC, and then shifting to various locations in Vancouver, beginning above a Vietnamese restaurant and taxicab office at Oak Street and Broadway and then moving to various locations in the Downtown Eastside.[17] And just as Lacan's—and indeed, psychoanalysis's—relation to academic institutions has always been fraught with rue—beginning with Freud's battles with anti-Semitism in Vienna at the turn of the last century and continuing with Lacan's critiques of the International Psychoanalytic Association in the 1950s and '60s, so too, the KSW's status was always ambivalent, including classes taught by academics (especially Peter Quartermain, on Stein and Zukofsky, in the 1980s), but also given as it was to situationist gimmicks like selling mock BA, MA, and PhD degrees for fifty dollars as a fundraising gesture.

Social collage

I am asserting a connection between Lacan's theory and the KSW's trope of social collage. What do I mean by social collage? By collage, I mean work that operates with a high level of disjunction, and by *social* collage I mean that this disjunction operates as a critique of the hegemonic role of meaning in late capitalist society. Collage, then, also signifies the breakdown of the signifying chain, whether at the level of the sentence (i.e., from sentence to sentence or phrase to phrase there is little narrative coherence) or at the level of the word/signifier/phoneme. As we saw before, the argument is that such writing constitutes an attack on how capital presents itself linguistically: that coherence is the ideological structure whereby capital interpellates the subject. Here, and with reference to an exchange between Steve McCaffery and Ron Silliman from the 1970s,[18] we can first of all make a distinction between issues of connectivity (syntax, narrative) and those of reference (variously, de-referential or post-referentiality). In what follows, I wish to use two different critical methodologies. First, I will treat brief excerpts from poems by Colin Smith, Dorothy Trujillo Lusk, Deanna Ferguson, and Jeff Derksen, and ascertain how their polysemy intersects with an anti-narrative stance. There are some references to and situating of these readings in terms of Lacanian theory. Then I take a detailed look at a single poem, Gerald Creede's "neglect is no bother," reading it more thoroughly in terms of Lacan's four discourses.

I am not interested in constructing a genealogy of disjunctive writing—such a tracing of its history in twentieth-century poetics from Stein and Zukofsky to Andrews and Davies has been done (most exemplarily in Andrews and Bernstein's *L=A=N=G=U=A=G=E Book* and Palmer's *Code of Signals*). Suffice it to quote two canonical statements:

Bernstein's "No 'death' of the referent—rather a recharged use of the multivalent referential vectors that any word has" (1986, 34: which is to say, polysemy) and Silliman's "Word's a sentence before it's a word—I write sentences" (1985, 57).[19] Andrews also contrasts two kinds of writing: the first of which has "assumptions of reference, representation, transparency, clarity, description, reproduction, positivism," and in which words "are mere windows, substitutes, proper names, haloed or subjugated by the things to which they seem to point" (1996, 16). The second kind of writing constitutes "a poetics ... of *subversion*: an anti-systemic detonation of settled relations, an anarchic liberation of energy flows ... an experimentalism of diminished or obliterated reference" (ibid., 17). I return to this question later, after a discussion of Jeff Derksen's "Interface."

Let's turn to the poets and the poetry. Here are some excerpts from four poems:

> I am not *chosen*
> but have applied for the job.
> I've always wanted to be a Government
> of Canada initiative. Starves his body down
> so his erection will be proportionally larger.
> (Colin Smith, from "Straw Man" in Klobucar and Barnholden 1999, 119)

> Forget it forget it & write about US. Despot a viscous mesh
> apparent; these walls return a favour—i.e. bum. Bum, I will
> meet him in 45 minutes my will disintegrate amen. Taken
> short shrift so change the lesser nouns, mewling—"Some
> job" i.e. weasel thrust apparent to talk around your ears "the
> world." Totems of thought. The gorge.
> (Dorothy Trujillo Lusk, from "Oral Tragedy," in Klobucar and Barnholden 1999, 139)

> Sometimes the subordinate clause is while you still have friends. Causality abets restless energy; ensues credit. If stool the size of an infant's head is removed from one's cadaver, it's a sign. Adjust connective degenerations. What appears to the eye and touch after twenty or thirty years is the same after forty or sixty, singing, cords, casts, stuck to the bottom.
> (Deanna Ferguson, from "Swoop Contract," 1993, 51)

> The Rocket Richard riots would be an example of spontaneous agency.
> "Jeanine is a living example of Noranda's attitude toward employees."
> China 6.3%
> This train.
> The residual anger resides here [points with right hand] and accumulates here [points with left hand], I'm still looking for the spigot.
> More American soldiers were killed by accidents during the build-up than by either the Iraqi army or so-called friendly fire.
> (Jeff Derksen, "Interface," in Klobucar and Barnholden1999, 203)

As discussed earlier (see page 38), there are two ways of thinking about work of this kind. We can locate this technique in terms of post-structuralist critiques of language (i.e., intertextuality, the "open" or "writerly" text, and language as a signifying chain). Or we can locate a politics in this technique, a politics at the level of *both* content and form. If these political gestures—both of form and content—place the poems in the realm of the hysteric's discourse, the structural polysemy does so in the realm of the university discourse.

Smith and starvation poetry

Colin Smith's text begins with the declaration that "I am not *chosen* / but have applied for the job." On the page before our excerpt, we read how "At home he makes an ornament sandwich, perambulates while chewing, you *would* live in a cube" [1999, 118]). And so, as with other pronouns in the poem, it is best to think of the poem's "I" in strictly linguistic terms as a *shifter*—Roman Jakobson's term[20] for signifiers in a message which refer to the sender or receiver of a message. Shifters, as the designation suggests, only possess a meaning in relation to the message being sent: here the "I" in "I am not *chosen*" refers to the speaker or writer of that message—not simply Colin Smith as the writer of the poem. Consider, for example, these lines from earlier in the poem: "I am Buster Keaton with neuralgia, Henry/Spencer with a poisonous erection" (ibid.). Given the rhetoric of the poem—the continual shifting references which mitigate against a strictly autobiographical reading—we must consider, alongside the possibility of someone saying this, its performative iterability. That is to say, we should neither Google "Buster Keaton + neuralgia" to check Smith's facts, nor assume his identification with the comedian; instead, we should reflect on the linguistic statement that leads us to consider doing those things.

This variable meaning continues in Smith: the "I" is not "*chosen*" but nonetheless has "applied for the job"—which is to say, the temporal narrative of the poem's sentence seems skewed. Wouldn't one normally say "I applied for the job but wasn't chosen"? Is this a *defeatist* poem? But there is humour here too, isn't there? The next lines read: "I always wanted to be a Government / of Canada initiative," suggesting an ironic identification with those large signs that appear on a subway or freeway construction site to let us know our tax dollars are at work. Here, the poem works in two different ways. First, there is the ludicrousness of identifying with government-speak, of having *always* had as one's ambition to be a government project, of even believing in such efforts. But we should also pay attention to the work of the line-break: "I've always wanted to be a Government" is its own phrasal or clausal meaning. It makes sense linguistically (I've always wanted to be a governing body) even if not actually. (What does it mean to want to be a government? A government of one? Here Smith's anarchism creeps in.) The line-break works to defer meaning, or to add another meaning, to the sentence. Smith's text works as a hysteric discourse: the irony disavows its very address to the master. Think, for example, of the upper half of the hysteric's discourse ($ [tab] S_1) in which the barred subject ($) is the subject of lack, the speaking subject, and could also be seen as the capitalist subject or the political protestor. But if the four discourses typically feature a disavowed "truth," *the hysterical discourse represents the truth of the master's discourse*; that is, the return of the repressed: the miserable subject of the master returns in reproach.

In part, what goes on in this style of writing, in this social-collage tendency of the KSW, is a disjunction both *in* the sentence and *between* sentences, and in this disjunction, we see the hysteric subject at work. The disjunction we've seen in Smith operates partly in terms of the line-break, but also between the three sentences that make up the verse-paragraph I've quoted from his "Straw Man." The first two sentences, for example ("I am not *chosen* / but have applied for the job" and "I've always wanted to be a Government / of Canada Initiative"), have some thematic continuity: the economics of looking for work, of government spending. We can also locate a politics in the subject position of the jobseeker, of the would-be recipient of government largesse (again, the hysteric beseeching the master). But there is also a greater disjunction between the second and third sentence, both in terms of content and linguistics. Now we suddenly jump from government initiatives to "Starves his body down so his erection will be proportionately larger." The "his" here is, of course, indeterminate—we are not to suppose that this is the same pronoun of previous lines: the "he" who is "Tempted to stick out / his ego" [Klobucar and Barnholden 1999, 118], or who "Goes to sleep / with cucumber slices all over his face" [ibid., 119]. Or, to be more precise, we should neither necessarily connect these possessive pronouns *nor* discount their connection. Dogmatic disjunction is as much an orthodoxy as dogmatic continuism. For we can also see connections of a thematic sort between this anorexic phallocrat and Henry Spencer (historically, a Victorian pornographer) with his "poisonous erection," and indeed, can also connect these with sticking out one's ego.

These formal concerns can also tell us something about the poem's title, "Straw Man." The title suggests first the "straw man" logical fallacy, or an argument in which one suggests an easily dismissed critique of one's own position. Or, the scarecrow in *The Wizard of Oz* with his head of straw. Or, to wax canonical for a moment, T.S. Eliot's well-known poem "The Hollow Men." But surely the shifters, the poem's shifting and indeterminate use of pronouns that aim at wrenching reference free from any monolithic meaning, and the poem's concomitant—and often hilarious—critiques of male self-importance, are also connected to this straw man, to this empty subjectivity, the pronoun's barred subjectivity: his *hysterical* subjectivity.

This disjunction is also paradigmatic of the university discourse. First of all, it effectively ditches the subjectivity of the poet as bourgeois artist: the barred subject is thus only the remainder, the excess. Then, disjunction reproduces and replicates at a formal level the gap between the expert (S_2: knowledge) and the subject (*a*: the subject either as subject-matter or student). This gap is present in all four discourses (between master and slave, hysteric and master, professor and student, analyst and patient); the gap between the rule of expert *qua* reader (a metonym for the rise of bureaucracies, non-democratic NGOs, and privatized police forces) and the democratic subject (student as client, as shifter, as consumer) is paradigmatic of the neoliberal state.[21]

Lusk and capital(s)

Disjunction works at a more fevered pitch in Dorothy Trujillo Lusk's "Oral Tragedy," which was first published in a chapbook of the same name by Tsunami Editions in 1988. The opening sentence of our excerpt demands not only that the reader "write about US" (which could be read as "write about the US"), but that s/he "forget it" not once but twice. This demand is modernist, and also Freudian—forgetting being a type of repression. And the repetition of the demand makes it both insistent and hectoring. Immediately, however, the next sentence retreats from sensibility or meaning: "Despot a viscous mesh apparent; these walls return a favour—i.e. bum." As discussed earlier (see page 39), this passage is replete with the punctuation marks of complex syntax—a dash, a semicolon—the sentences begin to flirt less with meaning than with sound. For walls to "return a favour" makes walls themselves into some kind of subject. In this way, Lusk's writing evacuates traditional subjectivity even while it shows how we attribute subjectivity to—how we anthropomorphize—the inanimate world around us. Again, here we can imagine leaning against a wall and perhaps the wall leaning against us or at least against one's bum; the meaning of that last word shifts as quickly as the next sentence begins. "Bum" is now an interpellation, as in "you bum." Is this bum the "him" that will be met "in 45 minutes"?[22] This next sentence ends with a paraphrase, perhaps, from the Lord's prayer: "my will disintegrate amen" instead of "thy will be done … amen." Subjectivity is evacuated and intentionality is eroded. But agency is restored, in a sense, with the beginning of the next sentence: "Taken short shrift." This skews the normal usage of "short shrift," as in "I was given short shrift": now, a lousy pittance is taken, perhaps without asking.

But, as earlier discussed, such reconstructions of meaning can blind us to how meaning never actually resides in the writing. Indeed, every sentence seems, as it meanders along, to have forgotten what it started talking about. Each sentence disintegrates under the force of association and the signifier; each sentence is given or takes short shrift.

Here, it is the text's rapid relay of signifiers—always with meaning continually dissolving and reappearing—that places us firmly in the realm of the university discourse. Again, the demand to know, to consume or produce meanings, to understand, however briefly, before moving on to the next signifier: a planned obsolescence of meaning. Too, the "forget it forget it write about US" may be read as simultaneously the hysteric and the university. The hysteric demands of the analyst that he write about her. Pay attention to me. Love me. The university discourse reading is to note the demand for more textual production, criticism, theses, essays, dissertations.[23]

This excerpt from "Oral Tragedy" should also be considered in the slightly expanded context of the poem itself, and especially in terms of two formal characteristics of Lusk's poem: its turn to capitalization as a form of emphasis, and its descent into non-signifying textualism. The use of capitalization is important to reading Lusk's work for a number of reasons. First of all, a comparison of variants of the poem (in *Oral Tragedy*, Lusk's 1988 Tsunami chapbook; in *Redactive*, her 1990 book from Talonbooks; and the 1999 appearance of the poem "Oral Tragedy" in *Writing Class*) shows us two different degrees of attention paid to capitalization. In the 1988 and 1990 versions, capitalized words are simply presented as such, while in the *Writing Class* version, most words are set in small caps,[24] while the majority of two-letter words are rendered in full-sized caps.[25] This variation is in some ways technologically (and therefore economically) overdetermined—the shift to a smaller font would have been more cumbersome for the

DIY moment of Tsunami chapbooks in the 1980s. But, arguably, as small caps make the capitalized words less jarring to the eye, their use in the *Writing Class* anthology mitigates the very purpose of such typography in the poem. The use of capitalized words in "Oral Tragedy," after all, is both a continuation of a new poetics strategy (at least since Olson, bissett, Gadd) and a critique of the disingenuously self-effacing strategy of the hippie poets to use the lower-case "i." But these strategies have now acquired different social resonances. With the rise of digital communication since the 1990s, when writing in capitalized words on email or discussion threads became synonymous with shouting (and, perhaps, being a "newbie" to some site or technology), and the use of the lower-case "i" and other affectations became part of how neoliberal capital spelled itself (from the "i" of Apple's various consumer products to the "camel case" spelling, also called medial capitalization, of the names of programs like WordPerfect).[26] If the latter showed that 1960s-era demands for inclusion could be met with a neoliberal fantasy, the former preserved, as it were, the anger that Lusk's orthography signals via the very misrecognition of the "newbie" or the bulletin board "flamer."

"Oral Tragedy" 's shift from fixed meaning into more indeterminate, metonymically linked, quasi-nonsensical meanings is also worth our attention. Consider these lines:

> Shiftless foci wont observe an onus & left to OWN loss,
> drawl & stick up our chins.
> (in Klobucar and Barnholden 1999, 134)
> Jar down mine own gritty polish & wonder when saliva
> segues patina. (135)
> First: appeared unlike any other—unbidden from out
> th'mist and all to convey a sense of 'to my home'. (136)
> Too broke to impress myself, the turnstile too intimate by
> HALF & not ethic either but LACK. (137)
> Litter spittle stubs bitter little grabby bugs ... As legs get

> tucked within thick spun lint knits & dubbin must, like salt prevention, be taught us. (138)
> Trash resistant crack repellant drone infectant broom retardant ('s disjunct as my rod and my staff—they contort &c. (139)
> There not so every passion as tactic as filmic sentience as cynic's catspaw as drone foil as tailor's chalk as what one gets as one another as one GET's through as municipal negligence as normal kid rash as an unidentified dominant life form as YOU as in sticking the ivories—that is, most gone suckered, deboned and unbidden. (140)
> About taxi Krakow to denim conspicuously around consuming union suited Mississauga scale lacking that provided trust squished beside punctuation entirely. (141)
> Caught up in sad tales wise up in due time shut up utterly. (142)

There are two variations in these sprees of textualism. There are those that work with some kind of repetition (either at the level of the word, as in "resistant ... repellant ... infectant ... retardant" [139] or syntax: "as tactic as filmic ... as cynic's ... as drone... as tailor's ..." etc. [140] and "Caught up ... wise up ... shut up..." [142]). And there are those that shift from one signifier to another based sometimes on sound (from "onus" to "OWN loss" [134] or "Litter spittle stubs bitter little" [138]). But then, as with "Too broke to impress myself, the turnstile too intimate by HALF & not ethic either but LACK" (137), meaning wavers between the direct and the associative. First of all, "Too broke to impress myself" offers us a clue to the reading practice demanded by Lusk's writing, suggesting as it does a split between the subject of the enunciation (the person making a statement) and the enunciated subject (the person in the statement: here, the "myself" of the utterance). That split subject is thus why the turnstile is too intimate "by HALF," for where and how the turnstile is too intimate is by its chrome caress of our genitals, "halfway" up or down the body. (The poem suggests, as well, the ideological phrase "too ... by half.") By "literalizing" the metaphor of what might be "too much by half," Lusk reminds us of how the phrase contains a common sense notion of excess and restraint: a notion that in true Gramscian sense is here made practical by this organic intellectual.

As we have seen, Lusk's writing frees the sentence from its own imprisonment, from the linear thrust of meaning in which meaning is finally something one has to "get" and then consume and then know. And this works specifically in terms of a concept I will elaborate upon below in my discussion of Deanna Ferguson: the idea of the signifying chain.

Ferguson and the reminder of the remainder

> Sometimes the subordinate clause is while you still have
> friends. Causality abets restless energy; ensues credit. If
> stool the size of an infant's head is removed from one's
> cadaver, it's a sign. Adjust connective degenerations. What
> appears to the eye and touch after twenty or thirty years is
> the same after forty or sixty, singing, cords, casts, stuck to
> the bottom.
> (Deanna Ferguson, from "Swoop Contract," 1993, 51)

As discussed earlier (see page 41), Jacques Lacan's notion of the signifying chain holds that language functions as a structure to give meaning to signifiers; and, further, that those signifiers constitute how memory works (or, in the case of repression, does not). In one formulation of the role of signifiers, things are remembered for the subject by the "signifying chain"—by words (Fink 1997, 20). Recall the ordinary sign: "Thank you for not smoking." We do not know what "thank you" means here until the end of the sentence, of the chain. "Smoking" gives meaning to "thank you."

Looking at Deanna Ferguson's excerpt, we earlier added a second meaning to the notion of the signifying chain: not only does a sentence only "make sense" once it is complete, but when sentences are removed from their context they do not make sense. The example given was how "stuck to the bottom" at the end of the Deanna Ferguson quotation would echo, for the reader of the entire poem, the line from its opening paragraph: "Failing tomato juice, macaroni stuck to the bottom, she squawked" (50). But that reference or resonance or echo does not mean that, literally, there is food or macaroni stuck to the bottom of a pot; what the reference does is indicate how meaning occurs by way of a technical or formal device of collaging in a phrase from earlier in the poem. Here, the stuff of the poem is drawn from itself as well as from other texts, other meanings. The text is an intertext; the text is dialogic. Meaning, in the sense of a fixed, definable essence, is resisted, is never arrived at.

It's also important to remember that it is not just this kind of poetry which is subject to the signifying chain—all language is. We can return to our earlier example of the "Thank you for not smoking" sign, for instance, and note that there are still further indeterminacies at work here: for not smoking *what*? Or for not smoking *where*? *When*? etc. These questions, this opening up of the signifying chain, which we ignore in our everyday use of language—or, Lacan would say, in the everyday use language makes of us—are what this writing is engaged with. And the refusal of meaning going on here is also, as we saw earlier, connected to how some critics have seen Lacan's own writing functioning. Recall Bruce Fink, who argues:

> [I]t is precisely insofar as understanding involves nothing more than situating one configuration of signifiers within another that Lacan is so adamant about refusing to understand, about striving to defer understanding, because in the process of understanding, everything is brought back

> to the level of the status quo, to the level of what is already known. Lacan's writing itself overflows with extravagant, preposterous, and mixed metaphors, precisely to jolt one out of the easy reductionism inherent in the very process of understanding ... Thus the gist of Lacan's claim that meaning (meaning as what you imagine you have understood) is imaginary. By assimilating something, you have the sense of being someone, or you imagine yourself as someone (an ego or self), who has accomplished a certain difficult task; you picture yourself as a thinker. (1997, 71)

Let us test this disavowal of the scholarly, first with a bibliographic note on this poem and Lusk's "Oral Tragedy." As I already noted for Lusk, both poems exist in various states: Ferguson's was published in the *East of Main* anthology as well as her 1993 collection *The Relative Minor*; Lusk's, as mentioned earlier, was published in her chapbook *Oral Tragedy*, her 1990 collection *Redactive*, and the *Writing Class* anthology. In both cases, minor punctuation mistakes or variations exist. Lusk's poem reads "ie. bum" in the chapbook and anthology, but "i.e. bum" in *Redactive*. Ferguson's poem reads "infant's head" in the anthology, but "infants head" in *The Relative Minor*. Now, these variations or mistakes, like the shifting small caps in "Oral Tragedy," locate the poems at a certain juncture or nexus of poetic, technological, and modes-of-production narratives. In terms of poetics, the incorporation of misspellings in contemporary poetry (and, in this case, mispunctuations) render the variations difficult to fix. Readers will not necessarily, in a book which includes titles like "iCS Fihing hol" (1993, 81), assume that "infants head" is a typo, missing the possessive apostrophe. Indeed, the missing apostrophe (if that's what it is, and not a revision by the author) could plausibly change the line to suggest that "head" is the predicate for the plural subject "infants"—as in, infants head for the exit. Then, in terms of technology, the typos also remind us that these poems were retyped, or re-entered on a keyboard, at a transitional space between the modernist typography of cold type and the contemporary (twenty-first-century) processes of scanning and uploading files.

Finally, the means, relations, and modes of production are also worth explicating. In Marxist theory, the first, *means of production*, refers to the machinery and material conditions of production: desktop publishing computers, offset presses. Then, *relations of production* asks us to consider who owns such means: the collectively owned Tsunami (publisher of *Oral Tragedy* and *The Relative Minor*) versus the petty bourgeois (such as New Star and Pulp, the publishers of the two anthologies, and Talonbooks, publisher of *Redactive*). Finally, *modes of production* refers to the larger societal organization of goods and profit: which is to say that this takes place under (late) capitalism.[27]

So let's return to Ferguson's excerpt, which begins with a meta-linguistic statement that rapidly becomes absurd: "Sometimes the subordinate clause is while you still have friends." The "subordinate clause" here is a noun phrase (as are my words "meta-linguistic statement"): ironically, this sentence does not have, at the level of the grammar itself, a subordinate clause. However, as discussed in Chapter One, the *frisson* of domination contained in the neutral linguistic marker "subordinate" is continued with the foreboding "while you still have friends." Speech is connected to the social. The declarative statement that follows suggests that these are descriptions of some pre-existing condition, be it linguistic, political, or physical: ideas of causality and energy suggest the latter, for instance. But the disjunction between and within the sentences makes us suspect that the text is to be read as non-referential: what "ensues credit," for instance? Rather, we are reading a certain tone or affect that then continues with the description of "stool the size of an infant's head" being removed from "a cadaver."

The medical language certainly reminds us that here we are in the realm of the university discourse—thus "stool" instead of *shit*, "cadaver" instead of *body* or *corpse*. Too, the very euphemistic nature of these nouns does nothing to hide the abject status of "stool" and "cadaver"—the body as *objet a* that is addressed by the university discourse: $\frac{S_2}{S_1}\ \frac{a}{\$}$. That scientificity, that university discourse, connects with other such words or phrases in the poem, including "proctitis" (inflammation of the rectum—*OED*), "the common cold," "professional muscle," "dirty-minded dentist," the obvious "we know medical companies are interested," (1993, 50) and "more and more medicine," culminating in "Cell formations on file dead on DNA" (ibid., 51). And so it goes, until the cool language is turned with the flat statement that, if all of this happens, "it's a sign." A sign in a medical sense, or a sign in a linguistic sense? Or, again, a meta-linguistic sign?

Once again there is play going on with the signifying chain: it's a sign *of what*? The passage then shifts registers slightly, to a demand: "Adjust connective degenerations" (again, demands abound in the poem: "Find suitable vents" [1993, 50], "Code functional disorders," "Test the theory" [ibid., 51], "Lunch forward," "Yell timbre," "Carry the baby," and "Forever calculate" [ibid., 52]). These medical resonances, these demands, soon return to the flat declarative and tautological sense of the beginning of the sentence, as "What appears to the eye and touch after twenty or thirty years is the same after forty or sixty." This is a form of entropy perhaps. But this sentence rapidly spirals out of meaning or control: "... or sixty, singing, cords, casts, stuck to the bottom."

In this poem, meaning is also overdetermined: that is, first of all, the sentences in Ferguson's poem keep sticking to the bottom, keep sticking to or coming unstuck at their ends. *The clause, is while you still have friends. Causality, ensues credit. Stool, is a sign. What connects, also degenerates. What appears the same, degenerates, or ensues, into something left over.* One way to think about what is going on here with this string of connective degenerations, of things removed from the body of the sentence, of things stuck to bottoms or stools, is that these are all remainders, reminders. These are the leftovers (the Canadian midnight snack, or that great meal made the day after, or the remaindered book). The remainder, in Lacanian theory, has two different resonances, the first to do with the *objet petit a*, that which is left over from the Real after the subject's entry into the Symbolic. If the Symbolic means language, the rational system of the Law, a system of signs that we all must navigate, then the Real is the unbearable nexus of pain/pleasure, a trace of which we all seek: the small "a" *autre*.[28]

So what disjunction does in the work of Ferguson and her colleagues is to open up language, the Symbolic, the Big Other, to what cannot be contained or symbolized or signified. This is the non-meaning that results from play with syntax, as in the paragraph's first sentence. The non-meaning that results from lack of referentiality, as in the "Causality" sentence. The break in the signifying chain that leads to the deflationary rhetoric of the cadaver sentence. The formal method that is commented upon with the impossible demand to "Adjust connective degenerations."

But, as explored earlier, these issues also connect to how poetry functions generally in our society, forever constituted in terms of the meaning which is its *objet petit a*. Poetry always lacks in meaning, lacks understandability—which is why, on the one hand, high school students are perpetually puzzled by it and, at the same time, write so much of it.[29]

In Ferguson's work, however, pleasure or *jouissance* is to be found in *not* getting "it." For the other sense of the remainder, in terms of the university discourse, is what is produced or lost in the bottom right of the formula: in this case, the split subject. We may, for example, attempt to reconstitute sentences for more conventional meaning: perhaps the first one would then read "Sometimes it's best to be nice to people while you still have friends." The second one might end "it's a sign of intestinal distress." The third might read "Adjust connective tissues." But this is only to show us what is *not* in the text.

Our pleasure in reading such a text lies in its *proximity* to meaning. And its lack of meaning is a trace of the Real in the sense that, in this example, Ferguson's poetry shows how words that possess meaning ("connective," "bottom") can be deployed without meaning: signifiers without signifieds.

Derksen and the statistic

> The Rocket Richard riots would be an example of spontaneous agency.
> 'Jeanine is a living example of Noranda's attitude toward employees.'
> China 6.3%
> This train.
> The residual anger resides here [points with right hand] and accumulates here [points with left hand], I'm still looking for the spigot.
> More American soldiers were killed by accidents during the build-up than by either the Iraqi army or so-called friendly fire.
> (Derksen, "Interface," in Kloburcar and Barnholden 1999, 203)

Let us now turn to the fourth poet whose work exemplifies the social collage: Jeff Derksen. I want to begin with his second sentence: "'Jeanine is a living example of Noranda's attitude to employees.'" The quotation marks in Derksen's text signal to the reader that this line is quoted from elsewhere; their usage also suggests that, by contrast, the lines in the poem that do not appear with quotation marks are Derksen's own, even while this appears unlikely. A few lines below, for instance, we read "More American soldiers were killed by accidents during the build-up than by either the Iraqi army or so-called friendly fire"—an observation about the first Gulf War that likely enough was sourced from news media or political analysis. But why, then, the quotation marks for the Noranda line?

Luckily for this critic, Derksen comments on precisely this line in his key essay "Sites Taken as Signs: Place, the Open Text, and Enigma in New Vancouver Writing." First published in the 1994 anthology *Vancouver: Representing the Postmodern City*, the essay ranges impressively over forty years of Canadian (and American) poetry.[30] Derksen begins the essay with our "Jeanine" line, noting that it came from a "Noranda TV ad" (144). He cuts to the chase: "In the face of corporate constructions of our subjectivity that reduce a person to a 'living example,' how can we assert a space for the subject that goes beyond the limited official versions? Even in poetry, which has potential to be an "unofficial" discourse, the position of the subject has been more or less taken for granted" (ibid.).

This provides one reading of the line—a reading that, in the context of Derksen's essay, jibes nicely with its overall argument with respect to how KSW texts refuse a monolithic subjectivity. But the line works differently in Derksen's "Interface." First of all, consider its place between the comment on the Rocket Richard riots and the China statistic. The Rocket Richard riots took place in 1955 when the Montréal Canadiens hockey player was suspended by NHL president Clarence Campbell: the riots are sometimes seen as an early precursor to the Quiet Revolution in 1960s Québec. In both cases—Richard's and Jeanine's—we have the spectacle of an employee being used by an employer. That is to say, remember Žižek's injunction to read the university discourse, or $\frac{S_2}{S_1} \; \frac{a}{\$}$, so that we have knowledge addressing the subject *qua homo sacer*, as bare life, the biopolitical. Both Richard and Jeanine are bare life. And both instances became "examples" in Derksen's poem. Does this mean that the poem should be read as a hysteric's discourse, as $\frac{\$}{a} \; \frac{S_1}{S_2}$?

Perhaps, but consider again the context in Derksen's poem, how the Jeanine line is followed by "China 6.3%,"[31] one of a string of statistics in the poem that indicate the percentage of military spending relative to the nation's gross domestic product (GDP). Others include "Soviet Union 24.9%" (1999, 197), "United States 18.3%" (ibid., 198), "Great Britain 17.1%" (200), "France 8.9%" (201), "West Germany 5.4%" (204), "Japan 3.5%," "Sweden 2.5%" (207), and "Poland 2.3%" (209). Does this succession of statistics in the poem, again, indicate the university discourse, the role of knowledge as agent?

To make this a stronger case, let us look at Derksen's poem "Interface." All of the following lines, I claim, point to the shift in political poetry from the hysteric to the university. The first series taken from the poem indicates an attitude toward self:

> I needlessly mapped an occasion, splitting my support, serving myself. (197)
> The structure I hate also hates me, but it makes me, and that's where the problem starts. (198)
> It was a way of thinking about myself that took in all perspectives and appeared not to damage the environment. (202)
> 'I'm a man—spell it *I apostrophe M*.' (204)
> I enter the artist's body of work by walking across Second and Cambie, becoming a flâneur in modernism at the shutter's click.
> (in Klobucar and Barnholden 1999, 207)

In all of these lines, then, we have the fully rationalized subject of late capitalism and neoliberalism. This is a subject that has mapped itself and possesses knowledge of the structure (and the attendant irony), that accounts for "all perspectives." This subject is fully aware of the disjunction between the "I" and the "man," and becomes, finally, the subject of an Ian Wallace photograph (Derksen refers, in the last excerpted line, to the Vancouver artist's *Heroes in the Street* series). This rationalized subject is then immersed in a world as the *objet a*, castrated and not knowing, apologized to but "still a little sore," located in a Canadian discourse:

> The return for refund where applicable part was never clear, but we continued, stopping at each gas station to ask. (197)
> Even though the ultra-sonic image of my testicle was on the split screen right in front of me, I felt detached, cube- or kiosklike. (199)
> The U.S. Navy did phone to apologize, making me feel even more like a nation, more unlike the United Nations, but still a little sore in the jaw. (205)
> Lieutenant-Colonel Butt phoned me at work to assure me of his regrets on the "unfortunate incident" and the strictness of the naval code. (206)
> 'A reader must face the fact that Canadian Literature is undeniably somber and negative, and that this to a large extent is both a reflection and a chosen definition of the national sensibility.' (208)

This rationalized discourse then not only denotes civil society, or culture, but also the triumph of culture over nature:

> The fish instinctively knew where the international boundaries are. (197)
> I was humped like a salmon. (198)
> 'Males have strange and elaborate paired crab-clawlike jointed appendages attached to the snout, which had a sexual function; the females are unencumbered.' (199)
> The bay curves past the family beach and pier, crosses the 49th Parallel, and terminates in an oil-tanker dock and naval base. (207).

The role of politics in this discourse, then, is to be simultaneously transparent and inconsequential—that is to say, pragmatic:

> A strike that tries to 'inconvenience the public as little as possible.' (199)
> 'It is only with plain talking, and a give and take on both sides, that will ensure there are forests in the future.' (200)
> Propaganda points to propaganda within a transparent frame. (200)

In this discourse, in the university discourse, the role of language is to act as a code which reveals nothing, refers only to itself, is historical by way of being archival or intertextual:

> 'Urgent Fury' wasn't the movie, but the code name: Grenada 1983. (200)
> There was a picture of him 'in the field,' notebook in hand, informant at knee. (201)[32]
> The language of war at this juncture is an aim, a name. (204)
> They wanted to argue generations but the past year is all archives. (205)
> A highly developed national sense of irony was in place by 1942: Canadian raid on Dieppe was code named Operation Jubilee. (205)
> 'Operation Comfort' lacks irony in not recognizing an alternative system: comparative literature without the *comparative*. (207)
> Operation Desert Shield, Operation Just Cause, Operation Rolling Thunder, Operation Success, Operation Martyrdom, Operation Should We Be Doing This? (209)

Most dramatically, of course, this succession of code-names for invasions and other war-like activities signals the elastic capacity of language itself to contain and represent the violent rupture of the Real.

As a way of substantiating my claim that Derksen's poetry posits the shift from the hysteric's discourse to the university discourse, consider the range of concerns in these lines: the self not as a victim; a universalizing discourse of bureaucracy (the military even apologizes); nature as part of scientific knowledge; a politics that is post-ideological; and language as always-already a code. Surely these conditions of Derksen's poem coincide in important ways with Žižek's view of Lacan, namely that the relation of Lacan's four discourses is constituted with respect to the two faces of modernity: "total administration and capitalist-individualist dynamics" (in Clemens and Grigg 2006, 110). But while "total administration" speaks to this essentially thematic reading of Derksen's work, "capitalist-individualist dynamics" speaks to form. That is to say, it is important to note that as is the case with, for example, Bob Perelman's work, Derksen's poetry is almost always grammatically correct: no Bruce Andrews-like disjunction here. In this sense, disjunction is not at the same level as we encounter in Lusk or Ferguson, and is closer to Smith or (as we will shortly see) Creede. Which is to say that, in Derksen's work, disjunction lies from line to line or verse to verse, as opposed to at the internal level of syntax. The collage is social because of the putative political content here, *and* because the disjunction means the reader must construct meaning. The social is a collage because that formal structure is held to bear a relation ("realism") with the social world.

But this agency of the reader is also problematic, as Derksen argued almost twenty years ago in "Sites Taken as Signs." There he critiqued the McCafferyesque valorization of the productive reader and a surface "disjunctiveness" that is merely "a kind of cut-up method that leaves the central subject intact and does not challenge how meaning is made socially" (in Delany 1994, 159). Crucially, that "central subject" is the neoliberal subject, the neoliberal citizen or reader who reads by clicking, makes meaning by turning the page, and abdicates social or political agency in favour of crowdsourcing. We can see how this claim holds up by tracing a quick trajectory of the "productive reader" in twentieth-century theory.

While the concept no doubt has some point of origin in Brecht's epic theatre and Benjamin's "author as producer" (see his essay of that title), the concept no doubt acquired a certain hegemonic status with Stanley Fish's notion of interpretive communities, which, like Wolfgang Iser's phenomenology of reading, can be placed into a context of anti-authorcentric interpretations. We can see, then, an etiology that might begin with the New Critics' (Wimsatt and Beardsley's) intentional fallacy, which argued that the author's intention should not be a constraint in interpretation and further, couldn't be, since the author's intentions didn't necessarily end up in the literary work. But this tradition really gets going in relation to Umberto Eco's idea of the open text from the early '60s, as well as Barthes' canonical "Death of the Author" and Foucault's "What is an Author?" (for post-structuralist variations). Fish's interpretive communities are useful not only for arguing, as Colin Davis notes, that any distinction in a text is only an "interpretive assumption which *produces* the effects it claims to describe" (2010, 83), but also that interpretive communities themselves are the products of earlier interpretations. In the 1980s, cultural studies continued this debate in at least two ways: first of all, with the distinction between mass and popular culture (the latter made by audiences from the former) and then with notions that the meaning of pop culture is not inherent in the works but in what use is made of them (especially through fan cultures or subcultures). Art world ideas extend this conversation—including both conceptualist theory, which argues against any meaning inherent in the art work, as well as institutional critiques, which, like Fish's critique of literary institutions, argue that museums and the gallery system itself are a network of power relations. More recently, this conversation has been extended through Derksen's theory of the productive reader, which sees the poem as a site for the reader to make meaning, rather than consume it (see his *Annihilated Time*), a Marxist idea itself ensuing from 1970s L=A=N=G=U=A=G=E writing.[33]

Creede and excess

When we turn to Gerald Creede's work, again we see that the play of language results in some ways from a collision between the intellectual and the street—that is, the dialectic I argued earlier when reading Creede's collaboration with Nancy Shaw is also internal to his writing. This reading of polysemic poetics as a counterpoint of the hysteric and the university discourses is relevant to understanding the place of the KSW in those discourses and to thinking about Lacan's system. That is, first of all, the KSW itself was both the hysteric in relation to larger university formations in Vancouver in the 1980s and constituted itself, in terms of the university discourse, as a "school" (in both the collective sense of an aesthetic group *and* in the pedagogic sense of a teaching institution—claims developed in Chapter Five). But let us run through a poem of Creede's first of all as a way of elaborating on these remarks.

In a loose way, Creede's "Neglect is no bother" narrates the morning after a drinking binge:

> I woke up in a basement
> not knowing where I was
> or how I got there.
> My head felt like
> an L.P. some drunk
> tried to centre
> after breaking the spindle.
> Sounded like it too.
> (in Wharton and Wayman 1989, 104)

The last sentence suggests a wit that is both occasioned by the hangover and not. Nonetheless, much of the poem tries to find metaphors for the bodily condition, either outlandish:

> My mouth
> tasted like the coloured tinfoil
> in a cheap kaleidoscope.
> My spine felt the sound of glass being shoveled. (105)

or descending into lurid, pulp-*noir* melodrama:

> A fist came
> from the blind
> side in my
> consciousness.
> I was weened over.
> From the floor
> on my back
> the ceiling
> seemed distant.
> (105)
>
> I let out a curd
> curdling scream &
> mumbled a few words over the useless carton:
> (106)

But then returns to the quotidian, the mundane:

> Drinking a mix of tea
> & leftover tonic that tastes like iced piss, flat,
> sweating summery summaries. The cranes move so
> slowly I've never seen them move. It's so hot you
> could fry x on the sidewalk. The traffic's distant
> boom reminds me of bourbon.
> (107)

Four of the five senses in as many sentences. The poem ends with both resolution—

> The last time I'll try
> Freezer burned vodka
> (108)

—and Beckettian dissolution:

> All day long I make the ice cube.
> Toting trays twixt sink & fridge.
> same. so. then. same. then. so.
> (108)

The "cube" here is both noun and verb. In this poem, arguably, it is the play between pulp description and bodily abjection that constitutes the counterpoint of hysteric/university discourse. The pulp-*noir* moments constitute the subject as hysteric—as divided, as victim—speaking to the master. Thus, in addition to the "fist" sequence above: "A boot swung in & / babied my teeth" (106) and

> He smelt like a cheese whip
> You could dip crackers in
> But a few days beyond
> His Best Before date
> (106)

First of all, these lines indicate a subjectivity that is both inside and outside: the fist comes "from the blind / side in my / consciousness" and a boot "swung in"—there is a blind side, a visual aporia, in the poet's consciousness, into which not just the fist but the boot swings. This shift to pulp signals the entry of another genre: earlier poems of Creede's are called "American Prose," or just "Prose," and half of his chapbook *Verbose* is made up of little narratives.[34]

These attempts to forge a description of the body as it endures a hangover constitute a university discourse because of how they relentlessly seek out knowledge, the knowledge of the metaphor especially: his head isn't just like a misplaced LP but sounds like it; his mouth tastes like not just "coloured tinfoil" but that found "in a cheap kaleidoscope"; his spine doesn't feel *like* "the sound of glass being shoveled" but "felt the sound" (the synasthesia of these two examples further extends the range); the assailant smelled not just like cheese whip, not just like *a* cheese whip, but one "a few days beyond / His Best Before date." This last example shows that instead of using the vernacular (a phrase like "he went bad"), Creede opts for the commodified jargon of consumer products, complete with the upper-case letters of "Best Before." And the poem's expansion of the field, of each metaphor, occurs both serially (that is, they are all attempts to convey the phenomenology of the hangover) but also particularly (each metaphor can conceivably expand infinitely) and so constitutes the university discourse in the following way: In this poem, knowledge is the speaking subject, the agent; knowledge is master, but supported silently by power; and, as Žižek remarks with respect to the university discourse (in *Iraq*), what is arguably addressed here is the abject body, the abject body of the alcoholic or hung-over subject.

My characterization of Creede's text might seem paradoxical or contradictory. Indeed, in texts like Ferguson's, Creede's, and Lusk's, with their poetics of the low, I am aware of a certain resistance to more common-sense ideas of the university discourse—its academic or ivory tower connotations. And haven't I just argued that the pulp and *noir*-ish description come from the abject? But two points are necessary to clarify things: first of all, the poem as a whole is being read as a counterpoint between the hysterical and university discourses—that is, the *noir* moments in Creede are *from the point of view* of the divided, or abject, subject. Also, as Žižek argues in an essay on Lacan's *Seminar XVII*, the upper level of the university discourse (S_2 directed at *a*) stands in for "the university knowledge endeavoring to integrate, domesticate, and appropriate the excess that resists and rejects it" (in Clemens and Grigg 2006, 108). So the poem attempts to take account of the excremental excess of the hangover—the "iced piss," the expired cheese whip, and the "Freezer burned vodka"—that is to say, it takes account of the decayed commodity, and also the decayed commodity *qua* the stain of language. Finally, it is not the abused body that is the subject matter here, nor even language as a vehicle for such description, but the commodity-form which, in the end, takes the form of exploitation, of class exploitation.

One last remark on this text—and on an interesting sub-theme of Creede's production. Creede appears in *Milk*, a 1984 lightbox photograph by Jeff Wall, another Vancouver artist, a colleague (and former student) of Ian Wallace's. In the picture, Creede squats in front of a brown brick wall, staring fixedly at the right as an arc of milk streams up from a carton in his hand. This may be referenced by the lines "I let out a curd / curdling scream & / murmured a few words over the useless carton" (1989, 106) and certainly by these, from "The Face Falls":

> Details such as the lack of shoelaces and socks, the lank, uncombed hair, the ugly polyester shirt rolled up on one arm but not the other, reveal the character as a low life, a derelict, unwilling or unable to care for his physical appearance and at the mercy of his impulses. (1986, 33)

In conversation with me some years ago, Creede admitted that this description of the photograph came from an unpublished essay by Peter Culley. On the Tate Modern website, Wall is quoted as saying: "Suffering and dispossession remain at the centre of social experience." (We will return to dispossession in the neoliberal moment at the conclusion of this book.)[35] Culley also comments, in an online essay, "Roy Arden's Fragments," on another photograph of Creede, this by Vancouver photographer Roy Arden:

> the subject, shirtless, awkwardly recumbent on a worn carpet, pivots nervously away from the ... merciless light ... the photographic portrait's conventional dialectic of subject (flesh), light and emulsion are out of balance, some unspoken contract between sitter and subject seems subtly violated. (Culley, n.d.)

It is no coincidence, I would argue, that these photographic representations (or their descriptions) are constituted around a hysterical subjectivity. To return to Creede's poem *qua* discourse: what mustn't be lost here is how the poem constitutes a barrier, a battery of signifiers *qua* knowledge, against *jouissance*, against the terrifying, transgressive pain-pleasure that is alcoholic oblivion.

Conclusion

Lacan's theory of the four discourses, first developed in his 1969–70 *Seminar*, has increasingly been read in terms of the possibilities for social critique. In *Iraq: The Borrowed Kettle*, Slavoj Žižek argues that the university discourse is a succinct model for how capitalism and the reign of experts function; and in particular, Žižek sees in this discourse the two forms of capitalist domination: the hysterical subject and the totalitarian bureaucrat.[36] In his essay "*Objet a* in Social Links," which discusses the analyst's discourse, Žižek remarks on a shift in Lacan's thinking, from the analyst as *Autre* or big Other to analyst as *objet a*. In the first, the analyst as big Other frustrates imaginary misidentification and misrecognition and thus gets the patient to recognize his or her place in the Symbolic. In the latter, analyst as *objet a*, it is the inconsistency of the big Other that is recognized. Further, in her essay "Fascism, Stalinism, and the Organization of Enjoyment," Jodi Dean argues that in the university discourse, "knowledge speaks" and thus we have "the rule of experts" (2007, 36); in this discourse, Dean continues, experts provide facts but not the values with which to assess them, which is why the divided subject $ is extra, production, surplus—that is, knowledge addresses the *objet a*, or *the subject as object*: "We see this in the way that capitalism undermines symbolic identities, how it undermines forms of attachment through the revolutionary force of ever expanding and intensifying markets. Instead of a symbolic identity of the kind provided by a Master, capitalism offers its subjects enjoyment (*objet petit a*)" (ibid.).

I must respond to two questions here: first, to make a final convincing statement on the relation of the four discourses to the KSW poets under discussion, and second, to address what seems to be an implication of that connection: that is, am I not arguing that social-collage poetics constitutes a continuation of late capitalism by other means?

To identify Derksen's or Ferguson's poetry with the university discourse means the following: that the formal methods of such poetry constitutes a dialectics of that discourse, a way in which such a discourse gives rise both to its own critique and to the pillaging of those methods. That is, Derksen's use of statistics[37] takes the paradigm of "knowledge speaking" and, by presenting those statistics anonymously, furthers the decontextualization by which statistics ontologically function (knowledge has no subjective value), as well as, finally, making such matter into the raw material of poetry. Elsewhere, as with Ferguson, the poetry operates by remainder. So, for example, when Ferguson's sentence—

> What appears to the eye and touch after twenty or thirty
> years is the same after forty or sixty, singing, cords, casts,
> stuck to the bottom. (1993, 51)

—appears in the midst of "Swoop Contract," it reminds us of the poem's opening verse-paragraph: "Failing tomato juice, macaroni stuck to the bottom of the pot, she squawked" (ibid., 50). This reminder/remainder constitutes the *objet a* not merely as a form of auto-intertextuality (or textual cannibalism) but also in the sense that in the university discourse, the $ or barred or split or hysterical subject is what is produced/lost/surplus: here figured as the "she" who "squawked," a "she" that then is *lost* in the second iteration of "stuck to the bottom" in Ferguson's poem.

But this still leaves the nagging suspicion that my reading of the social collage tendency in the KSW reduces a formally and politically radical poetics to a mere chorus for neoliberalism, cheerleaders for late capitalism, apologists for flexible labour and digital ennui. In answer to this, let us re-visit the brief quote from Jodi Dean previously, where she spoke of how capital "undermines forms of attachment through the revolutionary force of ever expanding and intensifying markets." This passage recalls another, more canonical moment in political theory: "Constant revolutionizing of production, uninterrupted disturbance of all social conditions, everlasting uncertainty and agitation distinguish the bourgeois epoch from all earlier ones. All fixed, fast frozen relations, with their train of ancient and venerable prejudices and opinions, are swept away, all new-formed ones become antiquated before they can ossify. All that is solid melts into air, all that is holy is profaned, and man is at last compelled to face with sober senses his real conditions of life and his relations with his kind." (Marx in Kamenka 1983, 207)

The authors of the *Manifesto of the Communist Party* had no doubt that capitalism was revolutionary—the admiration cannot even, in the rhetoric, be called begrudging—and their answer was for a communist revolution arising out of those very conditions. In the same regard, I would argue, the turn to a poetry of the university discourse in the formal machinations of the KSW constitutes a use of the tendencies in neoliberalism against their progenitors.

CHAPTER FOUR

Neo-Pastoral Red Tories

> I dreamt I was to use rags though a truck came along the street taking them off. I was looking at a river from sun windows where I saw apes that were giant—my knowing it wasn't usually seen and was germane to the rags—a giant ape that was male floating submerged on his back in very blue water, his genitals seen—floating gently as well. Some in the group stood up wearing the khaki clothes; them walking off into the town—it occurring to me, who would be interested in rags.
>
> —Leslie Scalapino 1998, 23

Overture

Two decades ago, readers in certain overlapping artistic and writerly urban subcultures in East Vancouver opened a book published by Tsunami editions—or perhaps heard a poet read at an artist-run centre or a local bar—and encountered the following lines, from the first section of the book, "How Pastoral: A Prologue":

> I needed a genre for the times I go phantom.... Ontology is the luxury of the landed. Let's pretend you 'had' a land. Then you 'lost' it. Now fondly describe it. That is pastoral.

(Robertson in Klobucar and Barnholden 1999, 108.)

A few years later, again, in East Vancouver, this time at the Portuguese Club on Commercial Drive, the present writer was handed a book by its author; opening it to a poem called "Winterreise," I read these lines:

> Low streak
>   of platinum
> edg'd with pewter, pumpkin hollow
>   forward straggle
> of quasi-suburban
>   foreground, graffiti
> outside Turku announces
>   *welcome to fucktown.*
> (Culley 1999, 176–77)

Poetry situated in the metropolis, poetry concerned with nature but also with its loss, poetry concerned with melancholy and with writing, whether in the form of the pastoral or graffiti (or graffiti as pastoral): ironic concerns, perhaps, but we will think about the possibility of irony in this work.

"This work" is, respectively, Lisa Robertson's *XEclogue* and Peter Culley's *The Climax Forest*. In this chapter, we will approach excerpts from each via a set of psychoanalytic concerns that have to do with the relationship of melancholy and loss (enunciated in a dialogue between Žižek, Freud, and Agamben) and the ideology of the utterance. I want to restrict my focus more here than in the previous two chapters; I want to only look at two poems of Culley's and at one of Robertson's, and I want by way of reading them to explain, perhaps, why this chapter deals with "Red Tories" and "neo-pastoralists."

Stolen land: Lisa Robertson's pastoral

Lisa Robertson's declaration in the "Prologue" to *XEclogue* is concerned with how it is possible to write a pastoral today. I want to call what she is doing the "neo-pastoral" for a couple of different reasons. First of all, I do not think that she is writing a modernist pastoral, and I do not think she is making a break with the pastoral. In her "Prologue," Robertson thinks about the pastoral as a genre (and here surely the work of Jerry Zaslove, the SFU anarchist professor who taught courses on Bakhtin in the Downtown Eastside, resonates with this social attention to questions of "genre," or what Bakhtin calls "speech genres"). Robertson makes a remark that connects the most ancient forms of genre with the most up-to-date—so up-to-date that they will not find expression commensurable with Robertson's until *after* the publication of *XEclogue*.

"Let's pretend you 'had' a land. Then you 'lost' it. Now fondly describe it. That is pastoral." Here—as with the quotes within quotes of Susan Yarrow's "From 'Not not'" or Jeff Derksen's "Interface"—the nesting of quotation marks render an indeterminacy between Robertson's words and those of the critic. But this indeterminacy also works the other way, for what the quotation marks indicate is the ancient resonance of such a claim (it is no accident that this section of her "Prologue" is signalled thus: "In deep sleep, my ancestress tells me a story"). For this definition of pastoral—the description of stolen land—is pretty much foundational to the Western pastoral, as it is to Virgil's *Eclogues*: thus in the first Eclogue, Meliboeus declares: "we leave our native borders and pleasant fields; we fly our native land" (Virgil 1950, 265), and in the ninth, Moeris: "O Lycidas, we live to have come to this, what we never feared, that an intruder in our little fields should say, These are mine; hence with you, old freeholders! Now crushed and sorrowing..." (ibid., 288).

And if the complaint of stolen land is to be found near the start of the Western pastoral, it continues past Robertson's historic moment, to the winter of 2010, when I was working on this chapter, and the slogan for protestors against the Vancouver Winter Olympics was "No Olympics on Stolen Native Land." The protest slogan as a pastoral, anti-colonial politics is wholly compatible with Western tradition.

But can Robertson have it both ways at once? Can her work be critical of the pastoral's melancholy for a land that was never really "owned," be a critique of Western property systems *and* be in solidarity with radical First Nations politics? Here it is useful to read Virgil with Marx, and to remember that the Eclogues were composed in specific historical circumstances. "The last phases of the civil war" between the older forces of the republic and the newer of an absolutist imperialism (Patterson 1987, 3) depended on land to reward its soldiers, which practice only continued a trend of, as Marx and Engels note in *The German Ideology*, "the concentration of private property, which began very early in Rome (as the Licinian agrarian law proves) and proceeded very rapidly from the time of the civil wars and especially under the Emperors" (1976, 45). So in this renewed historicist sense, Robertson's lines are not so much a critique of the pastoral as its continuation. But in order to see how this works more clearly, I will back away from her text for a moment, and return to that very simple text, the political slogan that began appearing at Vancouver demonstrations and as graffiti in 2007 (or perhaps earlier: see Lindsay 2007). For the anti-2010 slogan "No Olympics on Stolen Native Land" must be taken seriously, situated both in the history of the pastoral lyric, of poetry about nature, and in the Western tradition, as well as in the history of political protest. And I'll do this in terms of both a psychoanalytic reading and a postcolonial contextualization.

First of all we have to think about what Roger Farr calls "protest genres." These are speech acts that carry a double or even triple role: they must crystallize (or condense) political critique, they must perform a declaration of opposition, and they must exist as material signifiers. Thus "No Olympics on Stolen Native Land" situates a critique of the 2010 Olympics in terms of the history of colonialism in Canada, and especially in British Columbia, with its history of unceded Native land, of treaties not yet negotiated.[1] So here a critique is condensed into a few words, a phrase that is fairly unambiguous, if not uncontroversial (some activists, for example, thought the slogan was too specific for a broad-based movement: see Usinger 2010). Then, recalling my argument about "matter" in this book's title, the slogan also exists as a material signifier, the physical or substantial materiality of the signifier—this will exist as graffiti, or on placards, or on T-shirts, or on blogs; again, in Lacanian theory we also talk about the materiality of the signifier in terms of language, in terms of the sign or discourse.

And this materiality then connects the phrase or slogan back to the pastoral and thus, to Robertson and to Virgil. So now we have three texts—one by a canonized Western author, one by a contemporary feminist poet, and one that is perhaps anonymous, or collectively authored, or "crowd-sourced." In a psychoanalytic, but also postcolonial, reading, we can see that at the heart of Western culture is an anxiety about the Other, about the Other who steals something from us, who steals our land. The Other—the big Other—steals our enjoyment, and we have an anxiety about this in part because we hate our own enjoyment, our own pleasure. This reading takes a political slogan as seriously as literature and argues that a protest genre can be read alongside the Western canon and perhaps transforms that Western canon into something more critical of its heritage than previously thought. If the canon turns out to be subversive, and a slogan turns out to be literature, then the work we do as critics, as teachers, as readers, turns out to have implications for our everyday lives, as well as for the social world that we inhabit.

We still need, I think, to take a full measure of Robertson's critique of the pastoral, of the pastoral *qua* melancholy. Here some psychoanalytic theory, read via Freud and Agamben (and, later Žižek), may be helpful. In his essay "Mourning and Melancholia," Freud makes a distinction between healthy mourning—which is provoked by the death or eclipse of a loved one—and pathological melancholy—which is fixated on the loss of an object but turns back onto the subject. Focussing on how *rejection* becomes transferred to melancholia, Freud undertakes the following analysis:

> There is no difficulty in reconstructing this process. An object-choice had occurred, a bond had been formed between the libido and a particular person; through the influence of a real slight or disappointment on the part of the beloved person, that object-relation had been subjected to a shock. The result of this was not the normal one of withdrawal from this object and its displacement on to a new one, but another, which seems to require a number of different conditions in order to come into being. Investment in objects proved not to be very resistant, and was suspended. The free libido was not, however, displaced on to another object, but instead drawn back into the ego. But it did not find any application there, but served to produce an identification of the ego with the abandoned object. In this way the shadow of the object fell upon the ego, which could now be condemned by a particular agency as an object, as the abandoned object. Thus the loss of the object had been transformed into a loss of ego, and the conflict between the ego and the beloved person into a dichotomy between ego-criticism and the ego as modified by identification. (2006, 316)

So, to retrace Freud's analysis: we start with a bond, one that dissolves due to a shock, and instead of the normal transfer to a new object, the libidinal investment is suspended and draws back onto the ego, but it cannot latch on there and hence the ego is identified with the lost object. Freud's argument is that with the melancholic, self-loathing occurs because the original object of desire was itself in some ways a narcissistic object. Suppose I am in love with a woman and she does something to disturb or shock that affection—she turns out to be a heartless capitalist. But "The result of this was not the normal one of the withdrawal of the libido from this object and its displacement on to a new one" (Freud 2006, 316); that is, for some reason, I cannot fall for the next woman (or man) who comes along. My libido, my desire, is "instead drawn back into [my] ego," where it reminds me that I was in love with this woman because I identified with her in some way—I thought she was a hip, urban leftist like me. In Freud's memorable phrase, "the shadow of the object fell upon the ego." The ego is, of course, the primary narcissistic love object, and "the loss of object [is] transformed into a loss of ego." Because I'd really loved the woman for this unary trait—this inconsequential feature (enjoying the same band as I do or being a devotee of *rabble.ca*)—melancholy results. I hate what is in me more than I hate me, my narcissism, as Thing.

Then, Agamben argues in *Stanzas*, the causality may be skewed. It may be that we in fact lose our desire for the object—I fall out of love—*before* the objective historical change happens—*before* I find out she's a heartless capitalist. Melancholy, Agamben declares, "offers the paradox of an intention to mourn that precedes and anticipates the loss of the object" (1993, 20) or rather, "the object is neither appropriated nor lost, but both possessed and lost at the same time ... the object of the melancholic project is at once real and unreal, incorporated and lost, affirmed and denied" (21). We will pick up this argument later in this chapter with Žižek's elaborations, but for now the question is: how does it work? How does this notion of melancholy help us to read Robertson's lyric?

The title of Robertson's text is not simply "How Pastoral," but "How Pastoral: A Prologue"—with suggestions of those long, rambling, Renaissance poems that began with "prologues" and "arguments" and "dedications." A multivalent title, already. But the title also is a question. The title asks "just how pastoral is this poem?" The title is open-ended, open for debate: a question that immediately becomes a demand or, rather, a need. Too, this prologue is lyric, I would argue, in its insistent use of the first person pronoun, the "I." Like Robertson's reaching to the past, such a gesture already sets her work apart from many of her fellow-travellers in the avant garde, in the Kootenay School especially. This "I" has both a need (which is a genre) and a haunting quality (it needs genre for when it goes phantom—Derrida's "hauntology"). Genre here is a welcome constraint:

> I needed a genre for the times that I go phantom. I needed a genre to rampage Liberty, haunt the foul freedom of silence. I needed to pry loose liberty from an impacted marriage with the soil. I needed a genre to gloss my ancestress' complicity with a socially expedient code; to invade my own illusions of historical innocence. The proud trees, the proud rocks, the proud sky, the proud fields, the proud poor have been held before my glazed face for centuries. I believed they were reflections. (in Klobucar and Barnholden 1999, 108)

Genre is needed, but, following Lacan, it has also been enunciated, it has been made into a demand; here we can and should distinguish between need, demand, and desire.[2] In Lacan's account of the relation of the subject to the Other, the child's need, its originary need, if you will, is a biological one. The child needs to be fed, and therefore cries or screams. This noise communicates its need to another—the caregiver who, we hope, meets that need with milk. From then on, the *need* will be communicated in that way—but as a *demand*. And that demand will always have something extra left over—that something is called *desire*. There are two explanations for this process. On the one hand, when the child is fed for the first time, let us say, it not only ingests milk but quiets down. So the caregiver, relieved, coos at the child, comforts him or her: gives it love. This, to the child, is unexpected—as unexpected as how wonderful that milk felt going down. Such an unexpected pleasure is *jouissance*, a kind of pleasure that is never again attainable (for never again will that feeling of comfort be unanticipated). On the other hand—and this is from Dylan Evans' explication of Lacanian terminology—"because the object which satisfies the child's need is provided by another, it takes on the added significance of being a proof of the Other's love" (2005, 34–36), and so the demand is also and always a demand for love. In both explanations, then, the demand is articulated not only with respect to an actual need, but an unattainable desire. We are already in the land of melancholy.

What I am not saying here is that Robertson's text is infantile; such an analysis of need, demand, and desire is integral to Lacan's account of the analytic situation and, indeed, of how we interact with others. But the text's use of "need"—indeed, its repeated use of "need"—should signal for the reader two questions: first, why is this need so insistent that it must be repeated (and note that three of the four times "need" is used in the beginning of the "Prologue," it is "genre" that is needed); and second, can that need ever be met? These questions are deeply related: the genre that is needed here functions as a lost object, as lack, in much the same way that land functions as an occasion for the pastoral as a genre. *It is not the land that is missed here, but the genre of missing the land.*

The prologue also moves from genre *qua* genre onto notions of empire and class. Thus the genre was needed to alleviate or understand the narrator's "ancestress' complicity" and "to invade [her] own illusions of historical innocence." This is the work of culture, is it not? And so, "The proud trees, the proud rocks, the proud sky, the proud fields," are followed by "the proud poor," who "have been held before my glazed face for centuries." The face is glazed, not glossed—suggesting the personification of (glazed) porcelain, which figure becomes more vertiginous with Robertson's "I believed they were reflections."

These are the questions I wanted to begin with, though I will not answer them right now, preferring to first move fairly quickly through *XEclogue* in its entirety and map out some thematic and formal concerns of the poem/book. In so doing, I hope to show how the book's felicitous facility with language holds its genre—the pastoral—up to a mirror that is also a screen.

Here are some lines from Eclogue Ten ("Utopia"):

> If, under the cover of coherence, we were to applaud
> the irretrievable passing of that world through which we
> thought ourselves to be moving, to reconfigure our grief as a
> mocking epilogue, to become what we can no longer desire,
> and among these dispositions, to admit that we have been
> susceptible to charm and flattery ... (n.p.)[3]

And later on the same page:

> This tented evening will lend us the luxury of analysis.

And on the next page:

> When a boy walks into the philosophical, he's on a private
> earth.

And on the final page of the Eclogue Ten:

> Day of our Failed Desire.

Indeed, it is out of this very susceptibility "to charm and flattery" that I see Robertson's work trying to make its way; like Stewart's wary engagement with alphabetaries, like Strang's fucking with the medieval, like Culley's imbrication or bundling of the Romantic with grunge, *XEclogue* tries to re-imagine the Imaginary. For surely those first quoted lines are definitively in the realm of the Imaginary: being "under the cover of coherence" suggests that one's linguistic prowess is merely a guise (for the Other); applause is always for the Other, to show someone else that you approve; the world is one "through which we thought ourselves to be moving," a kind of passive-aggressive co-dependency that is firmly of the Imaginary; reconfiguring one's "grief as a mocking epilogue" is again the retooling of an affect in a neurotic way to disavow one's grief; and then to disavow, too, desire—which, *pace* Robertson, can never fail, for, according to Lacanian orthodoxy, desire is indestructible.

Here is a sampling of lines from different pages in Eclogue Nine ("History"), a seven-page poem:

> (Knowing memory only bruises the past, Lady M. scans the face of a feigned document whose ardent stammer she has already echoed, then languidly rejected.)
> [...] Lady M: *Who then would write the biography of their desires?*
> [...] Nancy: *If we were to imagine that contradiction as a landscape overwritten with vast, exhausted melancholy ...*
> *... we dream of the lustrous pitch of a truculent tissue ... We dream we are treading the sloping orthodox street etched with the scammed pride of hunger... We dream that their desires have become transparent to us .... we dream the night is far-spent ...*
> *Through the screen of grief we glimpse an ear's profane frill, luminous and insulting ... We wish to seize the real as a tissue, leave the milieux of the curious and enter that radiantly tortured grove.*
> *So again we draw on the opulent glove of sleep. We dream we have the will to think with the points of tiny scissors ... We dream of a bare and unbroken hunger blazing up in wild proportions, that we taxi through a wet night on thrumming streets ... We dream we are dilations of banality; it means we are the*

willing captives of their metaphor. (1993, n.p.)

In parsing this passage, I want to start first of all with the parenthetical introduction and in particular this: "Lady M. scans the face of a feigned document whose ardent stammer she has already echoed." There is a play of the textual and the subjective here—in not only the scanning of a "face," but "the face of a ... document," and "a feigned document" at that. What, then, of that document's "ardent stammer"? We can think of a stammer as one trace or trait of the voice, a remainder to the signified, to the meaning as communicated: like a foreign or regional accent, a stammer or lisp denotes something in the voice that cannot be assimilated into the symbolic. Žižek makes this argument in his discussion of one of Lacan's diagrams:

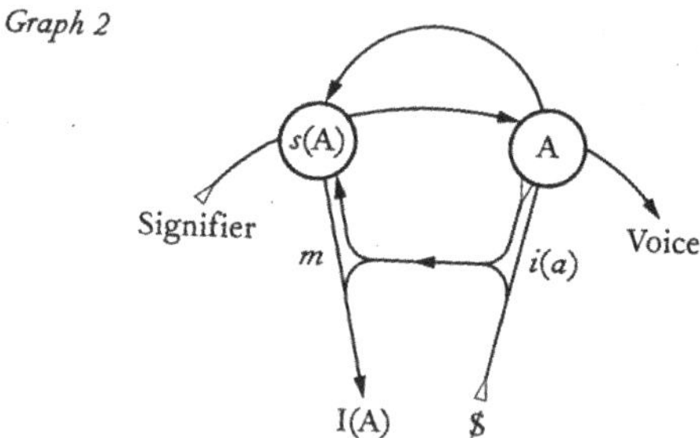

GRAPH 2. (Source: Lacan 2002, 684, Copyright W.W. Norton and Company, used by permission.)

As Žižek remarks in *The Sublime Object of Ideology* (initially of all referring to the first Lacanian diagram, reproduced earlier on page 70): "And why is the right, last part of the vector of the signifier S-S'—the part subsequent to the *point de capiton*—designated as 'Voice'? To solve this enigma, we must conceive the voice in a strictly Lacanian way: not as a bearer of plenitude and self-presence of meaning (as with Derrida) but as a meaningless *object*, as an objectal remnant, leftover, of the signifying operation, of the *capitonnage*: the voice is what is left over after we subtract from the signifier the retroactive operation of 'quilting' which produces meaning (1989, 115)."

Robertson's stammer, then, is voice as object; in this case, it is an "ardent stammer," a stammer that has been made lovely, made desirable, made into a fetish. So Robertson's line exemplifies the way in which Lacan's signifying chain works (the argument being that our meaning in language is only fixed retroactively by the Big Other, whom we are addressing). That is, in the sequence "Lady M. scans the face of a feigned document whose ardent stammer she has already echoed, then languidly rejected," the true meaning of the stammer is only apparent once the sentence has finished, once we learn the stammer has already been both echoed and rejected. But, again, like the failed desire that follows these lines a few pages later, we know that desire can never be rejected: rejection only sustains desire, gives it life.

To return to our concatenation of nature and the visual, let us look more closely at the following:

> *If we were to imagine that contradiction as a landscape overwritten with vast, exhausted melancholy ...*
>
> *Through the screen of grief we glimpse an ear's profane frill, luminous and insulting ... We wish to seize the real as a tissue*

The conditional mood ("*If we were to imagine...*") will destabilize any sure meaning, but then we have both (the contradiction of) "*a landscape overwritten*" and the desire to look or glimpse "*Through the screen of grief.*"

And returning to the Prologue: "I needed a genre to rampage Liberty, haunt the foul freedom of silence." The vocabulary is ramped up in Robertson's text; liberty is given a capital letter; alliteration is freely indulged. Genre is a welcome constraint precisely because of the liberty of postmodern poetics, in which anything goes; too, the speaker, a phantom, needs that constraint—the constraint of genre—in order to haunt, or bedevil, the paradoxically "foul freedom of silence." What does that last phrase mean? How is silence a freedom, and how is that freedom foul? Perhaps—if we are to give this a gendered or feminist reading—the silence of women's oppression, the silence that marginalizes women even in progressive poetic communities, is also a kind of freedom, but a dialectical freedom, both sweet and foul at the same time. Thus it must be haunted.

But this haunting, these phantoms, this liberty, are all "in the guise of an ambivalent expenditure," an expenditure not just of signifiers, of words, but of affect, of desire. In some ways, Robertson here is both in nostalgia—for "nostalgia can locate those structured faults"—and critical of it, critical of the "desuetude of nostalgia," of its having fallen into disuse (here I am almost quoting directly the Canadian *OED*'s definition of "desuetude"). The line is curious, isn't it—how does nostalgia fall into disuse? Is she nostalgic for nostalgia? Remember when we were nostalgic? She is longing for genre but longing to escape from it in a "melancholic mirror of sex" (and now we are near that narcissistic object, that "vapid twin"). As with the earlier question of genre, these queries all lead to what Žižek will say about melancholy, about nostalgia, but first let's wrap up how Robertson enunciates a Freudian or Agambenesque position. If, for Freud and Agamben, melancholy is the loss of the narcissistic love object, a loss that actually anticipates a loss, then for Robertson, the pastoral is the signifier of that loss: pastoral is not so much about loss of the object of the land, but of the unary trait of that land, of the fantasy of having had land—that fantasy that informs the pastoral as genre. And, again, "How Pastoral: A Prologue" is melancholic for the loss not of the land, but of the signifier: the loss of the pastoral *qua* pastoral.

Here, then, I would like to turn to how Žižek articulates these concerns in his 2000 essay "Melancholy and the Act," which was later to appear in revised form in *Did Somebody Say Totalitarianism?* (Žižek 2001, 141*ff*). Summarizing Freud, Žižek stresses that with melancholy, the "subject persists in his or her narcissistic identification with the lost object" (141) due to a confusion "between *loss* and *lack*" (143). The object-cause of desire (the "unary trait," that arbitrary signifier through which we identify with the other) always-already lacks, indeed, Žižek argues, *constitutively* lacks. That is, the pastoral is never anything more than what Robertson calls "fondly describ[ing]" the land, a "pining rhetoric [that] points to obsolescence." The object lacks from the very beginning, and we—as melancholics—misrecognize this lack as loss. The land always lacks, and we only possess its lack through the pastoral, through the signifier of that lack. The pastoral, read through Žižek *and* Robertson (and, we shall shortly see, Culley), is the signifier not of the land, but of the land as lack. And if a common misreading of the genre of pastoral is as some lyric of otiose shepherds and panpipes, so too is that reading built into the pastoral as form, in its constitutive moment—the Virgilian moment—of stolen land.

Culley and melancholic grunge

The full title of Peter Culley's poem is "Winterreise *after F. Schubert and W. Müller*" (1999)—indicating for the reader its lineage to the 1827 *lieder*-cycle that Austrian composer Franz Schubert (1797–1828) made from the poems by Wilhelm Müller (1794–1827).[4] But this "winter's journey" seems to end in late summer—if we are to trust the last line of the poem. And while it may begin on the Canadian West Coast with "its dear / and familiar contours" where arbutus trees "buttress / the hillside," it lingers at some point outside the Finnish town of "Turku," where graffiti "announces / *welcome to fucktown*." Time as well as space are indeterminate here. For all of the poem's classic Romanticism, magnetic north has "drifted a few degrees / off true," an "endless valley of rock / cools and twists" during the time of the poem, and there is "[a]necdotal evidence" of a surfer riding a tectonic plate across "the lake of fire." But more globally, at a macro level, the poem begins with lack (as opposed to loss: like Robertson, Culley makes no mistakes):

> Out of salt, iron
>   and out of iron, gold
> and out of gold,
>   along the chain
> of alchemical time reversals
> (1999, 175)

The poem begins with lack—"out of salt"—but also declaring that it is out of (or from) salt that we make iron, and so on. But the meaning of the first line is neither one nor the other: rather, via its repetition, the poem's meaning lies between the meanings, lies in the reader's move from one meaning to another. The poem's meaning is to have different meanings, and moves like the geological cooling of the valleys.

This lack is both given and taken away. The speaker (or the "he") of the poem "consults the compass" each day (i.e., needs some instrument to relate to nature, needs that unary trait, that signifier). And he finds what is again an ambiguous bit of information: "magnetic north / has drifted a few degrees / off true." This information is ambiguous because magnetic north is *always* off true[5]; that is, geographically, the magnetic north lies in a different location than true (or map) north—thus the variation between the two is itself variable according to where one is on the planet. The difference between the two, called variation or declination, is the subject of the old and sexist pilot's mnemonic (which I learned as an Air Cadet): "True Virgins Make Dull Company"—or True north plus Variation is Magnetic north, plus Deviation is Compass north (in which deviation denotes the difference caused by the steel superstructure in an airplane or boat). But it gets more complicated: for magnetic north does indeed change from year to year—by as much as a degree in northern locations like Yellowknife (though it isn't likely that the scenario described in the poem would occur). We have to also take into account whether Culley himself knows this information about the difference between magnetic and true north. Finally, it doesn't really matter, as the point of this issue in the poem seems to be twofold: first, that there is a lack of reliable mapping information about the earth; second, that the subject in the poem keeps making this discovery. For questions about Culley's intention, about authorial intention, we can look at what Walter Benjamin has to say about his *Arcades Project* in "[c]omparison of other people's attempts to the undertaking of a sea voyage in which the ships are drawn off course by the magnetic North Pole. Discover *this* North Pole. What for others are deviations are, for me, the data which determine my course.—On the differentials of time (which, for others, disturb the main lines of the inquiry), I base my reckoning." (1999, 456)

And it is this repetition of a discovery of lack—a lack which has to do with the north—that is so important to this poem. We see that importance in the connotative and symbolic power of the north to what Anthony Wilden calls *The Imaginary Canadian*[6] and we see it internally, in the poem's repetition—note, for instance, that the poem's spatiality shifts from the Canadian west coast to another "northern" nation, Finland.

So if the pastoral is about loss, what is lost—or rather, figured as lost—in Culley's "Winterreise"? In part, the poem is not so much about the difficulty of writing a pastoral lyric (the modernist lament) but what is left of that lyric, the remainder. We may have the occult and other Romantic tropes—the "alchemical time reversals"—but we also have the poem's closing reference to Caspar David Friedrich, perhaps to his 1808 painting *The Cross in the Mountains (Tetschen Altar)* in which Christ does, indeed, seem to be "writhing" (which is almost "writing") "in the warm searchlight / of late summer" (Culley 1999, 178). We have to turn to Culley's own version of the pastoral, the celebration of what Marx called rural idiocy, with the graffiti of the geologist as surfer:

Anecdotal evidence
   a mock tectonic plate
on which
   the hapless aspirant
stands as one
   upon a surfboard crossing
the lake of fire,
   a geologist
tut-tutting over
   a particularly disappointing
core sample—
(177)

The backyard barbecue as a religious rite:

Destroyed and sectioned
   tamarack into a crude
pyramid in the yard, floating
   ridge of fir indexed somewhere,
ready for the hot tip
   of the landlord's cigarette,
unreconstructed altar
   of cool brick and
rusted rack, a fat
   coot cracks
a dead branch.
(178)

And then among this pastoral detritus is what might be a late-modern pastiche, the allusion to Friedrich's painting:

from the narrow window
  Friedrich's Christ
just barely visible
  on his mountaintop, still
writhing in the warm searchlight
  of late summer.
(178)

I'd like to finish reading Culley's poem by tying together syntactical disjunction, the role of representation, and the relationship of the pastoral to loss. In the final lines of the poem, just quoted, it is not clear if we are outside looking through a window to see a painting in a house, or if we are inside, looking out "from the narrow window," in which case "Friedrich's Christ" is imputed to be there, in nature, on the mountaintop, in another late moment, not in the "thickened sun of late afternoon" (177) of slightly earlier in the poem (just after the surfing geologist), but in the "warm searchlight / of late summer," indeed, "still / writhing" in that light. And that ambiguity of whether one is looking into a house at a painting or looking out of the window at a writhing Christ is also matched by both sunlight-as-searchlight (a paradox, surely) and by the notion of Christ, on a cross, in late summer rather than in spring, indeed, inaugurating spring. If we then read back to the pyramid of broken tamarack, a similar mode of representation is doubly signified: the "floating / ridge of fir indexed somewhere" in the woodpile, the barbecue ("cool brick and / rusted rack") which is somehow an "unreconstructed altar."

Here "the hot tip / of the landlord's cigarette" is akin to the searchlight that warms Friedrich's Christ's writhing body, for it is uncertain if the lines refer to the notion of lighting the backyard barbecue, or a forest fire (in the "ridge of fir"). That same thematic indeterminacy is also at work in the syntax of the poem, indeed is determined by it. In the lines

Destroyed and sectioned
  tamarack into a crude
pyramid in the yard, floating
  ridge of fir indexed somewhere,
ready for the hot tip
  of the landlord's cigarette

for instance, there is a repressed "I" or "he" before "Destroyed," an assumed subjectivity discarded by the "floating" lines. These lines modify the pyramid, a certainty which is further dismantled as it is unclear what is ready for the "hot tip," the ridge or the pyramid. This recalls the lines earlier in the poem, in which we read:

Anecdotal evidence
  a mock tectonic plate
on which
  the hapless aspirant
stands as one
  upon a surfboard

and wonder if we are to think that "Anecdotal evidence" concerns "a mock tectonic plate" or *is* that plate—on which again, as with the indexed fir, we have a figure standing "as one / upon a surfboard." The loss that is not lost, then, the loss that is revealed to be lack as certainly as in Robertson's "Prologue," is the loss of nature, for here a lumpen-rural is revealed, revelled in, revelatory.

Take the opening page of Culley's "Greetings from Hammertown" (1995, 88–92):

Huge uproar lords it wide
  A tim'rous grader halts
Before an overflowing ditch, its
  big bad boy body slumped
As if thwarted at its gigging.

> In the shed's cartoon shadow
> Wee dinosaurs sport and romp, their urgent
> Territorial beefs
> Strangely comforting somehow. The missives
> of October
> Tonk against the upstairs windows
> like desperate and ancient flies …
>
> … fuck 'em.
> I tried to climb the glass mountain
> But I kept hitting
> the glass ceiling, so
> If you want to read
> "decay"
> Into this rocky heap
> of nasty moss, this
> Eggy newspaper intrusion, that's your
> quattrocento prerogativo—
> (88)

I want to look at two formal things going on in this excerpt. First, I want to look at the reflexive break between the two stanzas, that sudden and rude "fuck 'em." Second, I want to pause on the intervention at the level of the ideologeme that occurs in the lines that begin "If you want to" and end "prerogativo—." But to begin, a quick intertextual note: The lines, "I tried to climb the glass mountain / But I kept hitting / the glass ceiling" might refer to, or at least call to mind, P.K. Page's "Cook's Mountains":

> By naming them he made them.
> They were here
> before he came
> but they were not the same.

It was his gaze
that glazed each one.
He saw
the Glass House Mountains in his glass.
They shone.
(Page 1985, 71)

In writing that Culley's lines "might refer to, or at least call to mind" those of Page, I was not trying to avoid the question of influence (did Culley read Page—a well-known, modernist Vancouver Island poet?); rather, the notion of intertextuality is *not* a matter of influence hunting. Intertextuality, like dialogism, resides as much in the reader, in my spotting of the contiguous images, as in the author.

There are, then, two possible ways to read the break between Culley's opening stanzas: first, the "fuck 'em" is a rejoinder to the entire project of the first stanza, to its linkage of the pastoral and the mechanical (the "tim'rous grader" combines the poetic with the industrial); second, it is more specific, referring to the "missives / of October"—windblown leaves, perhaps—which strike the window like flies. The first reading would see the break in the poem as meta-poetic; the second as a reaction against the pastoral imagery itself. The second stanza also shifts to addressing the reader: first of all, the "I" tried to climb a glass mountain (continuing the imagery of the window in the first stanza, but also suggesting a slippery slope as it were), but hits "the glass ceiling," an interesting take on 1990s identity politics, since that phrase, "glass ceiling" ("an unacknowledged barrier to personal advancement" according to the Canadian *OED*) usually referred to barriers for "women and minorities" (according to the *American Heritage Dictionary*). That is, the term's definition and common usage left out class. And this, no doubt, is part of the meaning at work in Culley's poem, with its melancholic descriptions of Hammertown, a poetic geography of many a post-industrial or post-resource economy, but certainly befitting Vancouver Island's mill- and mall-town Na-

naimo, as the poem goes on to argue, with the "pheasant … nailed to the outhouse door" (Culley 1995, 88), "the banked woodfires / of the working class," "the few who walk … Hunched in the posture of exile," "the boarded laundromat," and "the birdshit-streaked copper eyes" of a local statue (89).

The speaker of the poem can't rise to the aesthetic occasion (not only is there a glass ceiling that keeps him from advancing, but the *very term*—the problematic—refuses to recognize that class, along with gender and ethnicity, can be such a determinant). What comes next is the intervention into the ideologeme of "If you want to read / 'decay' … that's your / quattrocento prerogativo—." Which is to say that in the poem, a class barrier is refigured as a challenge to cultural capital: I may be a rural bumpkin, says the poem's ideology, but I can reference the early Italian Renaissance (the fifteenth century or *quattrocento*). It is a political argument accomplished at the level of the signifier or, more precisely, at the level of the utterance. "That's your prerogative" becomes "that's your quattrocento prerogativo."

The utterance is a challenge to the reader—it is his or her privilege, the poem allows, to read what he or she wants to into the poem. But the poem also loads the dice: "decay" is placed in quotation marks as if to note its preciousness (i.e., a reading of a poem that sees decay everywhere). Concrete details—"rocky heap" and "nasty moss"—are torqued by an "Eggy newspaper intrusion" (which means, presumably, egg-smelling—the sulphur scent of a pulp and paper mill). So the privilege, the prerogative, lies in moving from the concrete to the abstract, from the sulphurous intrusions into the abstractions of ideology.

Interventions into the ideologemes of the utterances:

> Kevin Davies: "it's still anybody's meaningless post-Series
> tour of the new Axis/alliance" (2000, 40)

> Peter Culley: "that's your quattrocento prerogativo." (1995, 88)
>
> Nancy Shaw and Gerald Creede: "A soprano collapses and the opera calls a time out. // ... We always hung out in someone else's neighbourhood" (1992, 70)
>
> Dan Farrell: "Sovereign is he who gets off on being ungrounded. (1994, n.p.)

Here I want to return to utterances *qua* ideology, and explore the mechanics of these various interventions (above) in three senses: first, to understand the relationship between utterance and ideologeme; second, the relation between the politics of the gesture and its poetics; third and finally, to see how the self-reflexivity of the Creede/Shaw version makes it different from the others.

As Jameson argues in *The Political Unconscious*, one form of interpretation is to see the text itself as one giant utterance: "the individual text ... refocused as a *parole*, or individual utterance, of that vaster system or *langue*, of class discourse" (1981, 85). These utterances or ideologemes are seen as part of a class struggle carried out at the level of language. This notion of a text as an utterance is also close to Bakhtin's sense of the utterance in "The Problem of Speech Genres," where he distinguishes between primary and secondary utterances. The latter denotes "novels, dramas, all kinds of scientific research, [and] major genres of commentary" which "absorb and digest various primary (simple) genres that have taken form in unmediated speech communion" (1986, 62). But for Bakhtin, the primary utterances lose their specificity once taken up in the secondary ones: "[t]hey lose their immediate relation to actual reality and to the real utterances of others" (ibid.). We know what Bakhtin means here in an everyday sense (when a character in a novel says "I love you," no one is really being loved), but do utterances lose their politics in KSW texts?[7]

And this is where we come to the second part of this equation: Jameson's notion of the ideologeme, or the smallest possible unit of political belief or action that mediates "between conceptions of ideology as abstract opinion, class value, and the like" and literary materials (1981, 87). So what I am arguing here is that, at a close textual level, we can see this dialectic of the utterance and the ideologeme in the utterances that KSW texts intervene in, and then we can take that dialectic to another level and consider the KSW poem or text itself as an utterance (Bakhtin's secondary or complex utterance). In Culley's poem, then, the phrase "that's your prerogative" is, with the intrusion of *quattrocento*, intervened into. The Italian then further intervenes into the word "prerogative" itself, reshaping its expression to "prerogativo." "That's your prerogative" functions as an ideologeme, as a basic unit of ideology, as a form of passive-aggressive fetishistic disavowal (the weapon of the weak). It functions in dialogue (is dialogic) in that it depends on the speaker answering to another, answering with a critique that is less than a critique.

In the Kevin Davies line, "it's still anybody's meaningless post-Series tour of the new Axis/alliance," we have perhaps three ideologemes being mashed together: "it's still anybody's guess," the idea of the World Series, and the post 9/11 Bushism of the new Axis of evil.[8] But where such interventions also work is at the level of the phrase or sentence, at the level of rhythm, with the downward stress on "guess" being replaced by the rush to fit in "meaningless post-Series tour of the new Axis/alliance."

Nonetheless, you still have to reconstruct the "original" utterance to get a true sense of what is happening in such poetry: you have to "remember" or "know" or "Google" or "go back to" the phrases or ideologemes of "that's your prerogative" or "it's still anybody's guess." Or rather, when one does, when one uncovers that utterance in the poetic text, the difference between that "original" utterance and the poetry is what makes the poetry.

Let us continue this excursus, then, with the Creede/Shaw utterance.

> A soprano collapses and the opera calls a time out.
> We always hung out in someone else's neighbourhood

The first sentence is already meta-linguistic: it is a comment on the utterance of an umpire calling a time-out in a baseball or football game. Further, it is also a shift in register or value: from the high cultural status of opera to the lower cultural status of sports (or from the culturally valued and elite pursuit of opera to the devalued yet hugely popular and massively wealth-generating arena of professional sports). This shift is what is further commented on, as if to illustrate the heuristic value of this reading, in the second sentence. That is, the "time out" is hanging out, as it were, in the neighbourhood of "A soprano ... and the opera," or in the neighbourhood of high culture. But the intervention is still at the level of the utterance—for, before we get to this political or cultural capital reading, we must first traverse the broken syntax of the first sentence: the grammatical rupture which turns "the opera" into a speaking subject who "calls a time out."

Once more, in true Lacanian fashion, this is a case of the signifier's meaning being dependent upon what is to come. The causality implicit in the "and" is both naturalist and transformational: instead of the "and" leading to "the opera comes to a halt," the "and" leads to the opera itself (instead of the soprano) engaging in speech.

A different kind of ideologeme is intervened into in the example from Farrell's poem "Body," from *Thimking of You*. There, he also engages in other tweaks, such as "to find out who sings to the cast of *Shadow of a Double*" (1994, n.p.)—riffing, in this case, off the title of the Hitchcock film *Shadow of a Doubt*. Similarly, the line, "Sovereign is he who gets off on being ungrounded" also references a phrase or utterance, albeit one with a more academic provenance, Carl Schmitt's "Sovereign is he who decides on the state of exception" (2005, 5). It should be stressed that, as Susan Smith Nash has written of Dorothy Trujillo Lusk's work, the point here is not to control meaning or to generate cultural capital out of a proper reference (i.e., for those who "get it," who "spot the reference"). For one thing, since Schmitt's book was only translated into English in 1985 (Farrell's book was published in 1994), the reference was fairly obscure, even by the advanced standards of Vancouver's poetry and art world. But the intervention into the utterance as ideologeme also works in a manner similar to the earlier examples from Culley, Davies, and Creede/Shaw. Schmitt's phrase argues, in a compressed way, that true political leadership or subjectivity (sovereignty) lies in being able to step outside of political law, in making the exception. Farrell's switch, to "he who gets off on being ungrounded," continues the reflection on power (children being "grounded" or kept home as a punishment) and its subversion (the libidinal suggestion of "getting off" on or enjoying the punishment's end, the ungrounding). Farrell's line also makes an argument about the relationship between Schmitt's political theology[9] and the mundane, libidinally charged milieu of the family and the domestic, an argument that works here in poetry, in the ideologeme, in the intervention into the utterance.

These interventions into the ideologeme show how what is happening in Culley's or Robertson's texts is typical of the poetry in the KSW frame, where philosophical or political or theoretical statements are taken and retrofitted to the poetic, to a form of language that, in its formal practice, is about that language's own capabilities (always changing, always under erasure). But this is not to argue for a poetic exceptionalism (poetic is he ...): rather, à la Lacan's *point de capiton* or Freud's *Nachträglichkeit*, the meaning and ontology of language, of its use—whether in commodified commercial forms or rarefied philosophical genres—only finds its actual purpose once it has been translated into poetry.

At last: the Red Tory

So too it is with Robertson and the question of genre, an investment in a discredited form that can be understood via the Canadian political category of the Red Tory. This notion of the Red Tory perhaps should be explained, although most Canadians of my generation or older (i.e., born before the mid-1960s) will surely be knowledgeable about the phenomenon of Canadian Conservative politics before the Brian Mulroney era (which was properly neoconservative—or neoliberal—in a manner aping Reagan or Thatcher). But the history of the category reveals some interesting lessons both for thinking about poetry and for thinking about Canadian politics.

The term "Red Tory" was coined, experts agree, by Gad Horowitz, a young political science professor at McGill University, in a 1965 article in the radical socialist journal *Canadian Dimension*.[10] Writing in response to George Grant's *Lament for a Nation*, a key text of Canadian radicalism and nationalism in the 1960s, Horowitz argued that a Canadian political tradition of toryism (inherited from the British) was closer to socialism than to American-style "possessive individualism" (1965, 12; this last term comes from the Canadian political philosopher C.B. Macpherson). Horowitz thus writes:

> Since the tory and socialist minds have some crucial assumptions, orientations, and value in common, there is a positive affinity between them. From certain angles they appear not as enemies, but as two different expressions of the same basic ideological outlook. This helps explain the Canadian phenomenon of the red tory. At the simplest level, he is a tory who prefers the socialists to the liberals, or a socialist who prefers the tories to the liberals, without really knowing why. At a higher level, he is a conscious ideological tory with some "odd" socialist notions (R.B. Bennett, Alvin Hamilton) or a conscious ideological socialist with some "odd" tory notions (Eugene Forsey). (ibid., 13)

I do not want to get into the arcana of Canadian political history, nor do I want to go down the route that leads, in traditional Canadian literature, from Grant to such Canadian literary nationalists as Dennis Lee and Margaret Atwood, or, by more circuitous routes, Al Purdy. But before turning to what, in my argument, makes Robertson and Culley's poetry specifically Red Tory, I want to provide a further illustration of Horowitz's dialectic of the Red Tory with an important, and little-known, story from recent labour history. If by Red Toryism we mean the social-justice aspects of Canadian conservatism that died with the onslaught of Mulroneyism (and, more recently, the Reform-Harper juggernaut), no better example can be found than the Joe Clark government of 1979–80, and in particular, the first woman in Canada to be minister of External Affairs, Flora MacDonald.[11] In July 1979, a movement was building in Canada's Argentinian exile community to stop the shipping of nuclear materials to Argentina, due to the brutal human rights abuses and "dirty war" under the military dictatorship of General Jorge Videla (1976–81). Longshoremen at the Saint John, New Brunswick, docks honoured the ban, and even as the Canadian government was attempting to sell Candu reactors and heavy water abroad, MacDonald, who had only been in cabinet for a month, supported the actions of the Saint John local. As Jim Creskey tells the story, the work of a Red Tory cabinet minister meant that dock workers were *de facto* "architects of foreign policy" (2010, n.p.).

No doubt the notion of a conservative politician cooperating with organized labour is difficult to understand today, but here I would like to return to Robertson and Culley and make an argument that we can read their work as an example of Red Tory poetry. I mean this in the two following ways: first, their approach to the pastoral, to traditional forms and genres, suggests a willingness to engage with the poetic past that is different from the more sheerly disjunctive work of a Derksen, or a Lusk, or a MacLeod. Second, the formal contradiction to be found in Culley and Robertson's work, where the traditional form is brought into juxtaposition with a radically presentist content, is a dialectical continuation of the same contradiction that Horowitz found in the Canadian politics and political philosophy. But first, I will return to the discussion of melancholy and lack, sketched out above with respect to Agamben and Freud, as a way of drawing a more theoretical connection between the political Red Tories and the poets. To do this, we have to turn to *Did Somebody Say Totalitarianism?*

There, Žižek's discussion of melancholy and lack is introduced by his assertion that the Lacanian "big Other"—the Symbolic—is to be found not merely in the system of laws and regulations that is formally encoded, but also in unwritten *doxa*. One example of such an unwritten rule is the politically correct fetish of melancholy, which can be identified merely because in our postmodern, neoliberal climate of transgression and permissiveness, what is hegemonic is inevitably presented as a threat to hegemony. For the melancholic, then, "there is always a remainder which cannot be integrated through the act of mourning" and hence "[m]ourning is a kind of betrayal, the 'second killing' of the (lost) object" (2001, 141). On the contrary, Žižek refers to Hegelian sublation (*Aufhebung*) where the "notional essence" of a lost object is retained even while it is lost, whereas for the melancholic "the object resists its notional 'sublation'" (143). Thus—and this is where Žižek references Agamben's *Stanzas*—we have the confusion of loss and lack, "as if the object lacking were once possessed and then lost" and, furthermore, as the object was never there (and the subject is constitutively lacking), the object's "emergence coincides with its lack ... this object is *nothing but* the positivization of a void/lack, a purely anamorphic entity which does not exist 'in itself'" (144). Žižek gives as one of his examples of "politically correct" melancholy "the postcolonial-ethnic one" where, "under threat that their specific legacy will be swallowed up by the new global culture, they ... retain their melancholic attachment to their lost roots" (142).

So to read Žižek in tandem with Horowitz, on the one hand, and

Culley/Robertson, on the other, is to consider how these two bodies of work instantiate Žižek's key ideas: the remainder, or *objet petit a*; the question of mourning as betrayal but also as form of sublation; the post-colonial; loss versus lack; and the void or anamorphosis. For such "self-described" Red Tories as George Grant, the *objet petit a* or remainder is Canada's British heritage, which is its bulwark against the newer imperialism of the US. As a genre or form, George Grant's *Lament* is thoroughly melancholic, even as he is acutely aware of the same, allowing that "lamentation falls easily into self-pity" (1965/1970, 96). Horowitz, however, recognizes that "Grant's pessimism and determinism exude death. They ought to be rejected. Once they are rejected, he has a vital lesson to teach Canadian social democrats" (1965, 15). Horowitz's critique is Hegelian; he is talking about sublation or *Aufhebung*. This is why he can end his article with the claim that "A tory past contains the seeds of a socialist future." But here, in Horowitz's metaphor of the "seed," we can also see the remnant of another political theory that is contiguous to Lacan's *objet petit a*. Horowitz's theory is indebted to the American political scientist Louis Hartz, with whom he studied at Harvard in the 1950s, and who originated the "fragment" theory of political transmission, arguing that in postcolonial societies—particularly in such settler societies as the US, Australia, Canada, and South Africa—ideological "fragments" of the metropolitan nation would adhere to the settler colony. With the immigration of United Empire Loyalists to Canada after the American Revolution, a fragment of toryism survives in the Canadian milieu. This fragment then is akin to *objet petit a* in the following way: as Žižek argues in *Totalitarianism?*, "melancholy is not simply the attachment to the lost object but the attachment to the very original gesture of its loss"—that is, the postcolonial "double loss" of, in the Red Tory's case, the immigration to Canada. George Grant's lament is not for a nation, for an object that has been lost, but for that loss itself. This brings us to Culley and Robertson, whose work is trying to recapture "not the organic immediacy" of the pastoral but, in Žižek's words, "the organic-immediate experience of the loss itself" (2001, 144–45)—that is, loss of nostalgia, of the pastoral.

Here Žižek's use of Agamben is particularly lucid: "melancholia offers the paradox of an intention to mourn that precedes and anticipates the loss of the object" (Agamben 1993, 20; Žižek 2001, 146). A few pages later in *Stanzas* Agamben writes: "The imaginary loss that so obsessively occupies the melancholic tendency has no real object ... [t]he lost object is but the appearance that desire creates for its own courting of the phantasm ... what is real loses its reality so that what is unreal may become real" (25).

This is the postcolonial melancholy that the Red Tory embodies and the work of Robertson and Culley simultaneously inhabits and critiques. Indeed, it is the very difficulty of this dialectic, this *Aufhebung*, which makes their poetry so complex. The work is both mourning and melancholic at the same time, both radical and conservative, both "red" and "tory." In the semiosis of the poetry, nature is ruptured by industry and colonialism, which break leads to the pastoral; then, a post-industrial decay leads to the neo-pastoral of *XEclogue* or *Climax Forest*. Really it's not so much having lost the object, but having lost the desire for it—for it is not that the object is lost, but the object-cause of desire—and so "melancholy stands for the presence of the object itself deprived of the desire for itself. Melancholy occurs when we finally get the desired object, but are disappointed in it" (Žižek 2001, 148). Žižek claims that melancholy is "effectively ... the beginning of philosophy" in that it is the "disappointment at all positive, observable objects, none of which can satisfy our desire"; but melancholy is also the beginning of poetry (and let's say that Virgilian pastoral is close enough to the beginning for the West to count it as such). Thus the objects are structured around a void—which cannot be seen on pain of death—so one object occupies that void and is the *objet petit a*, meaning not so much that the void is embodied in that object (in the pastoral), but that the lack or void functions as that object. For our purposes, it is the pastoral (the land) that "keeps the gap of desire open" (ibid., 151).

CHAPTER FIVE

MY Archive Fever: the Material Cultures of the KSW

> As I study this age which is so close to us and so remote, I compare myself to a surgeon operating with local anesthetic: I work in areas that are numb, dead—yet the patient is alive and can still talk.
> —Paul Morand, in Benjamin 1999, 462

> The operation was a success but the surgeon died.
> —Gerald Creede 1986, n.p.

> What I give is a desultory analysis of the archive and not a detailed account of its numbers and specifics.
> —William Wood, "This is Free Money?" in Wallace 1993, 180n1

> Those who do not learn from history are doomed to research it.
> —Gerald Creede, in Lusk 1988, n.p.

> They wanted to argue generations but the past year is all archives.
> —Jeff Derksen, in Klobucar and Barnholden 1999, 205

> Out of kindness comes redness and out of rudeness comes rapid same question, out of an eye comes research, out of

selection comes painful cattle.
—Gertrude Stein 1984, 163

The KSW archives at Simon Fraser University's Contemporary Literature Collection comprises some seven bankers' boxes of documents—ranging from bank statements to emails, meeting minutes to class pamphlets, as well as numerous boxes of cassette tapes (recorded poetry readings), and files for *Writing* magazine. In the first box, lying on top, naked (not in a folder), is a double-sided eight-and-a-half by eleven-inch sheet of paper; on one side is a printed copy of an email to members of the KSW collective from Aaron Vidaver, which begins:

> Here are three nifty statements which may find a place somewhere in the counter-attack:
> "the organization does serve as an important source of literary information and author's resource."
> Standing Committee of Council on Finance and Administration, Report to Council, November 28, 1985
>
> "I would also like to take this opportunity to offer my deepest thanks to your organization for providing needed services and programs to Vancouver citizens in order to enhance and improve our quality of life. Your dedicated work contributes to the overall well-being of Vancouver."
> Sandra Wilking, Alderman
>
> Letter to Nancy Shaw, May 5, 1989
> "The office of Cultural Affairs remains supportive of the Kootenay School of Writing, recognizing the value of its role and potential within the city."
> Social Planning Department
> Report to Standing Committee of Council on City Services and Budgets
> April 9, 1996 [in reply to KSW appeal]

On the other side is a "definitive chronology of city grants," ranging from $1,000 in 1985 to $3,000 in 1997.[1]

The email from Vidaver is presumably from 1998 when, having been declined funding by Vancouver's Office of Cultural Affairs, the KSW resorted to such fundraising events as hosting a reading by Michael Ondaatje (with Lisa Robertson).[2] The email is interesting for two reasons: it was placed in the material archive (why did Vidaver, who helped assemble the archive,[3] put it there?), and it indicates the KSW's ongoing place in local institutional, social, and economic contexts. I will return to that latter question in the second part of this chapter. But first, I want to use this question of what is in the archive to consider why some things are or are not in the archive, as well as what those "things" are and, indeed, what the "archive" is. All this as a way to first think about how we can theorize archives and through that, reapproach the KSW archive and the KSW itself.

While the question of what is in, or belongs in, the archive, is not new, indeed may be fundamental to how we think about the archive,[4] a psychoanalytic approach may offer some new insights. Before elaborating on a specifically Lacanian approach, however, the broader question of the psychoanalytic archive can be situated via the work of Derrida[5] and Agamben. Here we begin with Derrida's *Archive Fever*. While much of this work is not concerned with the archive as such, and instead provides a reading of Yosef Yerushalmi's book on Freud's *Moses and Monotheism*, that discussion is framed by Derrida's famous thoughts on the archive in terms of state power and Freud's death drive. Derrida begins by stating that the archive is both the house and the public institution, a place of commencement and commandment, both conservative and revolutionary (1995, 1). Derrida sees Freud's ambivalence about consigning his work to paper, to the archive, as a matter of the death drive which "destroys in advance its own archive" (ibid., 10), since the archive, through its figure of repetition, "even when it summons memory … must also import there, *in the same stroke*, the death drive, the violence of forgetting" (ibid., 79). This linking of repetition to the death drive comes from Freud's *Beyond the Pleasure Principle* (originally published in 1920 as *Jenseits des Lustprinzips*). In that text, Freud wonders why sufferers of wartime trauma would dream of the moment of their injury—but he also observes his grandson at play, throwing and retrieving a wooden spool and acting out his mother's absences (he grouped both cases under "repetition-compulsion"). Freud came to argue that beyond simply pleasure, we have a capacity or desire for pain, indeed, for death. Derrida's comments should then be quoted more fully:

> The injunction, even when it summons memory or the safeguard of the archive, turns incontestably toward the future to come. It orders to promise, but it orders repetition, and first of all self-repetition, self-confirmation in a *yes, yes*. If repetition is thus inscribed at the heart of the future to come, one must also import there, *in the same stroke*, the death drive, the violence of forgetting, *superrepression* (suppression and repression), the anarchive, in short, the possibility of putting to death the very thing, whatever its name, which *carries the law in its tradition*: the archon of the archive, the table, *what* carries the table and *who* carries the table, the subjectile, the substrate, and the subject of the law. (1995, 79)

Derrida also comes to talk of the *mal d'archive*, the archive fever of his title, by which he means the desire for the document, for the singularity of some object or document in the archive, an "irreplaceable singularity" that is always doomed to being repeated, a *mal d'archive* that is "to burn with a passion … never to rest, interminably, from searching for the archive … to run after the archive … to have a compulsive, repetitive, and nostalgic desire for the archive" (1995, 90, 91). But if Derrida's archive fever is figural, a matter of psychoanalytic desire, it also turns out, in *Dust*, a hilarious riposte by Carolyn Steedman, to be an actual disease, the respiratory ailments and meningitis suffered by historians and men of letters who inhaled anthrax-infected spores from old books and documents. Hence my archive cough.

In the fall of 2010, after spending six hours one day in the KSW archives, I took the weekend off to travel into the BC Interior with my family to see the legendary spawning grounds of the sockeye salmon. The 2010 run of salmon had, beyond all predictions, and in spite of years of declining stocks, been the largest in almost a century: perhaps 30 million had returned to the mighty Fraser river system. A salmon spawning run is truly an example of the Freudian intertwining of *Eros* and *Thanatos*, of pleasure and death—of Lacanian *jouissance*. The fish have travelled thousands of miles, battered by current, by rock, and by each other. Their bodies are now coloured a lurid red, the males' mouths having shrivelled into a predatory hook. These sockeye salmon covered the Adams River near Chase, an hour or so outside the city of Kamloops. It was on this trip, a day after my visit to the archives, that I came down with my archive cough. With the worst cold I'd had in ten years.

Derrida and the substrate

But let us return to another materiality. That is, this question of how or why the Vidaver email would come to be printed off (whether on a double-sided sheet or single, in portrait or landscape format: how did this object come to exist in a material form separate from the digital?). As well, how and why did it come to reside on top of the material in the "first" box of the hitherto "unorganized" archive? The political and historical context of this archive we will turn to momentarily; Derrida's concept of archive fever is still located in the subject, in the dust of subject's desire. What we also have to understand is the question of the desire of the Other, the abyss of that desire, that is. For this question we can look at Lacan's 1960 talk "The Subversion of the Subject and the Dialectic of Desire in the Freudian Unconscious" (2002, 702) and Žižek's commentary on the same, in the third chapter of *The Sublime Object of Ideology*, "Che Vuoi?" (1989, 87–129). In what follows, I will talk about the archive in terms of its retrospective organization or constitution as an archive, and then address the question of what that archive wants. For these two ways of thinking about the archive, we can look at two of Lacan's graphs of desire.

In "The Subversion of the Subject" Lacan presented four graphs of desire,[6] as a way of mapping out the relationships between identification, subjectivity, and desire. The first graph, touched on in my second chapter, and based on the mechanics of speech and meaning, established the concept of the *point de capiton*. This linguistic operation is akin to Freud's *Nachträglichkeit*, the notion that a symptom only comes to have a meaning retroactively (in the canonical example, the Wolf Man witnesses his parents making love when he is an infant, but this only comes to acquire meaning when he develops sexually a few years later). Lacan's theory of the *point de capiton*, or "quilting button" or "button tie" (2002, 681) argues that, in any linguistic exchange, the meaning of a signifier only occurs retroactively when it is "fixed" or "quilted" or "tied down" (like a button on a cushion) by a master signifier.

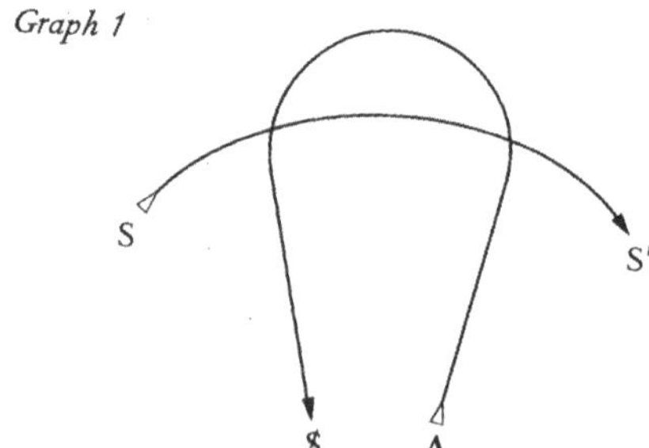

Graph 1. (Source: Lacan 2002, 681. Copyright W.W. Norton and Company, used by permission.)

Thus, in Vidaver's archival sentence quoted previously, "the organization does serve as an important source of literary information and author's resource," the word "organization" is free-floating, a sliding signifier, until its meaning is fixed by its being "an important source" and "resource." Or, as Lacan writes: "The diachronic function of this button tie can be found in a sentence, insofar as a sentence closes its signification only with its last term, each term being anticipated in the construction constituted by the other terms and, inversely, sealing their meaning by its retroactive effect" (2002, 682).

In Graph 1, while the subject may believe that meaning moves from S to S′, in a forward, linear manner, in (Lacanian) reality meaning moves backward on the line from the ¾ to $. Psychoanalysis works at the clinical, linguistic, and cultural levels, so the *point de capiton* has resonances not simply with respect to the symptom (as in Freud's Wolf Man case) or the sentence, but also in broader contexts. Žižek, for instance, drawing on Laclau and Mouffe's *Hegemony and Socialist Strategy*, uses it to argue for how ideological operations fix meanings: "Ideological space is made of non-bound, non-tied elements, 'floating signifiers,' whose very identity is 'open,' overdetermined by their articulation in a chain with other elements—that is, their 'literal' signification depends on their metaphorical surplus-signification ... *feminism* can be socialist, apolitical ...; even *racism* could be elitist or populist. The 'quilting' performs the totalization by means of which the free floating of ideological elements is halted, fixed—that is to say, by means of which they become parts of the structured network of meaning" (1989, 87).

In these Lacanian and Žižekian senses, then, the meaning of a sentence found in the KSW archive—namely, that "the organization does serve as an important source of literary information and author's resource," sent from the City of Vancouver Standing Committee of Council on Finance and Administration in its Report to Council, November 28, 1985, and quoted in a letter to the KSW—acquires additional layers. That is, retroactively, what was in 1985 a simple phrase of cultural value had, by 1998, become a "nifty statement" that could provide evidence for the KSW's "counter-attack" and defend its funding from the city. Note that I am using the concept of the *point de capiton* to describe the archival activity *already at work in the KSW archive*. The archive is already, when I am working with it in 2010, at work archiving itself—this is how I read and situate the double-sided email and chronology that Vidaver placed into the archive. The meaning of the archive does not lie in the inert, dusty files, in the sheets of paper and bank statements and funding applications and colloquium registration slips that appear to constitute the KSW archive. Rather, the meaning of what is in the archive—and to a degree this is an ontological argument as well as a hermeneutic one—lies in its being archived, in its being collected or constituted as a mass of material.

This retrospective organization of the archive, then, means that there is no original, organic archive—of the kind that is deposited by the author or his or her estate, collected over years by an acquisitions committee, or suddenly bequeathed to a university by a distant relative or generous poet. In terms of the KSW archive, the history is somewhat anecdotal: Tony Power, the librarian of the Contemporary Literature Collection at SFU, told me that one day "Ted and Mike" brought in the dozen or so bankers' boxes that, when I looked at the archive in 2010, and except for Vidaver's 1998 labour, still lay unsorted. "Ted and Mike" are Ted Byrne and Michael Barnholden, both longstanding members of the KSW collective, and both evidently have a desire to preserve that archive.

This brings us back to the question of desire, and also perhaps of subjectivity: who or what is the subject of the archive? Confining ourselves for the most part to literary archives, is it the author or writer who is the subject of the archive, whether or not he or she is the depositor? And what is the underlying desire—preservation? access? privacy? The writer's career or canonization or rescue from oblivion (from the "gnawing of the mice" as Marx described the fate of his and Engels' manuscript for *The German Ideology*)? What contradictions are to be seen in this desire? For, on the one hand, archives give access to researchers, but they also give some privacy, some repression of "bad history," whether personal failings, misalliances, or battles lost. Or is the subject of the archive the archivist herself? The staff at institutions (but also private archivists, small-town librarians, amateur collectors), have hierarchies and rivalries, rules and symbolic capital. Again, what plays out are desires for preservation, for institutional capital, for acquisitions, but not of everything (for collections must be curated, and this is never simply a matter of space or finances); for example, will the staff collect digital or physical copies and what of their overlap? Or is the subject the researcher? The academic or student (or, again, the amateur, perhaps researching an author or one's family history), the poet or political activist (or both)—and, again, what is his or her desire? Is it for access, use, for uncovering the hidden, discovering new material, something hitherto unpublished, the "archival jolt" (O'Driscoll and Bishop 2004, 2)? Or is it for one's own social or cultural or political capital? Again the contradiction: you have to share what you have found with the world.

To return to our archive; is the subject of the KSW archive the KSW itself, constituted as an institutional subject? Is it the figures we encounter in the minutes and grant applications of those early years: Tom Wayman, Colin Browne, Kathryn MacLeod, Calvin Wharton? Is it the Contemporary Literature Collection, first constituted by the late Charles Watts (after whom a library at the KSW is named) or its present-day librarian Tony Power? Is it Jason Wiens, who gives evidence of his work in the archive in his essay on the KSW and "Canonicity and Teachable Texts" or myself, as researcher?

These questions cannot be resolved merely by listing the material information that is found in the archive; such a turn to the empirical under the guise of history, like the historical datum of the email, only gentrifies the abyss of desire. What do I mean by this? To begin, the very question of who constitutes the subject of the archive—the very indeterminacy of that question, the difficulty that lies in pinning down subjectivity in one corner, in one actor or agent—demonstrates how the archive *qua* subject is located not so much in any of those places (a neoliberal, humanist notion that we all get to be subjects of the archive), but nowhere—there is no subject of the archive. Or, to take the notion further, the subject of the archive is a blank space, is a lack, a gap or void. The archive is terminable and interminable.

This is the argument of the Lacanian theory of the subject, and the relation of the subject to desire is further explicated in Lacan's third graph of desire, the graph that, shaped compellingly like a question mark or fish hook, asks *Chè vuoi?* What do you want? (2002, 690).

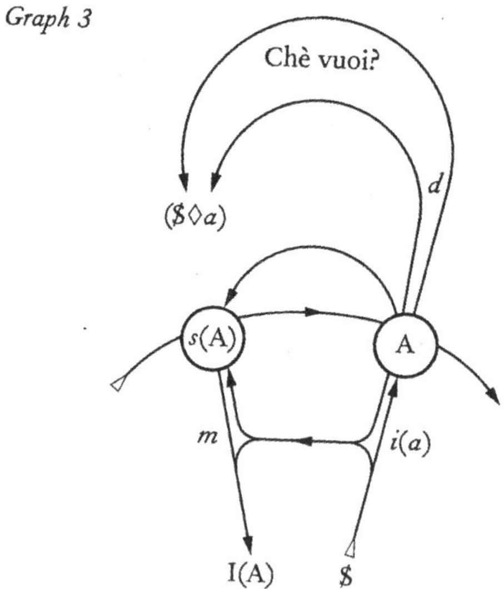

GRAPH 3. (Source: Lacan 2002, 690. Copyright W.W. Norton and Company, used by permission.)

We can see how much Lacan has elaborated on and complicated his graph since the elemental first diagram, but let us take it simply and concentrate only on a few aspects of this picture. The arrows that run between *s*(A) (signifier of the Other/Autre) and A (the Other/Autre) are the new version of the *point de capiton*: our signifiers, our speech, only acquire meaning in the Other—language is the discourse of the Other. Which is to say that we must communicate through a language that pre-exists us. The barred subject, the $ on the lower right of the diagram is constituted through the Other, but such subjectification always leaves an element of desire (the *d*)—the question of what the other wants from me. That question is "answered," or an answer is provided for the abyss of the Other's desire, by fantasy, the structure for which is ($◊*a*), or the barred subject in a movement to and away from the *objet petit a*.

Lacan elaborates thus: "For it is clear here that man's continued nescience [ignorance] of his desire is not so much nescience of what he demands, which may after all be isolated, as nescience of what he desires" (2002, 689). Here, first, then, is the distinction between demand and desire. Simply put, desire is what is left over when a demand has been met. If I go to the archive and request—ask for—demand—boxes five and six of the KSW archive, and a library assistant brings those out to a work table, my demand has been met, but my desire (what do I really want? what is my goal today? what do I hope to find? what bothered me on my walk over from my office?) remains.

Lacan then continues: "This is where my formulation that the unconscious is [the] discourse of the Other [*discours de l'Autre*] fits in ... But we must also add that man's desire is the Other's desire ... namely that *it is qua Other that man desires ...*" (2002, 690). This is where it gets tricky: my desire is not simply my own desire. Just as *my unconscious* is in the Other, and *my language* is in the other, so *my archive* is in the other. I don't just have remnants of my desire (the indivisible remainder, as Žižek puts it), but that desire is also the desire of the Other, of the archive, in the sense that "it is qua Other that man desires." Or to open this up a bit: my desire is the desire of the Other (of the archive) in the sense that I desire the archive, but I also want to be desired by the archive, and I want to have the same desire as the archive.

"This is why," Lacan declares, "the Other's question ... that comes back to the subject from the place from which he expects an oracular reply—which takes some such form as '*Chè Vuoi?*,' 'What do you want?,' is the question that best leads the subject to the path of his own desire" (2002, 690). Lacan then turns to clinical practice, where the analysand wonders of the analyst "What does he want from me?"

Referring to his diagram, it is this question, this open-ended question, this *Chè Vuoi?*, that Lacan calls "the outline of a question mark planted in the circle of the capital A." He continues, in full figural excess, asking "Of what bottle is this the opener? Of what answer is it the signifier, the master key?" (2002, 690). And this surely also denotes that archival moment, when, my "demand" met—the box brought to me—I open the box, take off the lid and, confronted with the double-sided email, with the "counter-attack," I ask, "What does he (Vidaver) want from me?" In asking, finally, what does the (subject of the) archive want, I am asking what I want.

And the answer to that question lies in fantasy: the archive as fantasy, as fantasy space. The archive as a space for dreams, for reverie, for that scholarly slumber on a hot, stuffy afternoon, surrounded by a jumble of papers, notes, one's laptop, perhaps a smuggled-in coffee.

That fantasy answers the question of desire, of what the archive wants, and it also protects us from that question: hence, in Lacan's graph, the structure for fantasy covers over the gap in the question mark—a gap that, like the signifier of the barred subject, $, denotes a split subject—"the moment of a fading or eclipse of the subject—which is closely tied to the *Spaltung* or splitting he undergoes due to his subordination to the signifier" (2002, 691). The subject is split because the subject is in language, the language of Being—the signifier—and that split, rendered in intersubjectivity as a subordination to desire, to the desire of the Other, is then papered over, or screened, by fantasy, by ($\$\Diamond a$).

But what is this fantasy of the archive? Is it simply, as I wrote above, a sublime slumber on an academic afternoon? Is it the fantasy that in the archive we will find the definitive object, the definitive material evidence—Derrida's archive fever? Or is it the post-structuralist dream of indeterminacy? Is the formula for fantasy that it, in Lacan's words, "is designed to allow for a hundred and one different readings, a multiplicity that is acceptable as long as what is said about it remains grounded in its algebra" (2002, 691)?

For help with some of these questions, let us return to Žižek's commentary on Lacan's graphs in *The Sublime Object*. First of all, Žižek connects the open gap in the *Chè Vuoi?* question to the *point de capiton*, which always turns out to be inadequate and "never comes without a certain leftover": After every 'quilting' of the signifier's chain which retroactively fixes its meaning, there always remains a certain gap, an opening which is rendered in the third form of the graph by the famous '*Chè Vuoi?*'—'You're telling me that, but what do you want with it, what are you aiming at?' The question mark arising above the curve of 'quilting' thus indicates the persistence of a gap between utterance and its enunciation ...' (1989, 111).

If the "utterance of the archive" is, say, Vidaver's declaration of a "counter-attack," then the "enunciation" is what archivists call the "substratum," the physical object, the double-sided piece of paper or email. The gap in the archive, the gap that gives rise to *Chè Vuoi?*, exists between two forms of materialism: the materialism of the signifier, of discourse, and the materialism of the object, of the thing.

Žižek continues, a few pages later, with a discussion of the role of fantasy, which "... functions as a construction, as an imaginary scenario filling out the void, the opening of the *desire of the Other*: by giving us a definitive answer to the question 'What does the Other want?,' it enables us to evade the unbearable deadlock in which the Other wants something from us, but we are at the same time incapable of translating this desire of the Other into a positive interpellation, into a mandate with which to identify" (1989, 114–15).

But this fantasy, it should be noted, does not comfort Žižek: fantasy does not satisfy our desire, but rather structures it and teaches us what to desire; indeed, in the end, becomes a defence against desire: "the desire structured through fantasy is a defence against the desire of the Other, against this 'pure', trans-phasmatic desire (i.e. the 'death drive' in its pure form)" (1989, 118). And this death drive, as we saw with Derrida (and with my archive cough, which conveniently enough came on when I was observing the death drive of the sockeye salmon), is in some ways constitutive of the archive.

Perhaps the archive needs to be thought of in a more doctrinaire, Marxist fashion. Perhaps the archive, or the archival item, is a commodity; or at least it is a commodity until it enters the archive. This was Benjamin's argument in *The Arcades Project* where, speaking of the collector, he said that "[t]o him falls the Sisyphean task of divesting things of their commodity character by taking possession of them. But he bestows on them only connoisseur value, rather than use value" (1999, 9). Thus the problem with the historical fantasy of the archive is that it isn't hysterical enough, it doesn't actually heed what Marx in another context called the essential mystery of the commodity, its strangeness. In *Capital*: if "there is nothing mysterious" about an object or thing "in so far as it is a use-value," once it emerges as a commodity "it changes into a thing which transcends sensuousness" (1990, 163), that is, it is no longer simply a matter of the substrate. Now we are in the realm of desire—of desire of the Other, of drive, of never achieving our desire precisely because it is the Other's.

Material conditions: the KSW qua *social institution*

The move of the KSW to Vancouver is both originary and shrouded in myth and obscurantism. Key questions surround the relation between place or space and the institution, the role of provincial as well as aesthetic politics, and the various social formations that constituted the KSW in Vancouver and to which it contributed.

Restricting ourselves to the archival record for the KSW's early years in Vancouver—from 1984 to 1990—we find records of the school's administration, including minutes from meetings, budgets, bank statements, and telephone bills. Files of clippings, minutes from articulation meetings, grant applications, logs of class attendance, course proposals, drafts of proposed anthology introductions and contents. One key insight we can glean from an examination of that record is the relationship between the KSW and other institutions, be they aesthetic, educational, or governmental. And we can also see the struggles, both internal and external, that the KSW underwent to constitute itself as a viable entity; struggles that resulted in a vibrant series of classes, workshops, and colloquia offered over these years, situated in a variety of aesthetic and poetic traditions.

Nelson, BC's David Thompson University Centre closed as an educational institution in April 1984[7]; the KSW ("Vancouver Centre") began weekly meetings on July 27, 1984 and started offering classes that fall. In the "interregnum," and even before the KSW had officially constituted itself as a collective organization, Fred Wah, who had been an instructor at DTUC, attended a creative writing articulation meeting at Douglas College in May 1984. The minutes of that meeting show Wah attempting to form a "Kooteney [sic] School of Writing," although it is not clear if this is to be located in Nelson or in Vancouver.[8] There is other evidence of attempted articulation or transferability with the University of British Columbia (including journalism classes), the University of Victoria, Simon Fraser University, and Lower Mainland boards of education and continuing education programs.[9] In the fall of 1985, and in response to a student query, the KSW applied for designation as an "Eligible Institution" under the Canada Student Loans Act and Alberta Student Loans Act, describing itself as a "faculty-run co-operative" founded in July 1984, with eighty-five students over the previous twelve months and eleven part-time faculty.[10] Almost all of these efforts were rebuffed, and while there is no record of the response on the part of the Alberta student loans program, one can imagine how unlikely it was that the KSW would become accredited.

Nevertheless, the grant applications (three successful, to the City of Vancouver, Province of British Columbia, and Canada Council for the Arts, and some unsuccessful, to private foundations) together with the record of classes organized and offered do not paint a picture of an unprofessional organization. A lot of energy was spent, and spent wisely, in the 1980s. And if major academic institutions were not amenable to working with the KSW, the same cannot be said for arts organizations in the city and province, most notably the visual arts. Thus in grant applications we see records and proposals to work with the Vancouver Art Gallery (for a Clark Coolidge residency as part of the Stan Douglas-curated Samuel Beckett exhibition)[11]; for readings and talks with the Coburg Gallery, with the Or and Western Front; with the Praxis filmmakers collective, with the Women & Words literary festival, with the R2B2 and Octopus East bookstores and, for the first few years of its operation, the KSW operated the Vancouver Literary Information Resource and published the Vancouver Literary Calendar.[12]

Most famously, the KSW was responsible (in part) for the establishment of Artspeak, an artist-run gallery that would eventually become independent of the KSW and is still in operation. Tom Wayman, in "Against the Smiling Bastards," his 2007 memoir about the KSW in both Vancouver and Nelson, explains the founding in this way: "One day a couple of recent graduates of Emily Carr's curatorial program showed up at KSW, and pointed out that our office and classroom were usually empty during the day. They wanted to launch their own exhibition space and convinced us this would complement our writing curriculum. Thus Vancouver's Artspeak Gallery began" (2007, 83–84).

Here we can supplement this work of memory by examining first the record of how that process—founding Artspeak—took place, and then the larger milieu of artist-run centres in Vancouver. In the KSW minutes for November 29, 1985, we see the following item: "8. Gallery—Jeff wants to use our small classroom as a gallery—he will talk to some artists if they want to curate." In the minutes for December 13: "gallery people looked at the room (101)." Then on January 31, 1986, we see "ArtSpeak" first used as a possible name for the space. In the minutes, Keith Higgins is mentioned (though it's unclear whether he attended the meeting), as well as details on the need to obtain track lighting for the "wall art," programs of local artists and book works, opening hours, a mandate for programming, and plans to open in March.

To anyone who has examined the minutes of grassroots arts organizations, the mix of the mundane and the aesthetic—seen in the lead-up to the establishment of Artspeak (or "ArtSpeak"), and throughout the KSW minutes over the five-year period from 1984 through 1989—is no surprise. Thus Wayman writes that the Friday afternoon meetings dealt with "every possible problem the fledgling operation encountered—from curriculum planning to the state of seminar tables to janitorial issues like the need to purchase more toilet paper" (2007, 84).[13] (Sara Diamond's essay on the Video Inn is exemplary in this regard, as is William Wood's archival account of the Western Front.) And so KSW minutes for April 4, 1986 (handwritten on yellow foolscap paper, like almost all the minutes from July 1984 until June 1985, after which the substratum varies), begin with the item "This week->" and include the following entries: "letter to Gwen Hoover re. Jane Rule; reg. sustenance stuff; photo-copier; Athena making a poster for Margaret's reading." And a little lower down, "next week->" includes entries on "Blue Pencil & Lit. Groc. following 2 Saturdays; Reading Sunday night." Further items include the discussion of the cost of a sign, a note on sending the "VLC" (Vancouver Literary Calendar) to the "Kits" (Kitsilano) neighbourhood or community centre; Community Arts money; a talk/letter on video censorship; reports on the co-sponsorship of the 3-Day Novel contest; the possibility of "Bob" Kroetsch visiting in July; a class by Barry McKinnon; and information on the Canada Council visiting foreign artists program. Attending were Colin Browne, Gary Whitehead, Jeff (whether Jeff George or Jeff Derksen is unclear), and Calvin Wharton.

What emerges in general from these minutes is, first, a representation of a self-governing organization determined to tap into existing funding sources as a way of carrying out poetic and literary programming as well as pedagogical functions, with little in the way of hierarchy or a division of labour (that is to say, tasks are assigned but there is little evidence that only one or two people did the work or that certain people did certain types of work). As well, the record consistently shows a wide variety of programming being proposed and pursued. This is also evident in the records of the classes taught, but especially in regard to the Artspeak initiative, it offers evidence not merely of the interdisciplinary nature of the KSW—a nature that was already in place due to cooperating with various other aesthetic institutions—but of the way in which such activities were themselves wholly self-starting.

The earlier reference to the research of Sara Diamond and William Wood, with respect to arts groups' archives, was not a digression. The move from the KSW proper to a visual arts organization or artist-run centre,[14] as well as the documentation of the KSW's collaborations with the Western Front, the Or and Coburg galleries, and the Contemporary Art Gallery indicates the need to situate the KSW's presence in Vancouver in the 1980s institutionally, in terms of other arts organizations.[15] Here critical-historical work by Sara Diamond, William Wood, and Keith Wallace is particularly instructive. Wallace's "A Particular History: Artist-Run Centres in Vancouver," in addition to providing such a history, focuses on a dialectic or contradiction between the need for artist-run centres to establish their autonomy from the market (as they were given to showing non-commercial art, often not even in a gallery itself) and the bureaucratization that came with accepting public monies. If galleries become "complacent with their marginality," they end up being subsidized by the very artists they are there to serve. If they succeed in attracting Canada Council for the Arts (or BC Arts Council) funding, this "suggests a move from a radical idea of 'alternative' to a more conservative one" (Wallace in Douglas 1991, 38). But Wallace is not wholly pessimistic, pointing out that the Vancouver tradition of curators possessing autonomy (whereas exhibition committees were, and are, common in other Canadian scenes) and arguing that "[m]odestly scaled exhibition spaces, characteristic of Vancouver, are another means of lessening bureaucracy" (39). This question of space—or scale—is a key link to the KSW, given that Artspeak began in a symbiotic relation to their "host," occupying classrooms that were otherwise unused during the daytime. That is to say, Artspeak's spatial relation to the KSW at the point of "origin" is akin to how the KSW and other grassroots organizations relate to the urban spaces they inhabit—more to follow on precisely that question of the urban.

Wood's and Diamond's accounts of artist-run centres and the aesthetics thereof are also useful as a way of situating both this research project in the archives and the relative status of the KSW in such a milieu or scene. In his essay in *Whispered Art History: Twenty Years at the Western Front*, Wood notes that while an "oligarchic" power structure (in Wallace 1993, 184, 187) at the Front ensured its longevity, there was also an absence of aesthetic criteria in its appeals for the funding needed to acquire technology (from video cameras and microphones to mixing boards and cables). Too, the location of the Front in the then "unsavoury locale" of Mount Pleasant (181) made its locked-down, bunker mentality all but inevitable given the artists' desire for the utopia of interdisciplinary media. That same location was part of its "embedding within the ... neighbourhood and the collection of artist-run centres in Vancouver" (186). With hindsight, it is now possible to argue that the Front contributed to the neighbourhood's gentrification.

Wood's essay proceeded from his "desultory analysis" of the archive, as noted in this chapter's epigraph, which expanded reads thus: "This essay is based on a reading of the Front's administrative archives; I will not note specific items with that *fond*. What I give is a desultory analysis of the archive and not a detailed account of its numbers and specifics" (in Wallace 1993, 181n). So too did Sara Diamond's essay on video aesthetics derive from a stroll through the archives of the "Video Inn Minutes" (in Douglas 1991, 58*ff*). Two concerns emerge in Diamond's text: first, the lack of aesthetic debate in the record and, second, the connection between video as a document and the documentation of video. Diamond begins her discussion of the "Video Inn Minutes (1973–1982)" with the observation that "Despite a strong interest in video, there is little evidence of theoretical or formal debates about the medium in the early days of the Video Inn" (ibid., 58). This is not to say the minutes did not display a range of material, from the "janitorial," as Wayman puts it, to matters of electoral politics. But, along with what Diamond calls "a desire to stay small, to function at a 'grassroots' level" (ibid.), there was interest in the power of the video as document (73*ff*). The same observations could be made of the artist-run centre archive, whether the archive of the Video Inn or the archive of the Kootenay School.

A final way in which to situate the KSW as an institution would be to place it within the social geography of Vancouver proper. That is, here we can think of spatializations of the city in terms of class (the east side versus the west side); ethnicity (the First Nations' aboriginal spaces and reserves, as well as Chinatown, Japantown, and Little India)[16]; sexuality (the West End and perhaps Commercial Drive as gay and lesbian neighbourhoods respectively); and waves of gentrification (the development of the West End in the 1960s, of Fairview and Kitsilano in the 1970s, of Mount Pleasant and Commercial Drive in the 1980s, and of Strathcona and the Downtown Eastside from the 1990s to today).[17] In this regard, the location of the KSW first at Oak and West Broadway above a Vietnamese restaurant ("Saigon") indicates the solidarity between the ethnic petit bourgeois and artists in terms of affordable rent. For the most part, after this, the KSW was located in various Skid Row or Downtown Eastside pockets of artist-run centres around the strip of West Hastings from Hamilton to Abbott.[18]

This urban practice—artists and other bohemians locating in undesirable neighbourhoods—is hardly unique to Vancouver, of course. Even just in the North American context, the artists' communities in San Francisco's SOMA and Mission districts, New York's SoHo, Toronto's Queen Street West, or Winnipeg's Exchange district all indicate the propensity for such subcultures to locate themselves in affordable urban zones. But questions of Vancouver's regions are also a matter of the KSW's aesthetics; the KSW's presentation of itself in terms of these debates and zones is perhaps most forcefully negotiated through the *East of Main* anthology, edited by Tom Wayman and Calvin Wharton and published in 1989. Here two forms of diversity predominate: one, of an ethnic/identity politics sort, via the book's cover; the other, of an aesthetic or poetic sort, via the book's contents.

I will come back to *East of Main* later, but before considering KSW production in the 1980s I want to finish this account of the archives with a brief consideration of the question of funding.[19] This is by no means a forensic audit, but some of the data available includes:

> 1984 budget (actuals): $5,439 expenditures /$5,463 income (donations, tuition)

1985 budget (actuals): $22,865 expenditures / $24,486 income ($500 community arts council, $7,725 Explorations CC, $500 Chevron Canada, $675 donations, $633 functions & office rent, $60 photocopier, $14,393 tuition)

1986 budget (actuals): $42,390 expenditures; $43,140 income ($19,450 Explorations CC, $2,000 Vancouver Civic Cultural Grants, $1,000 Koerner Foundation, $300 for box office tickets, $300 Community Arts Council, $750 functions, $1,440 donations, $15,500 tuition, $200 CAIMAW [union], $1,300 colloquium registration, $400 subscriptions to literary calendar; $500 photocopy fees)

1987 budget (actuals): (difficult to calculate as bookkeeping dates changed; but $14,250 from Explorations CC—final year; $3,000 Vancouver Civic Cultural Grants)

While the data is not consistent, we can see that even in these early years the KSW had some degree of success in acquiring public money. Additionally, the archives show there were repeated attempts to secure funding from private foundations—Leon & Thea Koerner (successful), but also Vancouver Foundation, Endeavour Foundation, Ford Foundation, Hamber Foundation, H.R. MacMillan Family Fund, Labatt Breweries, McLean Foundation, Richardson Century Fund, Samuel & Saidye Bronfman Family Fund, Witter Bynner Foundation, and the Woodlawn Arts Fund.[20]

If the KSW was rebuffed by academic institutions (including the universities, colleges, and adult education systems), made alliances with the artist-run centres, and had some success in grant-getting, that is, was constituted between the streets, the galleries, and the universities, what relation does this bear to its programming practices, to its production? Here we can make a few distinctions: between those activities that brought in revenue (like the literary calendar, classes, the colloquia) and those that mostly saw an expenditure of funds (readings, residencies); between the ephemeral (this is Wayman's term from a grant application: readings) and the documentary (publications such as *Writing* magazine); and within the readings themselves, between established and up-and-coming writers (again, the distinction is Wayman's[21]); and within the classes, between those on poetics and the more accessible workshops or "literary groceries."

Thus the Blue Pencil cafés and Literary Groceries workshops were a form of practical, pragmatic demystification: "The Blue Pencil Café provides the beginning and advanced writer with a critical evaluation of their work. Each writer receives a half hour assessment and discussion of their work with a Kootenay School of Writing Instructor ..." Instructors in fall 1984 included Jeff Derksen, Alicia Priest, Calvin Wharton, and Gary Whitehead; the fee was fifteen dollars.[22] The "Literary Groceries" workshop was "an information session on the publishing and financial aspects of the contemporary literary world. The topics explored that year included: preparation of manuscripts, how to submit for publication, where to send your work ..." The instructor was Tom Wayman; the fee was ten dollars.[23] Other courses in the fall of 1984 included "Listening to the Language" (with Daphne Marlatt); there were talks by Colin Browne, Gail Scott, and Brian Fawcett; a production workshop with Jeff Derksen and Calvin Wharton; and a journalism workshop with Tom Wayman.[24] A brochure for "SUMMER 1986 COURSES in Vancouver" includes courses on Introductory Creative writing (Dale Zieroth), Prose Fiction, How to Write What (Colin Browne), Poetry Workshop (Susan Musgrave), Zukofsky's 'A', Surviving as a Book and Theatre Critic (Alan Twigg), Marketing the Magazine Article (David R. Conn), a Blue Pencil café, and several Literary Groceries.[25]

What does this limited survey of the KSW's pedagogical practices tell us? First of all, I think the most important preliminary conclusion to be drawn is from the wide variety of aesthetic and discursive practices on offer here: that is, not only are there classes ranging from poetry and journalism to theatre criticism and "literary groceries," but the aesthetics represented by the teachers also ranges widely. Dale Zieroth (or such supporters of the KSW as Leona Gom) are best known for their anecdotal, lyrically based narrative poems; Susan Musgrave—who both read under the KSW banner and gave a course (both in 1986)—could hardly be further situated from the disjunctive poetics of the KSW and L=A=N=G=U=A=G=E in her hardcore, West Coast wiccan style. In a 1986 grant application, Wayman states that "[o]ur objective is to offer to the public the widest possible range of engagement with and instruction in current imaginative writing."[26] This question of aesthetic or programmed "diversity" also appears in Wayman's "wish list" or "dream sheet" from the collective's meeting at the end of the first year. There he lists "a rich diversity in offerings," including at the program level ("diploma program, community based courses ... graduate programs [i.e., new school of social research in NYC]"); in terms of disciplines ("artists-in-residence [not just writers], mix of artists and different kinds of courses supported by cash cows"); and, underlined to signal its magnitude, "potential for diversity important."[27] In his 2007 memoir, Wayman argues that that diversity has been lost, that while early in the KSW history, in the mid-1980s, Colin Browne stressed the importance of "many musics," that diversity was replaced by a "narrow focus" literary aesthetic.

From the archive to the chapbook

I think that Wayman's observation both is and is not the case—which is to say, we have to examine the historical record dialectically, and we could do this by turning from the archival and historical minutiae to the aesthetic record, looking at the publications and other practices of the KSW. That, of course, has been the practice of this book. In its opening remarks, this book situates the KSW in terms of a Vancouver social history, then locates readings of writers such as Kathryn MacLeod, Deanna Ferguson, and Dorothy Trujillo Lusk in their various publications, magazines, zines, and chapbooks. I want to finish this chapter, however, with a brief look at the various anthologies that appeared in the 1980s and 1990s, which, along with those magazines, chapbooks, and what were first books for many of the writers, flourished in Vancouver in this period. Other practices, less documented, would include the reading series that the KSW promoted, the classes themselves, and reading groups or other informal gatherings, including what Jeff Derksen has notoriously referred to as "a rather rigorous bar scene."[28]

Of the anthologies that collected writers associated with the KSW, then, we have *East of Main: An Anthology of Poems from East Vancouver* (edited by Calvin Wharton and Tom Wayman, 1989) and *Writing Class: The Kootenay School of Writing Anthology* (edited by Andrew Klobucar and Michael Barnholden, 1999)—both stand-alone books; and two issues of journals: the "New Vancouver Writing" issue of *West Coast Line* (24(1), 1990), and the "some Vancouver writers" issue of *Raddle Moon* (17, 1998). I've charted the distribution of writers as follows (writers who appear in more than one anthology are in bold):

East of Main	*West Coast Line*	*Raddle Moon*	*Writing Class*
Kathryn MacLeod	**Claire Stannard**	Christine Stewart	**Gerald Creede**
Gerald Creede	**Deanna Ferguson**	**Peter Culley**	**Kevin Davies**
Calvin Wharton	Colin Browne	**Colin Smith**	**Lary Timewell**
Dennis Denisoff	**Catriona Strang**	**Melissa Wolsak**	**Kathryn MacLeod**
Claire Stannard	**Nancy Shaw**	**Catriona Strang & Nancy Shaw**	**Dan Farrell**
Lary Timewell	Rhoda Rosenfeld	Maxine Gadd	**Lisa Robertson**
Colin Smith	**Calvin Wharton**	**Deanna Ferguson**	**Colin Smith**
Deanna Ferguson	**Peter Culley**	Robert Manery	**Dorothy Trujillo Lusk**

Nancy Shaw	Tom McGauley	**Dorothy Trujillo Lusk**	**Dennis Denisoff**
Jeff Derksen	**Gerald Creede**	**Kevin Davies**	Robert Mittenthal
	Steve Forth	**Lary Timewell**	**Nancy Shaw**
	Susan Yarrow*	**Jeff Derksen**	**Peter Culley**
	Dan Farrell	**Lisa Robertson**	**Judy Radul**
	Jeff Derksen	Meredith Quarter-main	**Jeff Derksen**
	Judy Radul	Edward Byrne	
	Paul Kelley	**Dan Farrell**	
	Adeena Karasick	Paul Mutton	
	Dennis Denisoff	Marie Annharte Baker	
	Dorothy Trujillo Lusk	David Bromige	
		Susan Clark*	

*Susan Clark also wrote under the name Susan Yarrow

A first set of observations might note that the *East of Main* anthology was fairly successful in predicting who would go on to produce work—to produce poetry that would continue to be anthologized; all of the poets in *East of Main* appeared in at least one of the collections that followed. Indeed, most of the poets are in at least three of the four collections: Creede, Denisoff, Timewell, Smith, Ferguson, Shaw, and Derksen. And viewed more globally, Robertson, Strang, Yarrow/Clark, and Davies are in at least two collections; Culley, Farrell, and Lusk feature in three of the four anthologies; and Shaw and Derksen are in all four.[29]

These numbers and comparisons only get us so far: such quantitative analysis should be joined by qualitative analysis. Here I propose to look at the editorial parameters of the collections. What we find is an extremely heterogeneous approach to socio-political contextualization—for the most part located in regionalism and urbanism—as well as varying levels of poetic characterizations. *East of Main* situates its anthologizing principles in terms of the micro-geographies of Vancouver, where Main Street has long functioned as a marker, dividing the city into the West Side and, variously, the East End (which often refers specifically to the Downtown Eastside and Strathcona/Chinatown), the East Side, and East Van/East Vancouver. The demarcation of city avenues into "east" and "west" officially happens at Ontario street (two blocks west of Main). But east of Main, or East Vancouver, has long been the criminalized, and Orientalized, and demonized zone of Vancouver, one that had fewer trees,[30] was farther away from the beaches, had more industry, is home to Vancouver's working classes and, according to an urban myth, a house just within its limits will sell for $100,000 less than one which lies a block from it, but on the other side of the divide.

East of Main sets its catchment area, then, in a marginal zone of Vancouver, with the express purpose of both illustrating thematic and formal concerns often neglected in "official" Canadian anthologies and critiquing what passes for Vancouver or Canadian writing:

> Since both editors of the present volume live in East Vancouver, we felt we could best show the variety and vibrancy of contemporary Canadian poetry by putting together an anthology that would indicate just how much literary activity is going on ... in only *one* part of *one* Canadian city. We wanted to compile an anthology depicting this so clearly that henceforth any reader would look more carefully at any collection claiming to represent 'Canadian' poetry, like Margaret Atwood's *Oxford Book of Canadian Verse*, or Dennis Lee's *The New Canadian Poets*. Similarly, we wanted to assemble a volume that would convincingly demonstrate the inadequacy of the two poetry anthologies issued to mark Vancouver's 1986 Centennial (the editor of one of these volumes being flown in from Montreal, the editor of the

> other residing in White Rock, BC). (Wharton and Wayman 1989, 10)

The choice of East Vancouver is thus both contingent (the editors just happened to live there) and overdetermined (they admit to "loading the dice a little"[ibid.]). But the real charm of the anthology is the alliance it poses between leftist, regionalist, ethnic, feminist, and working-class writing (Pauline Rankin's "Blackberries," Sandy Shreve's "Grievance Procedure," Michael Turner's "7:59 a.m.," Sadhu Binning's "Neighbours," etc.) and language-based writing. The latter is contextualized in the anthology's introduction with quotations from various American writers (Charles Bernstein, Ron Silliman, Bruce Andrews), making a case for writing that moves beyond "persona-centred, 'expressive' poetry" and attempts "openness rather than closure, expansion rather than reduction" (ibid.,12).

The introduction to *West Coast Line*'s "New Vancouver Writing" issue provides a briefer contextualization of the writing that is less Vancouver-centric and situated more in terms of the history of the Kootenay School, from its formation after DTUC was shut down to the cultural activities in Vancouver in the late 1980s. These activities included:

> ... a performance by Judy Radul at the Western Front, a George Stanley book-launching at R2B2 Books, an opening of Roy Arden photographs at the Or Gallery, a Jeff Derksen reading at the Coburg Gallery, Anselm Hollo at the KSW, a conversation with Al Neil on Co-op Radio's *radiofreerainforest*, the Downtown Eastside Poets at the Carnegie Centre, a neo-dadaist cabaret at the Clochard Gallery, a benefit reading for Nicaragua at La Quena, a lunchtime reading by Gerald Creede at ECCAD, text and music improvisation by Alex Varty and Peter Culley at the Glass Slipper or the Archimedes Club, a Susan Howe workshop, or the *Split Shift*

work poems of Tom Wayman and Calvin Wharton at Trout Lake Community Centre. (Bremner *et al.* 1990, 11)

So the *West Coast Line* introduction does the work of decentring Vancouver's cultural production, placing it in a network that includes bookstores (Renee Rodin's R2B2; Octopus East was another frequent venue); parallel galleries (the Or, Coburg, Clochard, the Western Front); community centres (the Carnegie, Trout Lake, Co-op Radio); and small-scale bars and cafés (La Quena, the Glass Slipper, Archimedes). The only academic institution mentioned is Emily Carr (then Emily Carr College of Art and Design; hence, ECCAD), and not SFU or UBC. Major cultural institutions such as the Vancouver Public Library are also out of the picture. This list is also notable for the sense it engenders, twenty years later, of loss, of nostalgia: R2B2, the Coburg and Clochard galleries, the Glass Slipper, and the Archimedes club no longer exist. This is also true of *all* of the like-minded publications *West Coast Line* situated itself amongst, including the long-running *Periodics, BC Monthly, JAG, Raddle Moon, Line* (subsumed by *West Coast Line,* after a merger with the *West Coast Review,* at the time of the introduction's writing), *(f)lip, Fissure Press, Tsunami Editions, Poptart, Anerca, Motel, Writing,* and the *East of Main* anthology (published by Pulp Press). Indeed, only *West Coast Line* survives.

Two other forms of cultural production—or perhaps genres—also exist from that period: the Tsunami Editions series of chapbooks and the initial book publications of many KSW writers. Here we see two qualitatively different series. The first is marked by material conditions (the chapbook as a saddle-stitched pamphlet, usually less than forty-eight pages), and the second by the authorial function (books proper assigned to KSW writers). Tsunami chapbooks ran in two series from *circa* 1986–89. The imprint's first series published work by Arni Runar Haraldsson, Peter Culley, Gerald Creede, Lary Bremner (who had changed his last name to Timewell by 1993), Jeff Derksen, and Kathryn MacLeod, while the second series released works by

Calvin Wharton, Nancy Shaw, Dorothy Trujillo Lusk, Peter Ganick, Susan Yarrow, Robert Mittenthal, Dan Farrell, and a reprint of the earlier Jeff Derksen chapbook.

Lary Bremner published the chapbooks, many of which measured approximately five-and-a-half by eight-and-a-half inches. While later editions were produced by professional printers (often credited to First Folio), the early ones, such as Creede's *Verbose* (1986), had a DIY feel to them, including two different rubber-stamped "Tsunami Editions" seals. The early works can thus be considered in terms of what was simultaneously, in the late 1980s, being theorized as the chapbook *qua* critique of the commodity in the Toronto small press milieu. That is, the Tsunami chapbooks should be seen less as a "farm team" try-out for writers who then graduate to major publishers, but as their own form or genre, a way for writers' production to take place in the contiguous fields of artist-books, avant-garde specialty publication, punk music, and experimental film and video. While all of these writers went on to publish other books, often including work from the chapbooks in their later publications, the Tsunami chapbooks might better be seen as a form in their own right. For if we merely consider the chapbooks in terms of the careers and conditions of their authors, a more complicated picture emerges. In part this has to do with the chapbooks themselves as material objects, with their historical status—which is a nice way of saying that they are dated.

What do I mean by this? First of all, that if we look at the colophons for various Tsunami chapbooks, for instance, we see that the typesetting is sourced out to CCWriter (Yarrow or Farrell) or Vancouver Desktop Publishing Centre (Wharton). This form of typesetting, of what was briefly called "desktop publishing," has already been historicized as a context for the production of variants between editions of Dorothy Trujillo Lusk's poetry (see page 100). And so Tsunami was absolutely contemporary in the later 1980s in using desktop publishing (as opposed to, say, fetishizing mimeograph) as a way of producing poetry chapbooks. But these chapbooks are also historical, are out-dated and, curiously, we have to be out of the archive, or in the neoliberal or privatized archives, in order to understand this. By the neoliberal or privatized archive, I refer to how often—and certainly this is more true outside of Canada—literary and other archives are now branded, privately owned and operated, and so on. More specifically, and pertaining to the KSW, research has to take place not only in the SFU special collections but in used bookstores. (Thus it was in Pulpfiction Books that I discovered a copy of *BC Monthly* with an early publication by Dorothy Trujillo Lusk.) Such bookstores often purchase extra sets of publications from SFU. But beyond that, I refer to the private or personal archive, the messy collection of texts that accumulate around any author. In order to find history, we have to leave the archive.

But what is also worth noting in looking at KSW literary production is, as noted above, the difference between the Tsunami chapbooks *qua* series and the later books, whether Tsunami or not, published by the central core of KSW writers. This difference itself is useful, for the shift to books was also accompanied, in some cases, by writers moving on to other Vancouver or Canadian (and, later, American or British) presses. So we have writers whose first books were with Tsunami, including Lisa Robertson, Gerald Creede, Kathryn MacLeod, Melissa Wolsak, Kevin Davies, Deanna Ferguson, Dan Farrell, and Colin Smith. Then Jeff Derksen's *Down Time* and Dorothy Trujillo Lusk's *Redactive* were published by Talonbooks. Peter Culley's first book was with the Vancouver-based Fissure, while Nancy Shaw and Catriona Strang published with Toronto's ECW, and Calvin Wharton, having shifted to short fiction, went with the Winnipeg-based Turnstone. Publishing soon became transnational: Lusk, Farrell, and Smith released books with the San Francisco-based Krupskaya; Davies, who moved to the US in the early 1990s, published with Washington, DC-based Edge; and Robertson went on to have books co-published with the British press Reality Studio. This series of descriptive notes indicates a spiralling out from the specificity of the Kootenay School in Vancouver in the 1980s. We can return to some of that specificity by returning to the archive, by returning to the material substrate and to questions of subjectivity.

Conclusions: An aesthetics of the archive

Let's conclude in a certain moment of history: May 30 and 31, 1985. The KSW has been having weekly meetings now since July 27, 1984. According to the minutes, they will continue to do so for the rest of the decade.[31] For the first few years, the meetings are recorded on yellow foolscap paper. For the entire five year period, they are handwritten, with the occasional typed financial record. Members in attendance are recorded at the top of the sheet: first name only, usually. For this—rare—two-day meeting, there is a "First Year Review." In attendance are Colin (Browne), Gary (Whitehead), Nancy S(haw), Calvin (Wharton), Tom (Wayman), Jeff (Derksen), Maureen, Athena (George), and Pete. The minutes begin with two questions: "What do we see for KSW in long terms? How do we see ourselves in this scheme?—See Dream Sheets" and "What concrete things are we prepared to do to achieve the goals? Two tools—1 a budget 2 an ongoing program of fundraising applications." The dreams on the next two pages range from the practical to the unlikely: from getting more room to having a graduate program, from spreading out the work to hiring an administrator to hustle grants. The archive of desire.

When I began to realize how complete the early years of the archive were (five years' worth of weekly meetings' minutes!), a certain tension entered my consciousness. *Would I find myself in the archive?* As mentioned earlier, I had participated in workshops in 1984 or 1985—I wasn't sure exactly when—and attended the 1985 New Poetics Colloquium. Then came an "archival jolt." In a list of participants in a

"Literary Groceries" workshop in November 1984, was my name—in my own handwriting. Proof, in a way, that "I existed" at that historical juncture. To be more complete, more archival: "Clint Burnham, (M) 32-1132 Johnson Street, Victoria V8O 3N8" appears on a sign-up sheet for the "Literary Groceries Workshop." Nov 24, 1984, Box 6, MsC 68, Kootenay School of Writing *fonds*. The "(M)" (indicating my gender) was not in my handwriting. Was it in the hand of Tom Wayman, whom I remember leading the workshop? And, on another day in the archives, in the New Poetics Colloquium files,[32] I came across a small envelope addressed to the KSW from my address in Victoria (32-1132 Johnson Street) and, separately but in the same file, a small form (two by four inches), filled out, and my name written in lower-case—again, my handwriting.

The small envelope reminds me of the letters my mother would write. Especially, for some reason, the letters she'd write to my father when he was on his various training courses in the Air Force. These were letters written in the evening from whatever military housing we were living in. (We were billeted in a series of duplexes known as PMQs or Permanent Married Quarters as opposed to the trailers which were TMQs—the housing temporary, not the marriages—though sometimes both.) The writing pad my mother would use, often from Safeway, came with a sheet of heavily lined paper to put under the writing sheet. I don't think—I don't know, of course—that any of those letters are in any archive. Perhaps my father has some. My mother has been dead for over nineteen years.

So these archival jolts, then—are they a matter of *jouissance*? As noted earlier in this chapter, I take the term from O'Driscoll and Bishop, where they use it to characterize some compelling moment in archival research, such as coming across William James being uncharacteristically timid, or Virginia Woolf's suicide note. In *The Intimate Archive: Journeys Through Private Papers*, Maryanne Dever describes the archival jolt in slightly different terms, as "a seemingly revelatory moment when one stumbles upon a piece that appears to resolve the puzzle" (2009, 46). And in another kind of jolt—a citation jolt?—Dever's footnote for the term leads back to Bishop, to his 2005 book *Riding with Rilke: Reflections on Motorcycles and Books*. There, in a chapter titled "Archival Jolt" (2005, 28–39), Bishop recounts the Woolf anecdote, connecting it to what Benjamin called "corporeal knowing," or the necessity of including "the tactile, the auditory, the gustatory, and not just the visual, in our scholarship" (ibid., 36). This is in the context of a visit to a Woolf archive at Washington State University, where, asked what he wanted in the archive, Bishop remarks to the reader that "The truth was I had come looking for the Archival Jolt" (33), adding that "Part of the reason we work in archives is, I'm convinced, for the archival jolt, a portal to knowledge and, in itself, an assurance that we have connected with something real" (36).

This jolt is thus the lost *and* the found object, a bit of the Real: that is to say, it is the *objet petit a*. The archival jolt is therefore constitutive to the archive *qua* fantasy, and nowhere is this so true as when we find ourselves in the archive. Discussing the intersubjective aspect of fantasy (again, the *Ché Vuoi?* moment), Žižek argues that "*objet petit a*, as the object of fantasy, is that 'something in me more than myself on account of which I perceive myself' as 'worthy of the Other's desire'" (2008, 9). So the "jolt," this little bit of *jouissance*, is not simply because, in Dever's formulation, it is a revelation, a piece of the puzzle of the archive, but instead it is the piece in the puzzle of who I am, of who I am to the Other, to the archive. The jolt is, as Bishop argues, the reason we work in archives, not as a portal to knowledge, but because it is a touch with the Real, with the fantasy that I am "worthy of the Other's desire." This is a fantasy because I can never know the Other's desire, the archive's desire.

Žižek argues that we can never escape fantasy; we can only exchange it for a better fantasy. In the fantasy of the KSW archive that I would like to propose here, then, "finding myself" in the archive stands in metonymically for a way to conceive of the KSW aesthetic in relation to the archive; I "deserve" to be working on the KSW archive because I am constituted in it, *not* because I am in sympathy with the poetics, with the disjunctive syntax of the writing, with the poetics conceived of in an idealist and ahistorical manner. In similar fashion, that very disjunctive aesthetic must be read against the background of an archive that is itself "beyond disjunction," that includes work writing (the Split Shift colloquium of 1986, the work writing section in *East of Main*, the role of Tom Wayman and Calvin Wharton in the 1980s) and other aesthetic forms and solidarities (thus classes taught by Susan Musgrave, Dale Zieroth, and the support of Leona Gom).

Comment on an epigraph

> Those who do not learn from history are doomed to research it.
> —Gerald Creede, in Lusk 1988, n.p.

In early November 2010, I remembered this quotation. What I did not remember was where to find it. I contacted Tony Power, the Contemporary Literature Collection librarian at SFU's special collections, for I thought that it perhaps was in one of Creede's books (I had his chapbook *Verbose* in my office, but not *Ambit*). Then again, I thought, it might be in Nancy Shaw's chapbook *Affordable Tedium* or her book *Scoptocratic*. I went over to the library and Tony had pulled those books for me. The quote was not in any of them. We looked through some of the other KSW authors' books in the collection. Was it in a Dan Farrell book or in Kathryn MacLeod's? I was pretty sure it must have been a Tsunami chapbook, but maybe it was one of the "actual" books, one of the Tsunami books with a "spine." No luck. That was a Friday morning and that afternoon I attended a seminar coordinated by Lisa Robertson as part of her project as writer-in-residence at SFU.

I asked her if she could think of where the quote might be and she suggested Dorothy Trujillo Lusk's work. The following week, sure enough, I checked my copy of Lusk's 1988 Tsunami chapbook *Oral Tragedy* and there was the quote. Those who do not learn from history are doomed to research it. The quote is not only illustrated by my research, but by my search for it (I had not learned from history that I should keep better track of quotations, so I had to research them). The process in turn illustrated the Freudian principle of the object being constituted by its search.

CONCLUSION

Resisting the Gentrification of the KSW

> So I know it's somewhere—two and a half to three hour time frame went by, but from my perspective it all went by very quickly. It took an inordinate long time to get from the mine office over to the church due to the crowds. And then at that point we went to the church. And it was my understanding that the families had been notified already. It wasn't until I walked into the church and looked out on the crowd and saw all those smiling faces and all the happiness that I realized that they had not been notified. So the news was broken. Just the opposite of the jubilation that had occurred three hours earlier occurred in that church. It was just gut-wrenching.
>
> —Mark Nowak 2009, 157

As I put the finishing touches to this book's manuscript in early 2011, a battle has erupted in Vancouver politics, one that, while hardly at the same level as the world-historical spectacle of the uprisings in the Arab world in January and February, is nonetheless part of the long history of gentrification in Vancouver. In this case, a city proposal to relax height restrictions on buildings in the Downtown Eastside met with vocal opposition from resident groups, who rightly saw the encroachment of condos and market-based housing as a threat to the low-income neighbourhood.[1] The term "gentrification," of course, has a specific history in urban politics and geography (for which see Neil Smith's *The New Urban Frontier*, as well as the Vancouver-specific studies cited in the previous chapter). More speculatively, Žižek has used the term to refer to attempts to disavow the political Real in cultural matters, as in *The Parallax View*, where he speaks of the "monstrous" Other that is minimally "gentrified" in the kind of humanism he argues is to be found in the work of philosopher Emmanuel Levinas (Žižek 2006c, 114). This example is not innocently chosen, it will soon become apparent,[2] but I want to use both the spectre of gentrification in Vancouver's DTES and Žižek's psychoanalytic notion of gentrification together as a way to introduce some concluding thoughts about the Kootenay School of Writing. Now, it is commonplace to argue that "artists are the stormtroopers of gentrification," and even to extend that analogy to universities—as in the role of artists' areas like SoHo in New York (and NYU or Columbia), or artist-run centres in Vancouver's Downtown Eastside (or SFU's new Woodward's campus). The argument goes that such cultural inroads into a neglected urban area prepare the way for the condos and market housing that are to follow, eventually squeezing lower-income residents out through a combination of higher-cost housing, lifestyle policing of the streets, harassment of street people, and so on. In this context, the history of the KSW as a collective that was spatially located in the Downtown Eastside for most of the past twenty years (as have been such artist-run centres as Artspeak, the Helen Pitt, the Or, and Access, etc.), has to be seen as connected in some way with the process of gentrification which, we can argue, is a structural process—i.e., it has little to do with the good intentions or the politics of the artists or writers involved.

But I would also argue that the KSW went through its own form of gentrification in the period that ran from its formation in 1985 to the publication of *Writing Class* in 1999—a gentrification that eliminated the more content-based class politics of work writing found in the *East of Main* anthology in favour of the formally based innovation *qua* intervention seen in much of the work I treat in this book. Most of the evidence for my claim can be found in the previous chapter, where I trace a history that begins with a loose, raw collective, scrambling for funding, trying to create a space for new forms of writing that are also political. But ten or fifteen years later, by the late 1990s, that writing has shed the work-writing tendency that was part of the original political make-up of the KSW, and settled into empty speech, social collage, and neopastoralism—a specific Vancouver brand of what is now called conceptual writing.[3] Now, it may be that I am falling into my own Žižekian paradox of mistaking *lack* for *loss*: I may be seeing the KSW as having lost what it never had, that leftist fantasy of a socially engaged, politically relevant culture. But I would like to explore this possibility, the possibility of there still being a way to read this early KSW work writing, not only with the psychoanalytic tools I have developed in this book, but alongside the very forms of disruptive, polysemic poetry that have been so important to the KSW program.

Consider Clark Coolidge's *Own Face* and Tom Wayman's *The Face of Jack Munro*. The first text concerns Floyd Collins, the Kentucky farmer who went missing in a cave in 1925 and touched off a brief national (US) sensation and seems to fit all the clichés of postmodern documentary poetry. That is to say, it is not about a world-historical Lukácsian event but a minor, marginal, pathetic one. The second text engages unabashedly with the role of labour in Canadian politics, its title poem taking full aim at BC labour leader Jack Munro and his sell-out of the province's broadly based Solidarity labour movement in 1983. And yet both—in their titles—flirt with the face. And it is through this face, as both thematic and structuring principle, that we can examine their work and assess how psychoanalysis can help in the project of reading political poetry.

Clark Coolidge's work is hardly concerned with thematic or content-based matters—except perhaps when it comes to jazz. The first poem in *Own Face* states the matter baldly, from the very title,

> "But it says nothing":
> But it says nothing. And one is as quiet
> as if to say nothing moves me. Then
> there is the chair. And one speaks of
> the chair sitting at the table.
> Scraping against surfaces, opening the mouth.
> (1978, 7)

Perhaps here we immediately have a rebuke of the face as a signifier of personality (it says nothing). And yet, four times in these opening five lines we have the notion of speech: twice to "say nothing" (or "as if to say nothing"), then "one speaks" or at least is "opening the mouth." The poem itself rebukes speech even as it talks about speech all the way to its closing lines:

> Least way it says nothing. And the
> thing is, it stays still before
> speaking of. The object of nothing, even
> speech.
> (7)

Samuel Beckett's "Text for Nothing XI" is quoted for the book's epigraph and, to be sure, the repetition here is mildly Beckett-like—a repetition that teases us with a suggestion of reference. But perhaps one way of reading this opening is to see the mouth that is open but says nothing as akin to the Kentucky cave into which Floyd Collins disappeared, a cave that, like a mouth, said nothing in the sense that nothing came out of it—which is to say, Collins did not. But it is Collin's "own face" that is on the cover of the book.

There is also a face on the cover of Tom Wayman's book: a drawing of Jack Munro's face (the cover art is credited to Gaye Hammond). At first, in this collection, reference appears to be less ambiguous:

> The supervisor delivering layoff notices,
> the tribunal refusing to hear the eviction appeal,
> the businessmen and women gloating over dinner
> at the news of the reduction of
> payments to the single unemployed
> —all share a face
> puffy with greed and fright and satisfaction,
> the face of
> Jack Munro.
> (1986, 122)

Wayman's poem is semantically richer in its politics, connecting a labour leader to the capitalist class. But just as Coolidge's poetry can conceal content beneath a patina of structural indeterminacy, so Wayman's argues for a more sophisticated reading than is at first apparent. The shared face here is the first clue: it is a metaphor for similar politics, but it is also where we can turn to Lacanian theory.

Read psychoanalytically, a face is both that obdurate, unknowable object that Coolidge's poem posits, and the appearance of humanity that Wayman's poem laments. This argument stems from the early Freud of his 1895 *Project for a Scientific Psychology*, through Lacan's *Seminar VII*, and thence to a collection of essays on *The Neighbor: Three Inquiries in Political Theology* by Kenneth Reinhard, Eric Santner, and Slavoj Žižek. For the ambiguity or contradiction or antagonism between Coolidge and Wayman can be seen at the very beginning of psychoanalysis, in Freud's *Project* (the *Entwurf*, or sketch, as it is called in German). There, discussing the infant's first perceptions, Freud characterizes these perceptions as presented with a *Nebenmensch* (also translated by Strachey as a "fellow human being"—Freud 1966, vol. 1, 331); the passage is worth quoting at length:

> Let us suppose that the object presented by the perception is similar to the [percipient] subject himself—that is to say a fellow human-being. The theoretical interest taken in it is then further explained by the fact that an object *of a similar kind* was the subject's first satisfying object (and also his first hostile object) as well as his sole assisting force. For this reason it is on his fellow-creatures that a human being first learns to cognize. The perceptual complexes arising from this fellow-creature will in part be new and non-comparable—for instance, its features (in the visual sphere); but other visual perceptions (for instance, the movement of its hands) will coincide in the subject with his own memory of quite similar visual impressions of his own body—a memory with which will be associated memories of movements experienced by himself. The same will be the case with other perceptions of the object; thus, for instance, if the object screams, a memory of the subject's own screaming will be aroused and will consequently revive his own experiences of pain. Thus the complex of a fellow-creature falls into two portions. One of these gives the impression of being a constant structure and remains as a coherent 'thing'; while the other can be *understood* by the activity of memory—that is, can be traced back to information about the subject's own body. (1954, 393–94)

Arguably Freud is talking about the mother or first caregiver here, and whether we buy his claim that the baby will distinguish between what in the fellow creature is both dissimilar (the face) and similar (the movement of the arms), that splitting of the neighbour into the recognizable and the Thing has had enormous resonance for psychoanalytic theory, not least in the work of Lacan and Žižek.

It is worth noting, too, that Freud makes cognate comments about the "mnemic image … of the mother's breast and a front view of its nipple" (1966, vol. 1, 328), a mnemic image that then becomes associated with desire (as described in *The Interpretation of Dreams* in 1966, vol. 5, 565–66) and, as is eventually worked out in his 1925 "Negation" essay: "The first and immediate aim, therefore, of reality-testing is, not to *find* an object in real perception which corresponds to the one presented, but to *refind* such an object, to convince oneself that it is still there ... [I]t is evident that a precondition for the setting up of reality-testing is that objects shall have been lost which once brought real satisfaction (1966, vol. 19, 237–38)."

This notion in Freud of the original object having once been lost, having always been lost—not to be found, but re-found—accounts, then, for the split that is in the Thing even as the Thing is the result of a split in the neighbour. The Thing that is part of the neighbour—which Lacan will retain in German as *das Ding*—I would argue, is what constitutes the *face* of the mother or caregiver. This face is what is new or different about the other, while its or her hands or arms would presumably be somewhat familiar to the child.

Lacan calls this "an original division of the experience of reality" (2007, 52), arguing it is always, then, a matter of trying to re-discover an original thing which is always lost, and is both the desired and the horrible: "*Das Ding* has, in effect, to be identified with the *Wieder zu finden*, the impulse to find again that[,] for Freud[,] establishes the orientation of the human subject to the object" (ibid., 58). But Lacan adds the following proviso: "since it is a matter of finding it again, we might just as well characterize this object as a lost object. But although it is essentially a question of finding it again, the object indeed has never been lost" (ibid.). Earlier, he explains, "it is to be found at the most as something missed" (ibid., 52). The split corresponds to the metapoetic split in Coolidge (the lost reference, and the lost Collins) and the trauma of a supposed "good father" (the labour leader) leading us astray in Wayman.

The essay collection *The Neighbor* contains essays by Kenneth Reinhard and Žižek that continue this stream of thought. In his "Toward a Political Theology of the Neighbour," Reinhard brings Freud and Lacan's work into dialogue with the conservative German thinker Carl Schmitt. Reinhard is especially useful for how he teases out the ambiguity of the *Nebenmensch* in Freud's *Entwurf*, arguing first that this "fellow creature" is "not, it seems, the parents, or a complete stranger, but perhaps, from the sounds of the scream, another child" (2005, 30). He then expands his conception of that fellow being: "To the extent that the *Nebenmensch* is the 'next person,' merely contiguous with the subject and its maternal source of both pleasure and unpleasure, it represents any and every other person to whom the subject is bound in a relationship of competitive similarity, an imaginary 'equality' enforced—more or less—as distributive justice in the social world by civil and moral codes" (ibid., 32).

In both of these definitions, Reinhard stresses the social solidarity embodied in the neighbour or *Nebenmensch*—and, I would argue, embodied in the face itself. Žižek also addresses the concept of the neighbour vis-à-vis the face in his essay "Neighbors and Other Monsters," one section of which is titled "Smashing the Neighbor in the Face" (142*ff*). Here Žižek takes issue with Emmanuel Levinas' claim that "a face 'can guarantee itself,'" arguing that this makes the face the ultimate fetish: "[T]his fetishization—or, rather, fetishistic disavowal—is discernable also in our daily relating to another person's face. This disavowal does not primarily concern the raw reality of flesh ('I know very well that beneath the face there is just the Real of raw flesh, bones, and blood, but I nonetheless act as if the face is a window into the mysterious interiority on the soul'), but, rather, at a more radical level, the abyss/void of the Other: the human face 'gentrifies' the terrifying Thing that is the ultimate reality of our neighbor" (2005, 146)

So in Žižek, we have a final splitting of the psychoanalytic theory of the face/Thing/neighbour: here the face is what covers up the Thing, whereas in Freud the face constituted the Thing. So let us return to Coolidge and Wayman and see how this series of antagonisms or dialectics is in turn reinforced, troubled, and thematized.

This thematization, I have already argued, occurs in Coolidge's book via the notions of speaking or expression itself, as well as the cave *qua* mouth. An even more blatant example might be the poem "Cares over the Thing" (1993, 17), which begins with "A butterfly lifter" and continues "With hands with. Have no neighborhood" and "Levers it up into an / old tank of American painting. Left-overs." Next, we lift the lines, "As to say, / what are they" and "Left out in the bulky sense," then move to the poem's conclusion, with "Stop listening, Glenn Gould." These extracts are chosen to display first the thematic continuity of the poem with our theoretic readings: from the title, "Have no neighborhood," to the strangeness of "what are they," especially since that phrase or sentence does not conclude with a question mark. As well, these lines show the materiality of its language: there is the homophonic repetition of "lifter," "Levers ... Left-overs," and "Left out," not to mention the metalinguistic, and Canadian, content of the closing lines "Stop listening, Glenn Gould."

In terms of the cave thematics and the face, a play of the signifier takes place throughout Coolidge's *Own Face*. For the cave thematics, see most notably "The Cave Remain" (Coolidge 1993, 47–50) but, on a more modest note, the poem "Floyd's Beancans" (ibid., 81). That poem begins with "Lasted beads" but also speaks of "a spatter adit" (an adit being a cave entrance), "time under the onyx," "let me out of this / crevice kitchen," "I barked / a crayon canyon in my thigh," and "if you go / all flat all out under the ridge / I will time you to death." The facing poem is "Mammoth Cave (again will I go there)" (80). Mammoth Cave is the Kentucky system of caves in which Collins died. In this poem, we read "I was born / in Gorin's Dome," the name of another cave. But faces also figure. In the same poem, we read, "This rock-hewn absence as much my source / as any face," a line which reminds us of the face as metaphor for a cave or mine wall. "Face the wall" is the title of one of the poems (52). The book ends with "At the Poem" (88), which again flaunts a metonymic parade of faces:

> You must gaze
> into the sun here to take your rest, suspend
> motion and speech on a point of
> zircon sand. The only articulate surfaces, they
> are also somehow sounds, are buildings which
> as you approach pour their facades at your feet
> in a rush of the purest substances.
> There are no faces to be seen since all
> that is human here is you.
> (88)

In this play of language, then, the face is a Thing, both in the sense that it is a signifier, a material signifier, but also because it is in some ways anti-human (or, rather, in the negation of the final sentence, the absence of the face attests to the human).

A different reading practice is demanded by Wayman's poem, which documents or narrates the political showdown in British Columbia during the fall of 1983 and, in particular, the rise and collapse of the Solidarity movement that also gave rise to the founding of the Kootenay School. As public- and private-sector workers, students, women, and other allied protest groups walked out in what was coming to look like a general strike, IWA president Jack Munro sat down as self-appointed labour representative in negotiations with BC premier Bill Bennett. Famously, the two men put their wallets on the table, as if negotiating to buy a used car:

> Then Jack Munro
> took out his wallet and placed it on a table.
> The other man
> took out his wallet, too,

and placed it beside Munro's.
The leather cases
were almost identical,
each thick with crisp bills
and uncashed cheques.
And while Jack Munro sat
and stuffed snacks into his fat jowls,
the two wallets
commenced negotiations.
Both wallets agreed
the moment was perilous,
that authority must be maintained
and that for this to occur
one side must win and the other lose.
(Wayman 1986, 119)

The personification of the wallets as a poetic trope cannot help but remind the reader of Marx's assertion, in *Capital*, that the capitalist is but a personification of capital:

> As the conscious bearer [*Träger*] of this movement, the possessor of money becomes a capitalist. His person, or rather his pocket, is the point from which the money starts, and to which it returns. The objective content of the circulation we have been discussing—the valorization of value—is his subjective purpose, and it is only in so far as the appropriation of ever more wealth in the abstract is the sole driving force behind his operations that he functions as a capitalist, i.e., as capital personified and endowed with consciousness and will. Use-values must therefore never be treated as the immediate aim of the capitalist; nor must the profit on any single transaction. His aim is rather the unceasing movement of profit-making. (1990, 254)

Now, the alert reader will object that neither Munro (a union leader) nor Bennett (a politician) were, strictly speaking, capitalists. But here, beyond the poetic device of personification, two aspects of Marx's analysis are germane to Wayman's poem. First, the notion that that personification endows upon capital both "consciousness and will" (what one might call the gentrification or humanization of capital). Second, an important argument throughout Marx's work sees capitalism beyond its immediate end. If the capitalist's aim is "unceasing movement of profit-making," then, too, the aim of the 1980s British Columbia government went beyond nastiness toward daycare operators or "municipal parks board employees" (Wayman 1986, 117) or "gill netters, instrument / technicians, welders / and geologists" (ibid., 120). Rather, the purpose of the "Restraint" budget was to facilitate that unceasing movement of profit-making (recall the epigraph to Chapter One). The wallets here have acquired a face and, like the obverse of Coolidge's face, it is the sign of the inhuman. Being personified, the wallets have become the Thing.

This assertion is borne out later in the poem, when Wayman writes that "What Jack Munro accomplished / now hangs over every hour" (121). Throughout, Wayman relies on Munro's face for his series of metaphors:

> the government spokesperson stares at us
> with the eyes
> of Jack Munro.
> At the bargaining sessions
> where negotiators from management
> demand we be punished, earn less,
> live less well,
> the employers' representatives speak
> using the voice
> of Jack Munro.
> The supervisor delivering layoff notices,

the tribunal refusing to hear the eviction appeal,
the businessmen and women gloating over dinner
at the news of the reduction of
payments to the single unemployed
—all share a face
puffy with greed and fright and satisfaction
the face of
Jack Munro.
(122)

Here two aspects of Wayman's poetics bear comment. First, the way in which proximity works as an ally of power (the boss as neighbour, let us say, but also the boss with a human face). Second, how his use of language here is so unlike Coolidge's. Just as Munro was close to the politician he negotiated with (in a "face-to-face meeting" as current business-speak has it—or, even, getting some "face time"), so the government spokesperson is close enough to "us" to stare with Munro's eyes, the employers' representative to speak "using the voice" of Munro, and the series of supervisors, tribunals, and businesspeople share a face. And just as that face is, finally, "puffy" (earlier in the poem, when the wallets got down to their business, Munro "stuffed snacks into his fat jowls" [119]), so too the language here is often flabby, stuffed, farcical. It's all bureaucratese and politically correct jargon: "government spokesperson," "businessmen and women" and, elsewhere in the poem: "only a prescribed amount" (112), "an embargo / on food allocated to the hungry" (113), "the removal of these detriments to the environment" (114), "data processors / from the government insurance bureaus" (115), "additional citizens" (116), "designated core of hospital workers" (117), "owners and company vice-presidents and personnel managers" (118), "in return for our compliance" (119), "non-debatable" (120), "kilometre by kilometre" (121), and "steering committees" (122). Language here is the language of neoliberalism, no doubt, and the material that Wayman has to work with: it is a Thing in a different way than the materiality of the text we see in Coolidge.

Coolidge's book can also be considered in the context of his larger *oeuvre*. It is both thematically and formally aligned with the works that followed *Own Face*, such as *Quartz Hearts* (1978), *Mine: The One that Enters the Stories* (1982), and *The Crystal Text* (1986). Here, three points of comparison are worth making: the subject matter of rocks, mines, and crystallography; the formal structure of collaged and metonymically jazzed writing; and the connection between metalinguistic *topoi* and the deconstruction of the subject. The last of these is evident in *The Crystal Text*:

> I still don't easily think of myself as a writer.
> I still don't think of myself. I look at the writing
> and sometimes see the self in there, out there, and wonder
> how I was somehow that self being written, writing
> itself out as if unwinding a spool of …
> I only see certain strands.
> (58)

These aspects of Coolidge's body of work lead back to our subject matter. The direction Wayman's own work writing takes is one concerned with the subject position of the worker, of the proletariat. In contradistinction to the "hard" rock of Coolidge's writing—both its difficulty and its concern with, literally, hard subjects—we might pit the "soft" feminism of, say, Lisa Robertson's project, the recuperation of softness evinced in her 2003 title *Occasional Works and Seven Walks from the Office for Soft Architecture*.[4] Finally, an impossible synthesis, perhaps, of Wayman's politics and Coolidge's poetics is seen in the found/appropriated technique of miners' testimony *qua* poetry in Mark Nowak's *Coal Mountain Elementary*, a text that collages that testimony in a way that, as the quotation at the beginning of this chapter demonstrates, can similarly deal with the indeterminacy, the fantasy, of the face.

But what Wayman's and Coolidge's works offer are variations on what has been made possible by the Kootenay School of Writing. That is, *contra* the all-or-nothing proposition offered at the beginning of this conclusion, when I posited the KSW's gentrification of its own class-based politics, it is equally important to assert continuities between forms of cultural production—in this case, poetry—that share a politics, if not a formal agenda.[5]

ENDNOTES

PAGE 5

1. Lisa Robertson, *XEclogue*, n.p.
2. Mancini and Smith, 100.
3. Paul Morand, *1900 A.D.* (1931), in Benjamin 1999a, 462.

INTRODUCTION

1. The internal quotation is from Offe, 11.
2. This is not to deny that there were, at various times in the collective histories, real tensions and struggles over questions of gender, representation, and politics. Three quite different accounts of this history/herstory can be found in interviews with Catriona Strang (268*ff*), Dorothy Trujillo Lusk (292*ff*), and Lisa Robertson (368*ff*), in Eichhorn, Kate, and Milne 2009.
3. It should be noted that Quartermain is especially arguing against feminist or lesbian readings that seek to fix the meaning of Stein's text (or decode it): see Englebrecht's essay for a more theoretically supple reading that also takes into account political identity.
4. Email from *English Studies in Canada* editor Cecily Devereaux, January 10, 2011.
5. See Klobucar and Barnholden 1999, from which much of this account is drawn; see also Magnusson 1984, from which this chapter's epigraph is drawn.
6. Various accounts of this period include Butling, Wah's "KSW: Origins," Wayman's "Against the Smiling Bastards."
7. See, in this regard, Douglas 1991 and Wallace 1993.
8. My association with the KSW goes back, over the past twenty-five years. In the mid-1980s I was living in Victoria, having left two different post-secondary institutions; a friend of mine, the poet Chris Robertson, was an émigré from DTUC in Nelson, and through her I heard about the KSW then emerging in Vancouver. I then saw, in the *Vancouver Sun*, a story about the KSW offering "blue pencil" workshops at the Kitsilano community centre. I was writing bill bissett-esque poetry at that time (had been since coming across his work in the late '70s in high school in Regina), and

I took the bus over to Vancouver and had a workshop with Calvin Wharton (who I thought looked like Fred Wah, whose book *Breathing My Name with a Sigh* I had read); I came over another time and had a workshop on filing your taxes as a writer with Tom Wayman. He told a great story about Mario Puzo being flabbergasted at the negotiations for movie rights for *The Godfather*. I was on the KSW mailing list and used to look enviously at workshops on Stein or Zukofsky (offered by Peter Quartermain?). I came back over to Vancouver for the New Poetics conference in the summer of 1985 in what is now the cafeteria at Emily Carr. I started reading *The L=A=N=G=U=A=G=E Book* and some of the American language poets. I went back to school that fall and, having been denied entrance to the creative writing program at UVic, took literature and especially became interested in literary theory.

Chapter One: A Tripartite Taxonomy

1. Key texts in the critical literature include Bowering; Butling and Rudy; Derksen's "Sites Taken for Signs" and *Annihilated Time*; Wah's review from *West Coast Line*, and Wiens' dissertation. The KSW also maintains an excellent online archive that includes histories, images, and reviews, at kswnet.org.
2. Here I refer to the best available edition of this poem in Klobucar and Barnholden 1999.
3. In the same interview, Davies half-jokingly referred to a psychoanalytic reading of the book: "Pause Button ... Pause Button ... Ah! Paw's Button! So, what is your relation to your father's button? Do you want to take it from him or share it with him? Or do you wish to destroy it utterly?" (2000, 5): the button of the father, which could presumably be extended to Lacan's concept of button-ties, the buttons on upholstery which hold together the imaginary and the symbolic, a.k.a. *point de capiton*. More on the *point de capiton* concept in Chapters Two and Five.

Chapter Two: Empty and Full Speech

1. Susan Clark published under two last names: Clark and Yarrow. She edited *Raddle Moon* under the name Clark and is better known in the community

by this name. In this chapter, the text I discuss was published under "Yarrow," so I will refer to Susan by that author-function.

2. By *lapproach* I mean a theoretical or interpretive strategy of reading, of engaging with language, that is not separate from the language itself, an approach that sits in the lap of language, as it were, one that laps from the bowl of language, is a lap dancer, but is also full of reproach. See Lacan's *lalangue*, often translated as "lalanguage," in *Seminar XX*.
3. *Raddle Moon* carried mailing addresses for both Sydney, BC (on Vancouver Island), and Vancouver for issues 8 through 14; from 15 on, it carried only a Vancouver street address (although not the west side address of 8–14; for issues 15–20 it also carried various website URLs). See Byrne's "*Raddle Moon*: a Talk" for more details on the career of the magazine.
4. *Writing* was published out of DTUC for issues 1–9 (Summer 1980–Spring 1984). The editors were David McFadden for the first five issues, John Newlove for 6, Colin Browne for 7–22, Jeff Derksen for 23–27. Issue 9 included the following note: "Although the provincial government has closed David Thompson University Centre and its School of Writing, *Writing Magazine* will continue to publish regularly. Your subscriptions are now more important than ever. Please send orders or submissions to our TEMPORARY ADDRESS: c/o 1871 EAST PENDER STREET, VANCOUVER, BC, V5L 1W6." While the mailing address was henceforth a post box, the magazine from issue 10 on was identified as published by the KSW, with addresses on 1045 West Broadway (issues 10–17; Fall 1984–January 1987) and then 152 West Hastings (20–22).
5. I remember Adeena Karasick, then an up-and-coming poet, arguing with me in 1989 or 1990 about the geographical determinism—or was it essentialism?—that excluded her from the anthology since she lived on the west side of Vancouver. See also Brian Fawcett's productive attack on the KSW titled "East Van Über Alles," in Fawcett 1991.
6. I put quotation marks around 1988 because while the Tsunami chapbook is not dated, its CCIP (Canadian Cataloguing in Publication) data indicates the years 1988 and 88 in the library codes: PS8561.A77A75 1988 and C88-091178-6.
7. In a colloquium edited by Clark in *Raddle Moon*, Abigail Child wrote that

"For Freud, Lacan and Hegel desire is always marked by an ontological lack which can only be filled with the other. In this tradition desire is negative, unfillable, an absence. In contrast, the tradition of Spinoza, Nietzsche, Foucault and Deleuze describe desire not as lack but as a positive force" (Child 1993, 17). Whether or not the latter four thinkers really thought of desire as such a vitalist "positive force," and even though for Lacan, at least, lack can never (or should never) be "filled with the other," Child's statement and its proximity to or perhaps sponsorship by Clark indicates that my Lacanian reading of Clark's work is hardly one that can be assumed to be supported by or agreed to by the author.

8. See my first footnote for the Clark versus Yarrow distinction/confusion.
9. In these quotations I have tried to preserve Yarrow's floating left margins.
10. The importance of this passage to Lacan's continuing sense of his work—i.e., from 1953, when the Rome discourse was first delivered, to 1966, when it was published in *Écrit*—is that Lacan notes "The preceding paragraph has been rewritten."
11. "[T]he psychoanalyst ... takes the description of an everyday event as a fable addressed as a word to the wise, a long prosopopeia as a direct interjection, and, contrariwise, a simple slip of the tongue as a highly complex statement, and even the rest of a silence as the whole lyrical development it stands in for" (Lacan 2002, 252).
12. As discussed on page 34, the ellipses' best-known appearance in twentieth-century literature is no doubt in the novels of Louis-Ferdinand Céline. Writing about style and language in Céline, Merlin Thomas commented on his use of what he calls the "three dots": "[T]hey divide his text into rhythmical rather than syntactical units, permit extreme variations of pace and make possible to a great extent the powerful hallucinatory lyricism of his style" (Thomas 1979, 89). This is in some ways what is going on in MacLeod's "The Infatuation." For a discussion of Emily Dickinson's syntax, see Howe 2007, especially p. 21.
13. Listing the textual sites for Kathryn MacLeod's written production above, I noted the 1986–87 Vancouver magazine *JAG*. What is interesting about that magazine—along with its promiscuous mixing of work writing, language poetry, feminism, etc.—is that the chatty introductions to the issues used

the same arbitrary line endings as does Farrell's poem (the *JAG* copy was done on a typewriter).

14. See Elisabeth Roudinseco's two biographies of Lacan for more on the variable length session: 1990, 253*ff*., esp 258–59; and 1997, 217–18.
15. See "Logical Time and the Assertion of Anticipated Certainty" (Lacan 2002, 197–213). With respect to *Nachträglichkeit*, a commonplace of Freud's theorizing is that a child's witnessing of the primal scene, for example, is not traumatic at the time, but later: see the Wolfman case ("From a History of an Infantile Neurosis") and also Lacan's commentary at various places including Lacan (2002, 256–57).
16. I expand on this dicussion in Chapter Five.
17. See Bowie, Chapter 3.
18. See Hurst's discussion of *différance*.
19. This comment really riled a reviewer of this manuscript. So, as if to meet my (Other's) desire, I recently found the Facebook email from Melissa Wolsak, which I reproduce with her permission:

> That Garcia Family was full—and empty, indeterminate and recklessly experimental, yet, i [*sic*] did want a couple of ideas to come across ... for instance the idea of a completely new way to slice 'commerce,' and that can speak for itself, however vaguely. There is an interview with Kent Johnson which mentions this if I remember correctly. *Vert* #6.
>
> http://epc.buffalo.edu/mags/vert/Vert_issue_6/cvrsix.html.
>
> Minnie was Minnie Mouse whose vision in many of 'her' cartoons where she was always applying lipstick in the most charming way, pooching out her lips, I had carried that around with me for years and writing it, inadvertently, was simply an instance of laying it down. Too, 'the Beagle Boys sped.' Just visions ... which was generally the oceanic feel of the book, what I was reading at the time, combined with jumpy surrealisms in an iconoclasts' smashing much of what was surrounding me.
>
> Literally, I had a wolf-malamute at the time whose fur would in the strangest way, align itself to make an appearance of—lines—on

his back and I used to ask out loud, how did he get his etc. small mysteries.

I had been reflecting after the book was out, on how so many things i [*sic*] said could have been interpreted as desire ... but the interesting thing for me was that that was—utterly unintended—for I had had 'other' things on my mind when writing, including not controlling the text which for me was the foremost point, the bodice ripper, so to speak ... But all that looped around so interestingly as I began to realize how the 'sexual' or 'desire' is so often—also ontological in expression (speech of same) and which is mentioned in *Maimonides Guide for the Perplexed* (which I had been reading at the time of writing *TGCo-M*) and subsequent looking around revealed other Jewish mystical thinkers/writers who delve into this most interesting territory. I have since dwelt there, still reflecting on this marvel ..."

(Facebook email from Melissa Wolsak, July 15, 2009)

Chapter Three: Social Collage and the Four Discourses

1. See Marianne DeKoven's groundbreaking *A Different Language* (1983) especially; but also, for example, Cynthia Merrill's use of Lacan's mirror stage to read *The Autobiography of Alice B. Toklas* (Merrill 1985).
2. More recent writings on L=A=N=G=U=A=G=E and post-L=A=N=G=U=A=G=E writing that make some (usually cursory) references to Lacan, Žižek, and/or Kristeva include S. Evans, Jarraway, Kellogg, Hoy, Nickels, Miller, Sussman, Frost, and Ngai. Evans' title ("That Sublime Object of Marginality") is a clear hat-tip to Žižek, and Jarraway's use of an epigraph from Lacan ("when you don't understand what you are being told, don't immediately assume that you are to blame; say to yourselves—the fact that I don't understand must itself have a meaning") could apply equally to Lacan and the KSW; however, Jarraway makes more use of Barthes' pleasure of the text and merely refers to, without expanding upon, Lacanian desire (1992, 330). Kellogg, too, foregrounds Lacanian desire, this time as lexical feature, in a range of contemporary poetry including that of Bob Perelman (1995, 411ff), whose 1998 volume, *The Future of Memory*, is the subject

of Nickels' sometimes Kristevan review essay; Watten similarly situates L=A=N=G=U=A=G=E writing in terms of Kristevan and Lacanian theory. Hoy references Žižek's infamous allegorical readings of toilet design as a way of critiquing flarf, or Google-sculptured poetry; Sussman uses the psychoanalytic notion of "introjection" to discuss Charles Bernstein's foregrounding of collage and method (2003, 11, 19, 21); and Ngai's chapter on "Stuplimity" moves from Stein and Beckett to method in the work of Dan Farrell and Kenneth Goldsmith, with a brief foray into Lacan on repetition.

3. Žižek often either refers to such a periodization to isolate a certain historically variable concept in Lacan, as in the "early" Lacan reading of the Oedipus myth in *The Ticklish Subject* (Žižek 2000, 180), or, in *How to Read Lacan*, to discuss "a shift in Lacan's development, from the early Lacan focused on the inter-subjective dialectics of recognition, to the later Lacan who puts forward the anonymous mechanism that regulates the interaction of subjects" (Žižek 2006a, 41) or, at his most radical, to use the late Lacan to re-read the early Lacan, as when he reads Lacan's seminar on Poe's "The Purloined Letter" in terms of the "stain of enjoyment" in *Enjoy Your Symptom* (1992, 22–23).
4. Useful commentary on *Seminar XVII* can be found in the following: Clemens and Grigg 2006, Fink 1997, Dean 2009, Žižek 2004, Mitchell and Rose 1985, and Jameson 1988.
5. For many years, MacCannell argues, it has been unacceptable to read Lacan's work in a historical context (in Clemens and Grigg 2006, 195). My situating of Lacan's work *away* from historicization, similar to my shift in reading KSW poetry and poetics, seeks to better determine the relationship between politics and form.
6. See also Johnston 2009 on the question of the shift in Lacan's work.
7. This is for the same reason, as Žižek argues in *The Sublime Object* (1989), that "the four subjects presumed to [know, believe, enjoy, desire] are not on the same level: the subject presumed to know is their basis, their matrix, and the function of the remaining three is precisely to disguise its troubling paradox" (1989, 213); the paradox or mystery is that, in the process of transference, "to *produce* new meaning, it is necessary to *presuppose* its existence in the other" (210). In the same way, then, the supposition of the subject

presumed to believe or desire or enjoy means that in order to produce new belief (to convert), or produce new desire, it is necessary to presuppose its existence in the other. This notion of transferential knowledge and meaning will be of great interest when we turn to the status of the open text.

8. See also Clemens and Grigg's introduction to their volume on *Seminar XVII*, in which they lay out the origins of the master's discourse in "an original matrix that characterizes the signifier that represents a subject for another signifier" (2006, 3).
9. This discussion of the mechanics of Lacan's "revolutions" owes much to a presentation by Chris Dzierzawa, Lacan Salon, Vancouver, BC, November 17, 2009.
10. In a nod to Deleuze, Jodi Dean talks about protestors' pleasure as "affective intensities." See her blog, I cite: http://jdeanicite.typepad.com/i_cite/
11. Žižek argues that the *objet a* in the university discourse, addressed by knowledge, is akin to Agamben's *bare life* or the biopolitical (2004a, 145).
12. And this dance with the popular holds not only in canonical modernism but also in its avant-garde or radical other: in Gertrude Stein's *Autobiography of Alice B. Toklas*, of course (and her writer's block after that success, one that was only resolved by writing another popular text, a mystery, *Blood on the Dining-Room Floor*); in her indifference toward, as Bob Perelman puts it, "general ideas of exactitude, efficiency, and 'good writing'" (1994, 131); in her "domestication of modernist art and writing" when she has Toklas declare "I always say that you cannot tell what a picture really is or what an object really is until you dust it every day and you cannot tell what a book really is until you type it or proofread it" (Stein 1998, 776); in Louis Zukofsky's use of what Peter Quartermain calls "stage Irish/Brooklynese" in Quartermain 1992, 81, not to mention the appropriation of Marx's *Capital* and his letters in the interests of exploring aesthetic value (the kernel of the antagonism between high and low modernism); and in Lorine Niedecker's New Goose poems from the 1930s which, as Jenny Penberthy writes, "explored folk models and, in particular, the short metrical rhymes of Mother Goose—poems of anonymous authorship, of proletarian origin, and of subtly subversive intent" (2002, 5). Too, not simply this enlarged canon, but the Black modernism of the Harlem Renaissance. See Langston

Hughes' alliances with popular music, as he writes in his essay "The Negro Artist and the Racial Mountain": "Let the blare of Negro jazz bands and the bellowing voice of Bessie Smith singing Blues penetrate the closed ears of the colored near-intellectuals until they listen and perhaps understand"; Zora Neale Hurston's beginnings in anthropology evidenced in the authorial voice as participant-observer in her study of Black folklore, *Mules and Men*; and Richard Wright's calls for a Sartrean engaged writing in his essay "Blueprint for Negro Writing." And if the high modernists sought to pump up their culture with the fresh air of the music hall and the minstrel show, the Black modernists sought to redeem their invocation of the popular with the academic gaze of the ethnographer, of the literary artist.

13. The metonymic slide from "archivist" to "anarchist" is properly Lacanian: see Collis 2006, 18.
14. See, in this regard, the interviews with Catriona Strang, Dorothy Trujillo Lusk, and Lisa Robertson in Eichhorn and Milne 2009. Cris Costa's 2010 article in *West Coast Line* about the politics of the KSW in the 1980s, published when my book was being edited, is also a thoughtful analysis.
15. See Culley 1993, 189–97; Douglas, 1991; O'Brian, 2007; and de Baere and Roelstraete, 2006.
16. Roudinesco 1997, 529.
17. See Klobucar and Barnholden 1999; since the early 1990s, the KSW office and performance spaces have clustered around Hastings and Cambie and have included shared spaces with Artspeak and the Or galleries; the list of locations in Vancouver was compiled by D. Mancini from KSW archives.
18. In a ca. 1976 exchange with Steve McCaffery, Ron Silliman provides a succinct definition of the relationship between meaning and capital: "going to go into the social origins of referentiality [which] are, of course, in the labor process of capitalism itself: referentiality is language serialized, its dual projection as product & commodity resolved by the repression of its product nature" (McCaffery, *et al* 1985, 64). Note that in the introduction to this correspondence, published in *Line* in 1985, McCaffery argues that while the "numerous contributors to *L=A=N=G=U=A=G=E* have been frequently lumped together as proponents of a de-referentialist 'school' of writing, this is not the case. Though many contributors conceived the

practice of writing to be primarily a social fact and saw the production of meaning as occupying, with a certain inevitability, a socio-political position within the politics of representation ... [t]he letters reveal many of the differences felt in the early struggles of post-referential conceptualization" (59).

19. Appropriately, while I am quoting from the authors' collections of essays, both statements first appeared in *L=A=N=G=U=A=G=E* magazine in the 1970s.
20. "Shifter" is borrowed by Jakobson from Otto Jesperson: see Fink 1997, 37–38.
21. See, in this regard, Dean 2009 and Harvey 2005.
22. Exactly contemporaneous with Lusk's poem's publication in 1988 is Leslie Scalapino's book-length poem *way*, which includes the "bum series" and various disjunctive meditations on homelessness: "the men / on the street who'd / died—in the weather—who're bums" (51). This synchronicity of texts indicates a social text, the social text of rising homelessness under neoliberalism.
23. As Žižek argues in "*Objet a* in Social Links," the university discourse means especially "the 'excluded' or 'damned' authors are the IDEAL feeding stuff for the academic machine" (108: he refers to Kierkegaard, Nietzsche, and Benjamin, but we could also add Lacan and Žižek himself—and, perhaps, the KSW).
24. OWN, SENTENCED (Klobucar and Barnholden 1999, 134), ALPO, AFTER (135), CANADA, SOUTH, MATTER, MOVED (136), HALF, LACK, HERE, OWN, PCB (137), PLENTY, WHAT (138), BLOODY, THIS, ONLY, CLEPT, EVER (139), LOOKS, 2D, GET, YOU, AGAIN (140), *WHY*, MINDING, NOT, WONDER (141), YET, STUFFED (142).
25. OK (Klobucar and Barnholden 1999, 134), PC, UNlike (136), OK, OR (137), NO, US (139), OK, MY (140).
26. See Caleb Crain's polemical essay "Against Camel Case."
27. Jameson delineates these distinctions nicely in his introductory essay on base and superstructure in *Valences of the Dialectic* (2009).
28. The *Autre*, what Žižek calls the big Other, is roughly analogous to the Symbolic, to the one we are trying to please, to figure out their desire—the parent, the teacher, the cop, the critic. Žižek reminds us, in *Contingency,*

Hegemony, Universality, that the big Other does not really exist; Žižek's materialist position is that, for example, "in order for interpellation ... to occur, material practices and/or rituals of real social institutions (schools, laws ...) do not suffice, that is, the subject has to *presuppose* the symbolic Institution, an ideal structure" (Žižek, *et al* 2000, 116). I return to this question of the big Other as Žižek articulates it in Chapter Four, when I discuss Red Tories and melancholy.

29. Hence the recent mock-genre of Teen Angst poetry—see http://www.teenangstpoetry.blogspot.com/.
30. Derksen (1994) quickly ranges over the work of Earl Birney, Pat Lowther, Brian Fawcett, Charles Olson, Gerry Gilbert, Fred Wah, and Phyllis Webb, by way of providing context for younger Vancouver poets such as Kathryn MacLeod, Dorothy Trujillo Lusk, Kevin Davies, and Gerald Creede.
31. China's military spending in 2008 was $59 billion US: see Drew 2008.
32. Refers to the cover of Clifford and Marcus's 1986 *Writing Culture*.
33. The letters of Steve McCaffery and also Ron Silliman (1985) are great sources here.
34. The full text of "American Prose" runs: "He needed a clear throat / 'Ahem.' he said / and put the barrel in his mouth." In *Writing* 16, the title "Prose" seems, again, to be a generic marker—the text is listed by that title on the cover of the magazine but, on the page, is also given the title "The Face Falls". This text includes a line very similar to the opening of "neglect is no bother": "I woke up in the basement."
35. See http://www.tate.org.uk/modern/exhibitions/jeffwall/infocus/section1/img5.shtm.
36. See Žižek 2004a, 131*ff*, esp. 156.
37. Various statistics (or at least such percentages as "Male 98%, married 92%") appear in "If History is the Memory of Time What Would our Monument Be" (Derkson 1993a, 60–74); the exchange rate for the Canadian and American dollars in "But Could I make a Living from It" (2003, 24–39); and exports of oil to the US from various countries in billions of barrels in "Compression" (2003, 103–110).

Chapter Four: Neo-Pastoral Red Tories

1. It should be noted that Farr is fairly critical of the efficacy of protest genres—of the slogan in particular—noting that many are actually intended for transmission through mainstream media. But the wide variety of material manifestations of the "No Olympics on Stolen Native Land" slogan/demand (and its various permutations) suggests that it did not suffer from that co-optation. Farr concludes that slogans are both ineffective (due to their commodification) and indispensable.
2. See Lacan 2002, 489–542, especially section 7, 514*ff*.
3. These quotations are from the book *XEclogue*, which is unpaginated (and not the excerpt in *Writing Class*).
4. As elsewhere in this book, when I resort to dates or give information I probably don't know, it comes from Wikipedia.
5. A detailed description of the differences between true, magnetic, and compass North can be found at the Government of Canada "Geomagnetism" website.
6. A book that should really have been called *The Canadian Imaginary*, but then it would have had to have been a different book.
7. Jed Rasula reminds us that Jameson argues for the pervasive, not to say residual, after-life of the ideologeme, which continues on like an "exoskeleton" (Jameson 1981, 151; Rasula 1996, 389).
8. The last phrase coined, lest Canadian readers get too smug, by Bush's Canadian speechwriter David Frum.
9. See Weber 2008, *Benjamin's -abilities*, for commentary on Benjamin, Schmitt, and Agamben (but esp. 176–210); see also Agamben's *State of Exception* and Žižek *et al.*'s *The Neighbor*.
10. See Dart 2010, English 1985, and Taylor 1982; Nelson Wiseman (2007) presents a critical survey of the concept as "bad history, poor political science" (23–24)—which sounds like an out-take from a Culley-Robertson collaborative b-side! (See also Wiseman's bibliographic survey of Canadian political theory with respect to the Red Tory [311–12].) Preece (1977) offers a rejoinder to Horowitz (1965) in "The Myth of the Red Tory." The Wikipedia entry for Red Tory also has an interesting section on "definition drift," or the tendency since the 1980s to use the category to refer to any

Conservative politician who is not a die-hard neoliberal; but even in 1985, English noted that this "popular term ... is used to refer loosely to the left wing of the Conservative Party."

11. Still in the Canadian political science literature on the "Red Tory," Preece's article is occasioned by journalists' use of the term "Red Tory" at the 1976 Conservative leadership convention; he notes that "[i]t is clear who the Red Tories in the Progressive Conservative Party are considered to be—Flora MacDonald, John Fraser and Gordon Fairweather are among the more obvious 'Reds'" (1977, 3); but Preece goes on to argue that Horowitz's use of the term is misleading, remarking of Robert Stanfield (leader of the Conservatives from 1967–76): "In truth, Stanfield is no Red Tory. Like other Canadian Conservatives he is a Whig but one who recognizes with Burke that unrestricted free enterprise, individual initiative and striving and the weak state will produce only chaos and destroy the security and stability of society, which are prerequisites of a society 'in which enterprise can flourish'" (ibid., 23).

Chapter Five: MY Archive Fever

1. Box 1, MsC 68, Kootenay School of Writing *fonds*, Contemporary Literature Collection, Special Collections and Rare Books, W.A.C. Bennett Library, Simon Fraser University, Burnaby, BC.
2. See http://www.kswnet.org/fire/resources-KSW.cfm for a chronology.
3. Accompanying the KSW archive is a "Records Inventory, Kootenay School of Writing, 1984–1994, Prepared by Aaron Vidaver, April 20, 1998." Box 1, MsC 68, Kootenay School of Writing *fonds*.
4. A useful recent survey of archive theory can be found in O'Driscoll and Bishop's 2004 "Archiving 'Archiving.'"
5. Marlene Manoff in a survey of "Theories of the Archive from Across the Disciplines," argues for the importance of Derrida's text in establishing the discourse on archival theory in the 1990s (11*ff*). Thanks also to Kim Minkus for her help in this regard.
6. The graphs were first presented in his seminar on the unconscious in 1957: see the headnote at the beginning of the "Subversion" essay (Lacan 2002, 671).

7. "Despite all our efforts," Wayman writes, "the buildings were padlocked on May 1" in "Against the Smiling Bastards," 2007, 82.
8. "CWRT Articulation Meetings" folder, Box 1, MsC 68, Kootenay School of Writing *fonds*. Articulation meetings are processes by which British Columbia college and university programs coordinate academic offerings and transferability. Present at the May 1984 meeting were representatives from the University of British Columbia, the University of Victoria, Kwantlen College, Douglas College, Malaspina College, Trinity Western College, Simon Fraser University, Capilano College, Vancouver Community College, Langara, and the Kooteney [*sic*] School of Writing. In his short memoir, "KSW: Origins, including Nelson," Wah writes that, "along with Pauline Butling, Paulette Jiles, Rita Moir, Irene Mock, Blake Parker, and others" he helped set up the KSW in Nelson, in the summer and fall of 1984 (2010, 142).
9. See minutes (April 26, and May 10, 1985), Box 4, MsC 68, Kootenay School of Writing *fonds*. Documentation in the archive of these continuing education classes include those run by Tom Wayman through the New Westminster system, for September 1985 and January 1986, and with the North Shore system, for November 1985. ("NW Continuing Education" and "North Shore Continuing Ed." folders, Box 5, MsC 68, Kootenay School of Writing *fonds*.)
10. "Canada Student Loan—Designated as 'Eligible Institution' App'n" folder, Box 1, MsC 68, Kootenay School of Writing *fonds*. The application was in response to an August 27, 1985 letter from a prospective student.
11. See Douglas 1988.
12. General documentation can be found in "Funding—City of Vancouver" file, Box 3, MsC 68, Kootenay School of Writing *fonds*. A poster for a readings series at the Coburg Gallery in the spring of 1986, "organized by The Kootenay School of Writing" and including Susan Musgrave, Peter Culley, Al Neil, Angela Hyrniuk, etc., is in the "Correspondence In" folder, Box 4, MsC 68, Kootenay School of Writing *fonds*. In an April 26, 1985 letter to Richard Holden, of the Explorations Program at the Canada Council, Tom Wayman describes at length the rationale for KSW replacing the Vancouver Literary Storefront with a Vancouver Literary Information Resource.

Letters of support dated from 1985 were received from Leona Gom, faculty member at Kwantlen College; Susan Lord, then a student at SFU; F.H. Eger of Pulp Press; Gloria Greenfield at West Coast Women & Words; and Percilla Groves, an SFU librarian and organizer of a reading series at Octopus Books—again, indicating the broad range of connections the KSW already had in the Vancouver literary scene. ("Explorations Program—Current App'ns." folder, Box 3, MsC 68, Kootenay School of Writing *fonds*.) More information about the KSW's role in establishing the Vancouver Literary Information Resource can be found in the 1985 and 1986 grant applications to the City of Vancouver's Civic Cultural Grants ("Funding—City of Vancouver" folder, Box 3, MsC 68, Kootenay School of Writing *fonds*.)

13. Indeed, as is so often the case with grassroots organizations—be they political, cultural, or some other formation—that very mix of the mundane and the aesthetic no doubt led to the attrition of the first generation of the KSW. Wayman relates, in his memoir, how "[b]y 1987, burnout arrived ... I recall poring over financial accounts in the office late one evening, trying to reconcile some balances, while in an adjacent classroom [Colin] Browne toiled at a grant application. Suddenly I heard a bellow from the room next door: 'What has any of this to do with *poetry*?'" (2007, 84).
14. See Wallace (in Douglas 1991, 43n1), for the classificatory nomenclature of the Canadian art world.
15. "In addition, we have co-ordinated our readings and talks series with various galleries in Vancouver who offer similar programs. Our reading series this winter is at the Coburg Gallery, for example, and in the past we have integrated our programming with that of the Western Front and the Contemporary Art Gallery." From a 1986 grant application to the City of Vancouver's Civic Cultural Grants ("Funding—City of Vancouver" folder, Box 3, MsC 68, Kootenay School of Writing *fonds*).
16. But also the Italian neighbourhood of Commerical Drive and the German and Polish settlements in Mount Pleasant and Cedar Cottage.
17. Please see, for general treatments of Vancouver's urban growth and gentrification, the popular history edited by Chuck Davis 1997 (especially the essays on various neighbourhoods by Bruce Macdonald and Jim Green); the geographers' collection edited by Wynn and Oke 1992, especially those

chapters by North and Hardwick, Ley, *et al*); the culturalist *Vancouver: Representing the Postmodern City* (edited by Paul Delany 1994); and Bill Jeffries *et al* 2005, *Unfinished Business: Photographing Vancouver Streets 1955–1965*. The literature on the Downtown Eastside is particularly rich and includes John Atkin's photo-history *Strathcona: Vancouver's First Neighbourhood* (1994); the oral histories *Opening Doors: Vancouver's East End* (Daphne Marlatt and Carole Itter 1979) and *Hastings and Main: Stories from an Inner City Neighbourhood* (edited Jo-Ann Canning-Dew 1987); the exhibition catalogue that accompanied Stan Douglas's panoramic photograph *Stan Douglas: Every Building on 100 West Hastings* (edited by Reid Shier 2002); *Woodsquat*, an issue of *West Coast Line* that documented a 2003 occupation of Vancouver's Woodwards building (edited by Aaron Vidaver 2003–04); and Boyd *et al* 2009, *Raising Shit!*, an account of the Vancouver Area Network of Drug Users' (VANDU) struggle against the war on drugs.

18. While some residents of the DTES don't particularly like the term "Skid Row," I use it in part as a historical reminder of the term "Skid Road," a logging term for areas on which timber was hauled—or skidded—down to the waterfront, and a reminder of the resource industry base of the city and neighbourhood.
19. All figures come from "Funding—City of Vancouver" file, Box 3, MsC 68, Kootenay School of Writing *fonds*.
20. These are the ones with responses: all in their respective folders, Box 3, MsC 68, Kootenay School of Writing *fonds*.
21. In both cases from "Funding—City of Vancouver" file, Box 3, MsC 68, Kootenay School of Writing *fonds*.
22. "KSW Fall 1984 Courses" brochure, Koerner Foundation folder, Box 3, MsC 68, Kootenay School of Writing *fonds*.
23. "KSW Fall 1984 Courses" brochure, Koerner Foundation folder, Box 3, MsC 68, Kootenay School of Writing *fonds*.
24. "KSW Fall 1984 Courses" brochure, Koerner Foundation folder, Box 3, MsC 68, Kootenay School of Writing *fonds*.
25. McLean Foundation folder, Box 3, MsC 68, Kootenay School of Writing *fonds*.
26. Dated 13 January 1986. Grant application to the City of Vancouver's Civic

Cultural Grants ("Funding—City of Vancouver" folder, Box 3, MsC 68, Kootenay School of Writing *fonds*.)

27. "KSW Minutes 27/07/84 up to Dec 31/1985" folder, Box 5, MsC 68, Kootenay School of Writing *fonds*.

28. Derksen, "Signs Taken as Wonders," (1994, 155). Further, early grant applications stressed a division in the readings: "two reading programs: one for more established writers and one for the best new talent in the city that we can identify." Too, a distinction was introduced between the readings and publication: "more portable and longer-lasting introduction to good new writing than public readings is provided by our triquarterly magazine, *Writing*"—1986 application to the City of Vancouver Civic Cultural Grants ("Funding—City of Vancouver" folder, Box 3, MsC 68, Kootenay School of Writing *fonds*).

29. But this is not the entire story; in each of my lists certain artists or writers are missing. *East of Main* actually included three groups of writers: in addition to the KSW-associated writers, there were those who write about East Vancouver (Pauline Rankin, Michael B. Turner, Mary Fong, Bud Osborn, Sandy Shreve, Jim Wong-Chu), and work writers (Sadhu Binning, Joanne Arnott, Brett Enemark, Jill Mandrake, Kate Braid, Cuba Dyer, Tom Wayman, Pam Tranfield, Evelyn Lau, Maxine Gadd, Geoff Inverarity). The cover, a representation of colourful East Vancouver neighbourhoods (including Chinatown, Little India, Hastings and Main, and Commercial Drive) is by Maggie Robertson. *West Coast Line*'s initial issue also features many artists, including a cover by Mina Totino, and work by Stan Douglas, Phil McCrum, Corinne Carlson, Victoria Walker, Kathy Slade, Sara Leydon, Jin-Me Yoon, and Roy Arden (and an omnibus review of Tsunami chapbooks by Fred Wah); *WCL* also included "statements on poetics" by Browne, Strang, McGauley, Yarrow, Denisoff, Farrell, Kelley, Karasick, and Derksen. Like *East of Main*, *Raddle Moon* has two other sections of writing: "Elsewhere" (William Fuller, Jean Day, Katrine Le Gallou, Jackson Mac Low, Gil McElroy, and Rae Armantrout) as well as "New Writing from Québec" (Cynthia Girard and Michael Délisle—both presented in the original French and translated). Finally, while the writers listed in my chart comprise all the contributors to *Writing Class*, that anthology's editors

also have a forty-seven page introduction (almost twenty-five percent of the 214-page book's length).

30. Former left-wing city councilor Bob Williams from a 2005 interview, talking about the 1960s: "I was on Little Mountain [Queen Elizabeth Park, in the centre of the city] one day looking out over the City and I was just flabbergasted when I saw the difference—the sea of greenery to the west of Little Mountain and this bloody rooftop empty landscape to the east" (Vaughan and Zaslove in Jeffries 2005, 266). Adrienne Burk (2005) has documented the activist work that went into creating an accessible beach (Crab Park) in the Downtown Eastside.
31. "KSW Minutes 27/07/84 up to Dec 31/1985" and "KSW Minutes Jan. 1/1986–Jan. 31, 1990" files, Box 5, MsC 68, Kootenay School of Writing *fonds*.
32. Box 7, MsC 68, Kootenay School of Writing *fonds*.

Conclusion

1. Please see Jean Swanson's article (2011) in the *Vancouver Sun* for a well-argued critique of gentrification plans for the Downtown Eastside. For a response to the City of Vancouver's proposed legislation, see "SFU, UBC Professors" (2011).
2. Žižek's use of "gentrified" occurs in his discussion of Levinas' concept of the face, where Žižek argues that we should "restore to the Levinasian 'face' all its monstrosity: the face is not a harmonious Whole of the dazzling epiphany of a 'human face', the face is something a glimpse of which we get when we stumble upon a grotesquely distorted face, a face in the grip of a disgusting tic or grimace" (2006c, 113). This is the face, of course, we see in Tom Wayman's poem "The Face of Jack Munro."
3. This can be seen, specifically, in the shift from the more inclusive politics/poetics of *East of Main* to the more formally determined poetics of the *West Coast Line*, *Raddle Moon*, and *Writing Class* collections.
4. Christine Stewart notes, in her interview with Lisa Robertson and Catriona Strang, that during the feminist intervention into the late 1980s KSW, "Writers like Bruce Andrews, Barrett Watten, and Clark Coolidge, for example, were put aside in an attempt to locate something else. Robertson's

reading and writing practice proposed that there might be very different texts to be read, to be reread, and different readers and different readerly communities to be reconfigured" (2010, 134).

5. In a forthcoming essay in *Canadian Literature*, Alessandra Capperdoni reads the humanist/lyrical writing of Pat Lowther and Gwendolyn MacEwan alongside the deconstructive works of Daphne Marlatt, Nicole Brossard, and Dorothy Trujillo Lusk.

REFERENCES

Agamben, Giorgio. 1993. *Stanzas: Words and Phantasm in Western Culture.* Translated by Ronald L. Martinez. Theory and History of Literature, 69. Minneapolis: University of Minnesota Press.

———. *State of Exception.* 2005. Translated by Kevin Attell. Chicago: University of Chicago Press.

Andrews, Bruce. 1996. *Paradise & Method: Poetics & Praxis.* Evanston: Northwestern Univeristy Press.

———. "Constitution/Writing, Politics, Language, the Body." 1982. *Open Letter* 5 (1); *L=A=N=G=U=A=G=E* 4 (Winter): 154–65.

Andrews, Bruce and Charles Bernstein, eds. 1984. *The L=A=N=G=U=A=G=E Book.* Carbondale, IL: Southern Illinois University Press.

Antliff, Allan. 2004. *Only a Beginning: An Anarchist Anthology.* Vancouver: Arsenal Pulp Press..

Armstrong, John. 2001. *Guilty of Everything.* Vancouver: New Star.

Atkin, John. 1994. *Strathcona: Vancouver's First Neighbourhood.* Vancouver: Whitecap Books.

Ayers, David. 2004. *Modernism: A Short Introduction.* Oxford: Wiley-Blackwell.

Bakhtin, Mikhail. 1986. "The Problem of Speech Genres." In *Speech Genres and Other Late Essays.* 60–102. Translated by Vern W. McGee. Austin: University of Texas Press.

Benjamin, Walter. 1985. *The Origin of German Tragic Drama.* Translated by John Osborne. London: Verso.

———. 1999a. *The Arcades Project.* Translated by Howard Eiland and Kevin McLaughlin. Cambridge: Belknap Press.

———. 1999b. "The Author as Producer." In *Selected Writings,* edited by Michael W. Jennings, Howard Eiland, Gary Smith, translated by Rodney Livingstone, *et al.* Vol. 2: 768-782. Cambridge: Belknap Press.

———. 1999c. "The Task of the Translator." In *Selected Writings,* edited by Michael W. Jennings, Howard Eiland, Gary Smith, translated by Rodney Livingstone, *et al.* Vol. 1: 253–63. Cambridge: Belknap Press.

———. 2006. *Berliner Kindheit um Neunzehnhundert.* Frankfurt: Suhrkamp.

Bernstein, Charles. 1986. *Content's Dream: Essays 1975–1984*. Los Angeles: Sun and Moon.

———.1992. *A Poetics*. Cambridge: Harvard University Press.

Bishop, Edward. 2005. *Riding with Rilke: Reflections on Motorcycles and Books*. New York: Norton.

Bowering, George. 1994. "Vancouver as Postmodern Poetry." In *Vancouver: Representing the Postmodern City*, edited by Paul Delany, 121–43. Vancouver: Arsenal Pulp Press.

Bowman, Paul and Richard Stamp, eds. 2007. *The Truth of Žižek*. London: Continuum.

Bowie, Malcolm. 1991. *Lacan*. London: Fontana.

Boyd, Susan, *et al.* 2009. *Raise Shit! Social Action Saving Lives*. Halifax: Fernwood Publishing.

Bremner, Lary, *et al.* 1990. "Preface." *West Coast Line* 24(1): 10–11.

Burk, Adrienne. 2005. "Speaking Between the Lines." In *Unfinished Business* by Bill Jeffries, *et al*, 116–24. Vancouver: Burnaby; Presentation House Gallery: *West Coast Line* 47 (Fall).

Butling, Pauline. 2001. "Writing as Social Practice (review of *Writing Class: The Kootenay School of Writing Anthology*). *XCP* 9: 85–92.

Butline, Pauline and Susan Rudy. 2005. *Writing in Our Time: Canada's Radical Poetries in English (1957–2003)*. Waterloo: Wilfrid Laurier University Press.

Byrne, Edward. 2008. "The Women (First Reel): On Susan Clark." In *Antiphonies: Essays on Women's Experiemental Poetries in Canada*, edited by Nate Dorward, 7–26. Toronto: The Gig.

Canning-Dew, Jo-Ann. 1987. *Hastings and Main: Stories from an Inner City Neighbourhood*. Vancouver: New Star.

Carroll, William K. 1984. "The Solidarity Coalition." In *The New Reality*, edited by Warren Magnusson, *et al.*, 94–113. Vancouver: New Star. Child, Abigail. [n.d.] "Active Theory." *Raddle Moon* 13: 12–33.

Child, Abigail. 1993. "Active Theory." *Raddle Moon* 13: 12-33.

Clark, Tom. 2000. *Charles Olson: The Allegory of a Poet's Life*. Berkeley: North Atlantic Books.

Clemens, Justin and Russell Grigg, eds. 2006. *Jacques Lacan and the Other Side of Psychoanalysis: Reflections on* Seminar XVII. (SIC 6). Durham, NC: Duke

University Press.

Clifford, James and George E. Marcus, eds. 1986. *Writing Culture: The Poetics and Politics of Ethnography*. Berkeley: University of California Press.

Coolidge, Clark. 1978. *Quartz Hearts*. San Francisco: This.

———. 1982. *Mine: The One that Enters the Stories*. Great Barrington, MA: Figures.

———. 1986. *The Crystal Text*. Great Barrington, MA: Figures.

———. 1978/1993. *Own Face*. Lenox, MA: Angel Hair Books; reprinted by Sun & Moon Classics, 39. Los Angeles: Sun & Moon.

Collis, Steve. 2006. *Through the Words of Others: Susan Howe and Anarcho-Scholasticism*. Victoria, BC: University of Victoria Department of English (ELS).

Copjec, Joan, ed. 1993. *Shades of Noir*. London: Verso.

Costa, Cris. 2010. "Neoliberalism and Literary Discourse: Collectivity, Agency, and the Kootenay School of Writing." *West Coast Line* 67 (Fall): 26–35.

Crain, Caleb. 2009. "Against Camel Case." *New York Times Magazine*. November 29, 18.

Craven, Louise. 2008. *What Are Archives?: Cultural and Theoretical Perspectives: A Reader*. Aldershot: Ashgate Publishing Group.

Creede, Gerald. 1983. "American Prose." *British Columbia Monthly* 30 (June/July): n.p.

———. 1986a. "The Face Falls." *Writing*. 16 (October): 33–34.

———. [1986b.] *Verbose*. Vancouver: Tsunami.

———. 1987. "faluables." *Raddle Moon* 5: 95–99.

———. 1989. "neglect is no bother." In *East of Main*, edited by Calvin Wharton and Tom Wayman, 104–08. Vancouver: Arsenal Pulp Press.

———. 1990. "resumé." *West Coast Line* 24 (1): 61–69.

———. 1993. *Ambit*. Vancouver: Tsunami.

Creede, Gerald and Nancy Shaw. 1989. "Close to Naked." *Writing* 23/24 (Fall/Winter): 18–22.

Creskey, Jim. 2010. "Dock Workers as Architects of Foreign Policy." *Embassy* (March 24). http://www.embassymag.ca/page/view/creskey-03-24-2010.

Culley, Peter. 1993. "Because I Am Always Talking: Reading Vancouver into the Western Front." In *A Whispered Art History*, edited by Keith Wallace,

189–97. Vancouver: Arsenal Pulp Press.

———. 1995. *The Climax Forest*. Vancouver: Leech Books.

———. 2002. "Roy Arden's Fragments: A Poem Containing History." *Oakville Catalogue*. The Centre for Contemporary Canadian Art: The Canadian Art Database, Canadian Writers Files. http://www.ccca.ca/c/writing/c/culley/cul005t.html.

———. 1999. "Winterreise *after F. Schubert and W. Müller*." In Andrew Klobucar and Michael Barnholden, eds. *Writing Class: The Kootenay School of Writing Anthology*. Vancouver: New Star Books, 175–78.

Dart, Ron. 2011. "Red Tory." *The Canadian Encyclopedia*. Historica Foundation. http://www.thecanadianencyclopedia.com/.

Davidson, Michael. 1983. "Discourse in Poetry: Bakhtin and Extensions of the Dialogical." In *Code of Signals*, edited by Michael Palmer, 143–50. Berkeley: North Atlantic.

Davies, Kevin. 1992. "From *Meanstreak*." *Raddle Moon* 14: 57–63.

———. 1995. *Thunk*. New York: Situations #2.

———. 1999. "From *Overkill/a protocol*." *Raddle Moon* 17: 80–89.

———. 2000. *Comp*. Washington: Edge Books.

Davies, Kevin, and Diane Ward. 2000. "Interview." *PhillyTalks* 15 (January 18): 1–8.

Davis, Chuck, ed. 1997. *The Greater Vancouver Book*. Surrey, BC: Linkman.

Davis, Colin. 2010. *Critical Excess: Overreading in Derrida, Deleuze, Levinas, Žižek, and Cavell* Stanford: Stanford University Press.

Dean, Jodi. 2007. "Fascism, Stalinism, and the Organization of Enjoyment." In *Did Somebody Say Ideology: Slavoj Žižek and Consequences*, edited by Fabio Vighi and Heiko Feldner, 21–40. Newcastle, UK: Cambridge Scholars Press.

———. 2009. *Democracy and Other Neoliberal Fantasies: Communicative Capitalism and Left Politics*. Durham, NC: Duke University Press.

De Baere, Bart and Dieter Roelstraete, eds. 2006. *Intertidal: Vancouver Art and Artists*, exhibition catalogue. Antwerp; Vancouver: Museum van Hedendaagse Kunst Antwerpen; Morris and Helen Belkin Art Gallery.

DeKoven, Marianne. 1983. *A Different Language: Gertrude Stein's Experimental Writing*. Madison: University of Wisconsin Press.

Delany, Paul, ed. 1994. *Vancouver: Representing the Postmodern City*. Vancouver: Arsenal Pulp Press.

Derksen, Jeff. 1987. "Blind Trust." *Raddle Moon* 5: 66–74.

———. 1990a. *Down Time*. Vancouver: Talonbooks.

———. 1990b. "Exploded View." *West Coast Line* 24 (1): 144–45.

———. 1990c. "Solace." *West Coast Line* 24 (1): 85–98.

———. 1993a. *Dwell*. Vancouver: Talonbooks.

———. 1993b. *Selfish*. Vancouver: pomflit 5.

———. 1994. "Sites Taken as Signs: Place, the Open Text, and Enigma in New Vancouver Writing." In Delany, ed., 144–61.

———. 1998. "From International Muscle Cars." *Raddle Moon* 17: 92–99.

———. 2003. *Transnational Muscle Cars*. Vancouver: Talonbooks.

———. 2009. *Annihilated Time: Poetry and Other Politics*. Vancouver: Talonbooks.

Derksen, Jeff and Roy Arden. 1989. "Through." *Raddle Moon* 8 (November): 33–57.

Derrida, Jacques. 1995. *Archive Fever: A Freudian Impression*. Translated by Eric Prenowitz. Chicago: University of Chicago Press.

Dever, Maryanne, Ann Vickery, Sally Newman. 2009. *The Intimate Archive: Journeys Through Private Papers*. Canberra: National Library of Australia.

Diamond, Sara. 1991. "Daring Documents: The Practical Aesthetics of Early Vancouver Video." In *Vancouver Anthology*, edited by Stan Douglas, 47–83. Vancouver: Talonbooks.

Dorward, Nate, ed. 2008. *Antiphonies; Essays on Women's Experimental Poetries in Canada*. Toronto: The Gig.

Douglas, Stan. 1988. *Beckett: Teleplays*, exhibition catalogue. Vancouver: Vancouver Art Gallery.

———, ed. 1991. *Vancouver Anthology: The Institutional Politics of Art*. Vancouver: Talonbooks.

Drew, Jill. 2008. "China Military Budget Reported at $59 Billion." *The Washington Post*. March 5. http://www.washingtonpost.com/wp-dyn/content/article/2008/03/04/AR2008030401345_pf.html.

DuPlessis, Rachel Blau. 2001. *Genders, Races and Religious Cultures in Modern American Poetry, 1908-1934*. Cambridge: Cambridge University Press.

Eichhorn, Kate and Heather Milne, eds., 2009. *Prismatic Publics: Innovative Canadian Women's Poetry and Poetics*. Toronto: Coach House Press.

English, John. 1985. "Red Tory." *The Canadian Encyclopedia*. Edmonton: Hurtig, vol. 3, 1554.

Engelbrecht, Penelope J. 1990. "'Lifting Belly is a Language': The Postmodern Lesbian Subject." *Feminist Studies* 16(1) (Spring): 85–114.

Evans, Dylan. 2005. *An Introductory Dictionary of Lacanian Psychoanalysis*. London: Routledge.

Evans, Steve. 1998. "That Sublime Object of Marginality." *Jacket Magazine* 2 (January). http://jacketmagazine.com/02/evans.html.

Farr, Roger. 2002. "Protest Genres and the Pragmatics of Dissent." Manuscript, Kootenay School of Writing: Studies in *Practical Negation* 8 (May 26).

Farrell, Dan. [1988]. *ape*. Vancouver: Tsunami.

———. 1994. *Thimking of You*. Vancouver: Tsunami.

Fawcett, Brian. 1991. "East Van Uber Alles?" In *Unusual Circumstances/Interesting Times: And Other Impolite Interventions*. 91–102. Vancouver: New Star Books.

Feltham, Oliver. 2006. "Enjoy Your Stay: Structural Change in *Seminar XVII*." In *Jacques Lacan and the Other Side of Psychoanalysis*, edited by Justin Clemens and Russell Grigg, 179–94. Durham, NC: Duke University Press.

Ferguson, Deanna. 1993. *The Relative Minor*. Vancouver: Tsunami.

Fink, Bruce. 1997. *The Lacanian Subject: Between Language and Jouissance*. Princeton, NJ: Princeton University Press.

———. 2004. *Lacan to the Letter: Reading* Écrits *Closely*. Minneapolis: University of Minnesota Press.

Freud, Sigmund. 1954. *The Origins of Psychoanalysis: Letters to Wilhelm Fliess, Drafts, and Notes: 1887–1902*. New York: Basic Books.

———. 2001. *The Standard Edition of the Complete Psychoanalytical Works*. Edited and translated by James Strachey, *et al.* 24 vols. London: Vintage/Hogarth Press/Institute of Psycho-Analysis.

———. 2006. "Mourning and Melancholia." In *The Penguin Freud Reader*, edited by Adam Phillips, 310–26. London: Penguin.

Frost, Elisabeth A. 1995. "Signifyin(g) on Stein: The Revisionist Poetics of

Harryette Mullen and Leslie Scalapino." *Postmodern Culture*. 5(3). http://pmc.iath.virginia.edu/text-only/issue.595/frost.595.

Ginsberg, Allen. 2006. *Howl: Original Draft Facsimile, Transcript, and Variant Versions, Fully Annotated by Author, with Contemporaneous Correspondence, Account of First Public Reading, Legal Skirmishes, Precursor Texts, and Bibliography*, edited by Barry Miles. New York: HarperPerennial.

Government of Canada. [2008]. "Geomagnetism." *Natural Resources Canada* website. http://gsc.nrcan.gc.ca/geomag/index_e.php.

Grant, George. 1969. *Technology and Empire: Perspectives on North America*. Toronto: House of Anansi.

———. 1965/1970. *Lament for a Nation: The Defeat of Canadian Nationalism*. Ottawa: Carleton University Press.

Green, Jim. "DERA." In Chuck Davis 1997, 791–92.

Hansen, Ann. 2001. *Direct Action: Memoirs of an Urban Guerrilla*. San Francisco: AK Press.

Harvey, David. 2005. *A Brief History of Neoliberalism*. New York: Oxford University Press.

Hartz, Louis, *et al.* 1964. *The Founding of New Societies: Studies in the History of the United States, Latin America, South Africa, Canada, and Australia*. New York: Harcourt, Brace & World.

Hebdige, Dick. 1979. *Subculture: The Meaning of Style*. London: Methuen.

Hejinian, Lyn. 1984. "If Written is Writing." In *The L=A=N=G=U=A=G=E Book*, edited by Bruce Andrews and Charles Bernstein, 29–30. Carbondale, IL: Southern Illinois University Press.

Hoens, Dominiek. 2006. "Toward a New Perversion: Psychoanalysis." In *Jacques Lacan and the Other Side of Psychoanalysis*, edited by Justin Clemens and Russell Grigg, 88–103. Durham, NC: Duke University Press.

Horowitz, Gad. 1965. "Tories, Socialists and the Demise of Canada." *Canadian Dimension* 2 (4) (May): 12–15.

———. 1968. *Canadian Labour in Politics*. Toronto: University of Toronto Press.

Howe, Susan. 1993. *The Nonconformist's Memorial*. New York: New Directions.

———. 2007. *My Emily Dickinson*. New York: New Directions.

Hoy, Dan. 2006. "The Virtual Dependency of the Post-Avant and the Problematics of Flarf: What Happens when Poets Spend Too Much Time

Fucking Around on the Internet." *Jacket Magazine* 29 (April). http://jacketmagazine.com/29/hoy-flarf.html.

Hurst, Andrea. 2008. *Derrida Vis-à-vis Lacan: Interweaving Deconstruction and Psychoanalysis*. New York: Fordham University Press.

Jakobson, Roman. 2008. "Linguistics and Poetics." In *Modern Criticism and Theory: A Reader*, third edition, edited by David Lodge and Nigel Wood, 141–64. Toronto: Pearson Longman.

Jameson, Fredric. 1981. *The Political Unconscious: Narrative as a Socially Symbolic Act*. Ithaca, NY: Cornell University Press.

———. 1988. "Imaginary and Symbolic in Lacan." In *The Ideologies of Theory: Essays 1971–1986*, Vol. 1. *Situations of Theory*. Theory and History of Literature Series, 48, 75–115. Minneapolis: University of Minnesota Press.

———. 2006. "Lacan and the Dialectic: A Fragment." In *Lacan: The Silent Partners*, edited by Slavoj Žižek, 365–97. New York: Verso.

———. 2009. *Valences of the Dialectic*. New York: Verso.

Jarraway, David R. 1992. "'My Life' through the Eighties: The Exemplary L=A=N=G=U=A=G=E of Lyn Hejinian." *Contemporary Literature* 33 (2) (Summer, Special Issue: American Poetry of the 1980s): 319–36.

Jeffries, Bill, *et al.* 2005. *Unfinished Business: Photographing Vancouver Streets 1955–1965*, exhibition catalogue. North Vancouver; Burnaby: Presentation House Gallery; *West Coast Line* 47 (Fall).

Johnston, Adrian. 2009. *Badiou, Žižek, and Political Transformations: The Cadence of Change*. Evanston, IL: Northwestern University Press.

Keithley, Joe. 2004. *I, Shithead: A Life in Punk*. Vancouver: Arsenal Pulp Press.

Kellogg, David. 1995. "'Desire Pronounced and/Punctuated': Lacan and the Fate of the Poetic Subject." *American Imago* 52 (4) (Winter): 405–37.

Klar, Malte and Tim Kasser. 2009. "Some Benefits of Being an Activist: Measuring Activism and Its Role in Psychological Well-Being." *Political Psychology* 30 (5): 755–78.

Klobucar, Andrew and Michael Barnholden, eds. 1999. *Writing Class: The Kootenay School of Writing Anthology*. Vancouver: New Star Books.

Lacan, Jacques. 1991. *The Seminar of Jacques Lacan: Book II: The Ego in Freud's Theory and in the Technique of Psychoanalysis, 1954–1955*, translated by Sylvana Tomaselli. New York: Norton.

———. 1997. *The Seminar of Jacques Lacan: Book VII: The Ethics of Psychoanalysis 1959–1960*, translated by Dennis Porter. New York: Norton.

———. 2002. *Écrits*, translated by Bruce Fink. New York: Norton.

———. 2007. *The Seminar of Jacques Lacan: Book XVII: The Other Side of Psychoanalysis*, translated by Russell Grigg. New York: Norton.

Laclau, Ernesto, and Chantal Mouffe. 1985. *Hegemony and Socialist Strategy: Towards a Radical Democratic Politics*, translated by Winston Moore and Paul Cammack. London: Verso.

Levinas, Emmanuel. 1969. *Totality and Infinity: An Essay on Exteriority*, translated by Alphonso Linguis. (Duquesne Studies Philosophical Series, vol. 24). Pittsburgh: Duquesne University Press.

Ley, David, *et al.* 1992. "Time to Grow Up? From Urban Village to World City, 1966–91." In *Vancouver and its Region*, edited by Graeme Wynn and Timothy Oke, 234–66. Vancouver: University of British Columbia.

Lindsay, Hillary Bain. 2007. "Stolen Games." *The Dominion* 44 (4 April). http://www.dominionpaper.ca/articles/1099.

Lusk, Dorothy Trujillo. [1988]. *Oral Tragedy*. Vancouver: Tsunami.

———. 1990a. *Redactive*. Vancouver: Talonbooks.

———. 1990b. "Sentimental Intervention." *Writing* 25: 24–30.

———. 1990c. "This Story." *West Coast Line* 24 (1): 122–126.

———. 2000a. "Decorum (Typical)." In *Four Poems*. Kamloops: Monoecious House Folios 4: n.p.

———. 2000b. *Sleek Vinyl Drill*. Vancouver: Thuja.

———. 2001. *Ogress Oblige*. San Francisco: Krupskaya, 2001.

MacCannell, Judith Flower. 2006. "More Thoughts for the Time of War and Death: the Discourse of Capitalism in *Seminar XVII*." In Clemens and Grigg, 195–215.

McCaffery, Steve. 1984 "From the Notebooks." In *The L=A=N=G=U=A=G=E Book*. edited by Bruce Andrews and Charles Bernstein, 159–62. Carbondale, IL: Southern Illinois University Press.

McCaffery, Steve, Ron Silliman, Charles Bernstein. 1985. "Correspondence: May 1976–December 1977." *Line* 5 (Spring): 59–89.

MacLeod, Kathryn. 1986. "Circus Darkness." *Writing* 16 (October): 19–22.

Macdonald, Bruce. 1987. "3 Poems" ("Scrim," "Overqualified," "Vile, Moral").

Raddle Moon 5 (September): 32–38.
———. 1989a. "From *Houseworks.*" *Writing* 23/24 (Fall/Winter): 7–12.
———. 1989b. "Scrim," "Vile, moral." In Wharton and Wayman, eds. 99–103.
———. 1990. "From *Houseworks.*" *Motel* 3 (Summer): 23–32.
———. 1991. "The Infatuation." *The Capilano Review* 2 (6/7) (Fall): 151–54.
———. 1992. "Oh, theory," "Asylum." *Raddle Moon* 11: 33–40.
———. 1996. *mouthpiece*. Vancouver: Tsunami.
———. 1997a. "Fairview." In *The Greater Vancouver Book* by Chuck Davis, 93. Surrey, BC: Linkman.
———. 1997b. "Grandview." In *The Greater Vancouver Book* by Chuck Davis, 92. Surrey, BC: Linkman.
———. 1997c. "Mount Pleasant." In *The Greater Vancouver Book* by Chuck Davis, 94–95. Surrey, BC: Linkman.
———. 1999. "The Infatuation," "Asylum," "One Hour Out of Twenty-four." In Klobucar and Barnholden, eds., 76–88.
Magnusson, Warren, *et al.*, eds. 1984. *The New Reality: The Politics of Restraint in British Columbia*. Vancouver: New Star Books.
Mancini, Donato and Colin Smith. 2010. "Versus the Atomizations of Power: A Dialogue about The Kootenay School of Writing, Friendship, and Collectivity." *Open Letter* 14 (3) (Summer): 93–122.
Manoff, Marlene. 2004. "Theories of the Archive from Across the Disciplines." *Libraries and the Academy* 4(1) (January): 9–25.
Marlatt, Daphne and Carole Itter, eds. 1979/2011. *Opening Doors in Vancouver's East End: Strathcona*. Madeira Park, BC: Harbour Publishing.
Marx, Karl. 1976. *The German Ideology*, edited by C.J. Arthur. New York: International.
———. 1990. *Capital*, translated by Ben Brewster. Harmondsworth, UK: Penguin.
Marx, Karl and Friedrich Engels. 1983. *Manifesto of the Communist Party*. In *The Portable Karl Marx*, edited by Eugene Kamenka. Harmondsworth, UK: Penguin, 203–41.
McGrath, William J. 1986. *Freud's Discovery of Psychoanalysis: The Politics of Hysteria*. Ithaca: Cornell University Press.
Merrill, Cynthia. 1985. "Mirrored Image: Gertrude Stein and Autobiography."

Pacific Coast Philology 12 (1/2) (November): 1–17.

Miller, Tyrus.1999. "Avant-Garde and Theory: A Misunderstood Relation." *Poetics Today*. 20 (4) (Winter): 549–79.

Mitchell, Juliet and Jacqueline Rose, eds. 1985. *Feminine Sexuality: Jacques Lacan and the école freudienne*. New York: Norton.

Mulvey, Laura. 1999. "Visual Pleasure and Narrative Cinema." In *Film Theory and Criticism: Introductory Readings*, edited by Leo Braudy and Marshall Cohen, 833–44. New York: Oxford University Press.

Nash, Susan Smith. 1992. "Review of *Redactive* (Dorothy Trujillo Lusk)." *Witz* 1 (1). http://wings.buffalo.edu/epc/ezines/witz/witz_1.1.html.

Ngai, Sianne. 2005. *Ugly Feelings*. Cambridge: Harvard University Press.

Nickels, Joel. 2001. "Post-Avant-Gardism: Bob Perelman and the Dialectic of Futural Memory." *Postmodern Culture* 11 (3) (May). http://pmc.iath.virginia.edu/text-only/issue.501/11.3.r_nickels.txt.

North, Robert N., and Walter Hardwick. 1992. "Vancouver Since the Second World War: An Economic Geography." In *Vancouver and its Region*, edited by Graeme Wynn and Timothy Oke. 200–33. Vancouver: University of British Columbia Press.

Nowak, Mark. 2009. *Coal Mountain Elementary*. Minneapolis: Coffee House Press.

Offe, Claude. 1980. "The Separation of Form and Content in Liberal Democratic Politics." *Studies in Political Economy* 3: 5–16.

O'Brian, Melanie, ed. 2007. *Vancouver Art and Economies*. Vancouver: Arsenal Pulp; Artspeak.

O'Driscoll, Michael and Edward Bishop. 2004. "Archiving 'Archiving.'" *English Studies in Canada* 30(1) (March): 1–16.

Olson, Charles. 1958. *Call Me Ishmael: A Study of Melville*. San Francisco: City Lights.

———. 1972. *The Maximus Poems*. New York: Jargon/Corinth.

Page, P.K. 1985. *The Glass Air: Selected Poems*. Toronto: Oxford University Press.

Palmer, Michael, ed. 1983. *Code of Signals: Recent Writings in Poetics*. Berkeley: North Atlantic.

Patterson, Annabel. 1987. *Pastoral and Ideology: Virgil to Valéry*. Berkeley:

University of California Press.

Penberthy, Jenny. 2002. "Life and Writing." In *Lorine Niedecker: Collected Works*, edited by Jenny Penberthy. 1–11. Berkeley: University of California Press.

Perelman, Bob. 1994. *The Trouble with Genius: Reading Pound, Joyce, Stein, and Zukofsky*. Berkeley: University of California Press.

Pound, Ezra. 1986. *The Cantos*. New York: New Directions.

Preece, Rob. 1977. "The Myth of the Red Tory." *Canadian Journal of Social and Political Theory* 1 (2) (Spring/Summer): 3–28.

Quartermain, Peter. 1992. *Disjunctive Poetics: From Gertrude Stein and Louis Zukofsky to Susan Howe*. Cambridge: Cambridge University Press.

Rasula, Jed. 1996. *The American Poetry Wax Museum: Reality Effects: 1940–1990*. (Refiguring English Studies) Urbana, IL: National Council of Teachers of English.

Reinhard, Kenneth. 2005. "Toward a Political Theology of the Neighbor." In *The Neighbor*, by Slavoj Žižek, *et al.*, 11–75. Chicago: University of Chicago Press.

Robertson, Lisa. 1993. *XEclogue*. Vancouver: Tsunami.

———. 2003. *Occasional Work and Seven Walks from The Office for Soft Architecture*. Astoria, OR: Clearcut.

Roudinesco, Elisabeth. 1990. *Jacques Lacan & Co.: A History of Psychoanalysis in France, 1925–1985*, translated by Jeffrey Mehlman. Chicago: University of Chicago Press.

———. 1997. *Jacques Lacan*, translated by Barbara Bray. New York: Columbia University Press.

Scalapino, Leslie. 1988. *way*. San Francisco: North Point.

Schmitt, Carl. 2005. *Political Theology*, translated by George Schwab. Chicago: University of Chicago Press.

Schroeder, Jeanne Lorraine. 2008. *The Four Lacanian Discourses: or Turning Law Inside Out*. Abingdon, UK: Birkbeck Law College.

"SFU, UBC professors concerned about effect of height review on Downtown Eastside." 2011. *The Georgia Straight*. January 19. http://www.straight.com/article-368944/vancouver/sfu-ubc-professors-concerned-about-effect-height-review-downtown-eastside.

Shaw, Nancy. 1992. *Scoptocratic*. Toronto: ECW Press.

Shier, Reid, ed. 2002. *Stan Douglas: Every Building on 100 West Hastings*. Vancouver: Contemporary Art Gallery; Arsenal Pulp Press.

Silliman, Ron. 1985. *The New Sentence*. New York: Roof.

Smith, Colin. 1997. *Multiple Poses*. Tsunami: Vancouver.

———. 1999. "Untitled." *Raddle Moon* 17: 24–28.

Smith, Neil. 1996. *The New Urban Frontier: Gentrification and the Revanchist City*. New York: Routledge.

Steedman, Carolyn. 2001. *Dust*. Manchester: Manchester University Press.

Stein, Gertrude. 1984. *Tender Buttons. Look at Me Now and Here I Am: Writings and Lectures 1909–45*, 161–206, edited by Patricia Meyerowitz. Harmondsworth, UK: Penguin.

———. 1998a. *The Autobiography of Alice B. Toklas*. In Stein, Gertrude. *Writings 1903–1932*, edited by Catherine R. Stimpson and Harriet Chessman. 653–913. New York: Library of America.

———. 1998b. "Lifting Belly." In Stein, *The Autobiography of Alice B. Toklas*, 410–58. New York: Library of America.

Stewart, Christine. 2010. "Aroused by Unreadable Questions: Interviews with Lisa Robertson and Catriona Strang." *Open Letter* 14(3) (Summer): 133–40.

———. 1993. "From 'Taxonomy.'" *Raddle Moon* 13: 66–70.

———. 2003. *From Taxonomy*. Sheffield: West House.

Stoller, Paul. 1997. *Sensuous Scholarship*. Philadelphia: University of Pennsylvania Press.

Strang, Catriona. 1993. *Low Fancy*. Toronto: ECW Press.

Sussman, Henry. 2003. "Prolegomena to any Present and Future Language Poetry." *MLN* 118 (5) (December Comparative Literature Issue): 1193–1212.

Swanson, Jean. 2011. "Condo Towers Do Not Provide Affordable Housing to Residents." The *Vancouver Sun*, February 1. http://www.vancouversun.com/business/Condo+towers+provide+affordable+housing+residents/4201021/story.html.

Taylor, Charles. 1982. *Radical Tories: The Conservative Tradition in Canada*. Toronto: House of Anansi Press.

Taussig, Michael. 1993. *Mimesis and Alterity: A Particular History of the Senses*.

London: Routledge.

Thomas, Merlin. 1979. *Louis-Ferdinand Céline*. New York: New Directions.

Usinger, Mike. 2010. "East Van Olympic Torch Protestors Need to Get a Life." *Georgia Straight* blog, February 12. http://www.straight.com/article-289364/vancouver/mike-usinger-east-van-olympic-torch-protesters-need-get-life.

Vaughn, Annabel and Jerry Zaslove. 2005. "Bob Williams on the History of Planning in Vancouver." In *Unfinished Business*, edited by Bill Jeffries, 266–83. North Vancouver: Burnaby; Presentation House Gallery: *West Coast Line* 47.

Vancouver: Art and Artists 1931–1983, exhibition catalogue. 1983. Vancouver: Vancouver Art Gallery.

Vidaver, Aaron. 2003–2004. *Woodsquat: West Coast Line* 41 (Fall/Winter).

Virgil. 1950. *Virgil's Works*, translated by J.W. Makail. New York: Modern Library.

Wah, Fred. 1990. "Tsunami Editions: A Review." *West Coast Line* 24 (1) (Spring): 147–51.

———. 2010. "KSW: Origins, Including Nelson." *Open Letter* 14 (3) (Summer): 141–44.

Wallace, Keith. 1993. "A Particular History: Artist-Run Centres in Vancouver." In *Vancouver Anthology*, edited by Stan Douglas, 23–45. Vancouver: Talonbooks.

———, ed. 1993. *Whispered Art History: Twenty Years at the Western Front*. Vancouver: Arsenal Pulp Press.

Watten, Barrett. 1982. "Method and Surrealism: The Politics of Poetry." *Open Letter* 5(1); *L=A=N=G=U=A=G=E* 4 (Winter): 129–40.

Wayman, Tom. 1986. *The Face of Jack Munro*. Madeira Park, BC: Harbour.

———. 2007. "Against the Smiling Bastards." *The New Quarterly* 101 (Winter): 76–89.

Weber, Samuel. 2008. *Benjamin's -abilities*. Cambridge: Harvard University Press.

Wharton, Calvin and Tom Wayman. 1989. *East of Main: An Anthology of Poems from East Vancouver*. Vancouver: Arsenal Pulp Press.

Wiens, Jason. 2001. *The Kootenay School of Writing: History, Community, Poetics*.

PhD Diss. University of Calgary.

———. 2010. "Canonicity and Teachable Texts: A Response to Christian Bök's 'TISH and KOOT.'" *Open Letter* 14 (3): 162–69.

Wiseman, Nelson. 2007. *In Search of Canadian Political Culture*. Vancouver: University of British Columbia Press.

Wolsak, Melissa, 1994. *The Garcia Family Co-Mercy*. Vancouver: Tsunami.

Wood, William. 1993. "This is Free Money? Western Front as Facility, Institution and Image." In *Whispered Art History*, edited by Keith Wallace, 179–87. Vancouver: Arsenal Pulp Press.

Wynn, Graeme and Timothy Oke, eds. 1992. *Vancouver and its Region*. Vancouver: University of British Columbia Press.

Yarrow [Clark], Susan. 1990. "From 'Not not'." *West Coast Line* 24(1): 76–81.

Žižek, Slavoj. 1989. *The Sublime Object of Ideology*. London: Verso.

———. 1992. *Enjoy Your Symptom! Jacques Lacan in Hollywood and Out*. London: Routledge.

———. 2000. *The Ticklish Subject: The Absent Centre of Political Ontology*. London: Verso.

———. 2001. *Did Somebody Say Totalitarianism?* London: Verso.

———. 2004a. *Iraq: The Borrowed Kettle*. New York: Verso.

———. 2004b. *Organs Without Bodies: On Deleuze and Consequences*. New York: Routledge.

———. 2005. "Neighbors and Other Monsters." In *The Neighbor* by Slavoj Žižek, *et al.*: 134–90. Chicago: University of Chicago Press

———. 2006a. *How to Read Lacan*. London: Granta.

———. 2006b. "*Objet a* in Social Links." In *Jacques Lacan and the Other Side of Psychoanalysis*, edited by Justin Clemens and Russell Griggs, 108–28. Durham, NC: Duke University Press.

———. 2006c. *The Parallax View*. Cambridge: MIT Press.

———. 2008. *The Plague of Fantasies*. London: Verso,

Žižek, Slavoj, *et al.* 2000. *Contingency, Hegemony, Universality: Contemporary Dialogues on the Left*. London: Verso.

———. 2005. *The Neighbor: Three Inquiries in Political Theology*. Chicago: University of Chicago Press.

CREDITS

Page 14: By Nancy Shaw, from *Scoptocratic*. Reprinted by permission of ECW Press.

Page 30–31, 59, and 68–69: By Dan Farrell, from *Ape* and *Thimking of You*. Reprinted by permission of the author.

Page 33–34, 65: By Kathryn MacLeod. Reprinted by permission of the author.

Page 37, 94 (bottom), and 101–102: By Dorothy Trujillo Lusk. Reprinted by permission of the author.

Page 38, 95 (top), 103, and 122: By Deanna Ferguson, from *The Relative Minor*. Reprinted by permission of the author.

Page 49: By Catriona Strang, from *Low Fancy*. Reprinted by permission of ECW Press.

Page 53: By Rachel Blau DuPlessis, from *Genders, Races and Religious Cultures in Modern American Poetry, 1908–1934*. Reprinted by permission of Cambridge University Press.

Page 89: By Susan Howe, from *The Nonconformist's Memorial*, copyright ©1993 by Susan Howe. Reprinted by permission of New Directions Publishing Corp.

Page 94 (top): By Colin Smith. Reprinted by permission of the author.

Pages 121, 126, 140, and 142–145: By Peter Culley. Reprinted by permission of the author.

Page 195: Excerpt from *Coal Mountain Elementary* (Coffee House Press) is reprinted by permission. Copyright © 2009 by Mark Nowak.

Page 199, 204 (bottom)–207: By Tom Wayman, from *The Face of Jack Munro*. Reprinted by permission of the author.

INDEX

CLINT BURNHAM is a professor of English at Simon Fraser University in Vancouver. His previous books include *Smoke Show* (Arsenal Pulp Press) and *The Jamesonian Unconscious* (Duke University Press).